A FAMILY FROM FLANDERS

A FAMILY
FROM FLANDERS

JOHN PETERS

COLLINS
8 Grafton Street, London W1
1985

William Collins Sons and Co. Ltd
London · Glasgow · Sydney · Auckland
Toronto · Johannesburg

BRITISH LIBRARY CATALOGUING IN PUBLICATION DATA

Peters, John
A family from Flanders.
1. Huguenots—England—History
I. Title
284'.5'0942   BX9458.G7

ISBN 0-00-217346-8

First published 1985
© John Peters 1985

Photoset in Sabon by
Rowland Phototypesetting Ltd
Bury St Edmunds, Suffolk
Made and printed in Great Britain by
William Collins Sons and Co. Ltd, Glasgow

CONTENTS

Acknowledgements   vii
Preface   xi
Prologue   1

PART I
Protestants and Outlaws
1500–75

1   The Family from Flanders   9
2   Flanders in The Golden Age   20
3   The Reformation in Flanders under
    Charles V 1520–55   31
4   The Protestant Recovery in Flanders
    1556–66   44
5   The Troubles: The Coming of Alva and
    the Council of Blood 1566–75   61

PART II
The Great Migrations
1560–1635

6   The First Exodus from Flanders 1560–75   81
7   The First Walloon Communities in
    England   97
8   The Second Exodus from Flanders
    1580–1600   113
9   Armistice and Recovery: Gorne Found   128
10 The de le Pierre Family Joins the Third
    Exodus 1625–35   143

PART III

Home from Home
1635–1700

11 Toil and Trouble 1635–50   155
12 Commonwealth, Restoration and
    Prosperity 1650–70   173
13 Brief Lives   185
    Epilogue   192

APPENDIX: Family Network in the
Walloon Refugee Communities   197

Select Bibliography   209
Index of Northern French
    and Walloon Names   213
Index of Places   217

ACKNOWLEDGEMENTS

As an amateur historian I owe a great deal to the help and indulgence of those who know more than I do about every subject touched on in this book: most of all to my own father who (as will be clear) did most of the work fifty years ago, and to Mr Frank Tyler who provided him with expert advice. They and I received the usual generous help from the keepers of diocesan, parish and civil registers in this country, especially at Canterbury, and I am grateful to the archivists at the Public Record Office in London. In the more specialised field of Protestant history, many nineteenth-century scholars rescued scraps of information in the nick of time, and their work is preserved in the proceedings and publications of such bodies as the Huguenot Society of London; I am particularly indebted to the Society and especially to Mr Marmoy, its honorary librarian, for frequent access to its splendid collection of manuscript and printed material at University College, London. In Brussels, the Bibliothèque Albert Premier and its helpful staff have provided valuable material: the publications of the *Commission Royale d'Histoire* are particularly scholarly and well produced. In the Netherlands, historians whether amateur or professional have cause to bless the staffs of the Universities, especially in my case those of the *Bibliothécaires* at Leyden; and family historians depend on such organisations as the Central Bureau voor Genealogie at the Hague. In France, the director and staff of the Services d'Archives of the Département du Nord at Lille and of the Département du Pas-de-Calais at Arras, which inherited from the Habsburg rulers the records of Artois and the other *pays* restored to France by Louis XIV, reply with unwearying patience and skill to the importunities of family historians; it is thanks to them that my own place of origin was pinned down at last. To these, and to the historians whose work is mentioned in the following pages and in the bibliography, I offer my sincere thanks for being able to include their expert opinions in my unprofessional narrative: including Dr Geoffrey Parker, Professor G. R. Elton, Rosi Briggs, Mr Alistair Horne, Mr John Keevil, Dr Alan Macfarlane, Monsieur Jean-Michel Pardon, Mr A. L. E. Verheyden; and – last in alphabetical order, first woman elected to the Académie Francaise – Marguerite Youcenar, whose interest in her own family history in Flanders has found expression in typically delightful books.

JOHN PETERS

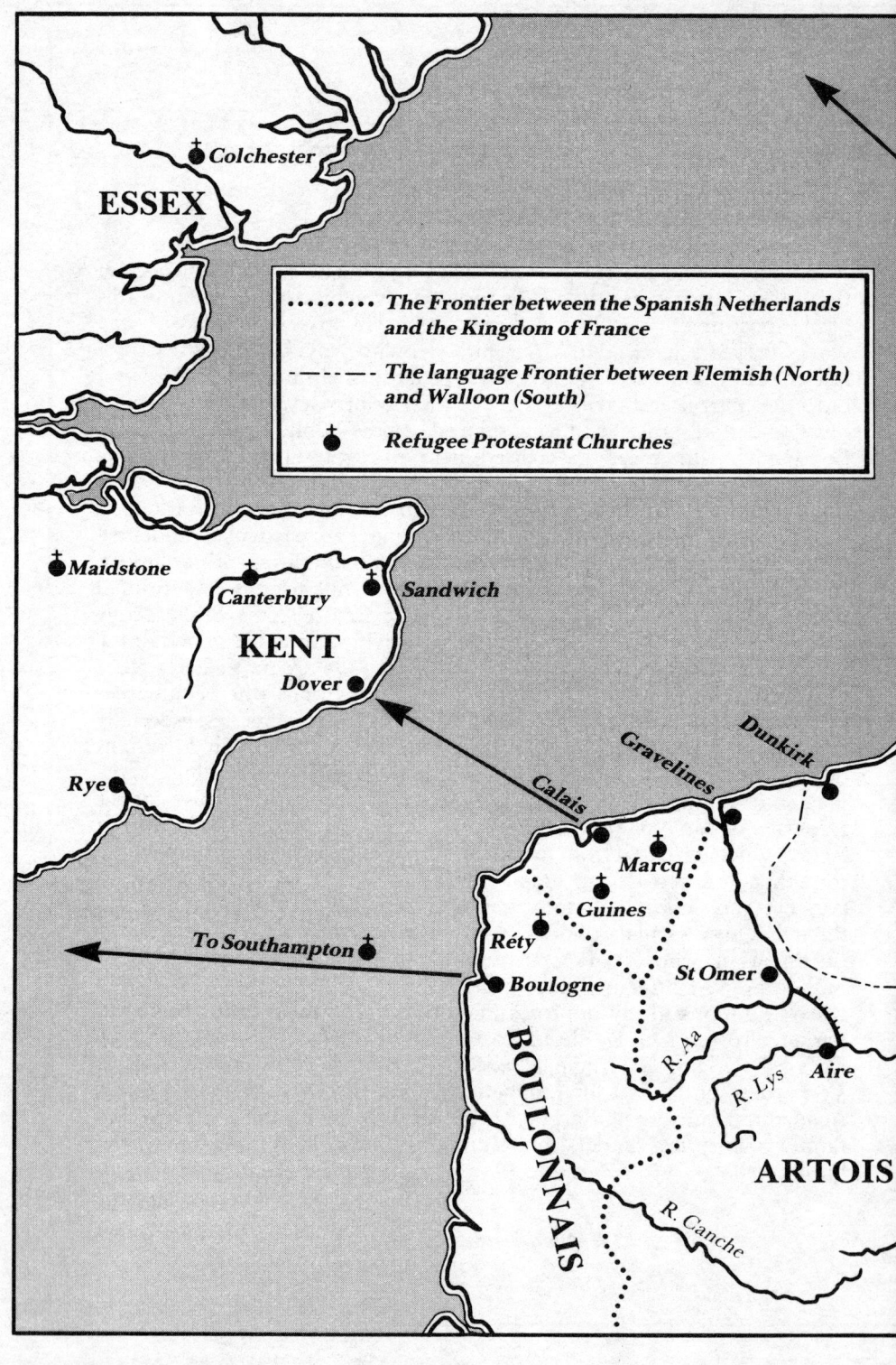

Colchester

ESSEX

The Frontier between the Spanish Netherlands and the Kingdom of France

The language Frontier between Flemish (North) and Walloon (South)

Refugee Protestant Churches

Maidstone

Canterbury   Sandwich

KENT

Dover

Rye

Calais

Gravelines

Dunkirk

Marcq

Guines

To Southampton

Réty

St Omer

Boulogne

BOULONNAIS

R. Aa

R. Lys   Aire

ARTOIS

R. Canche

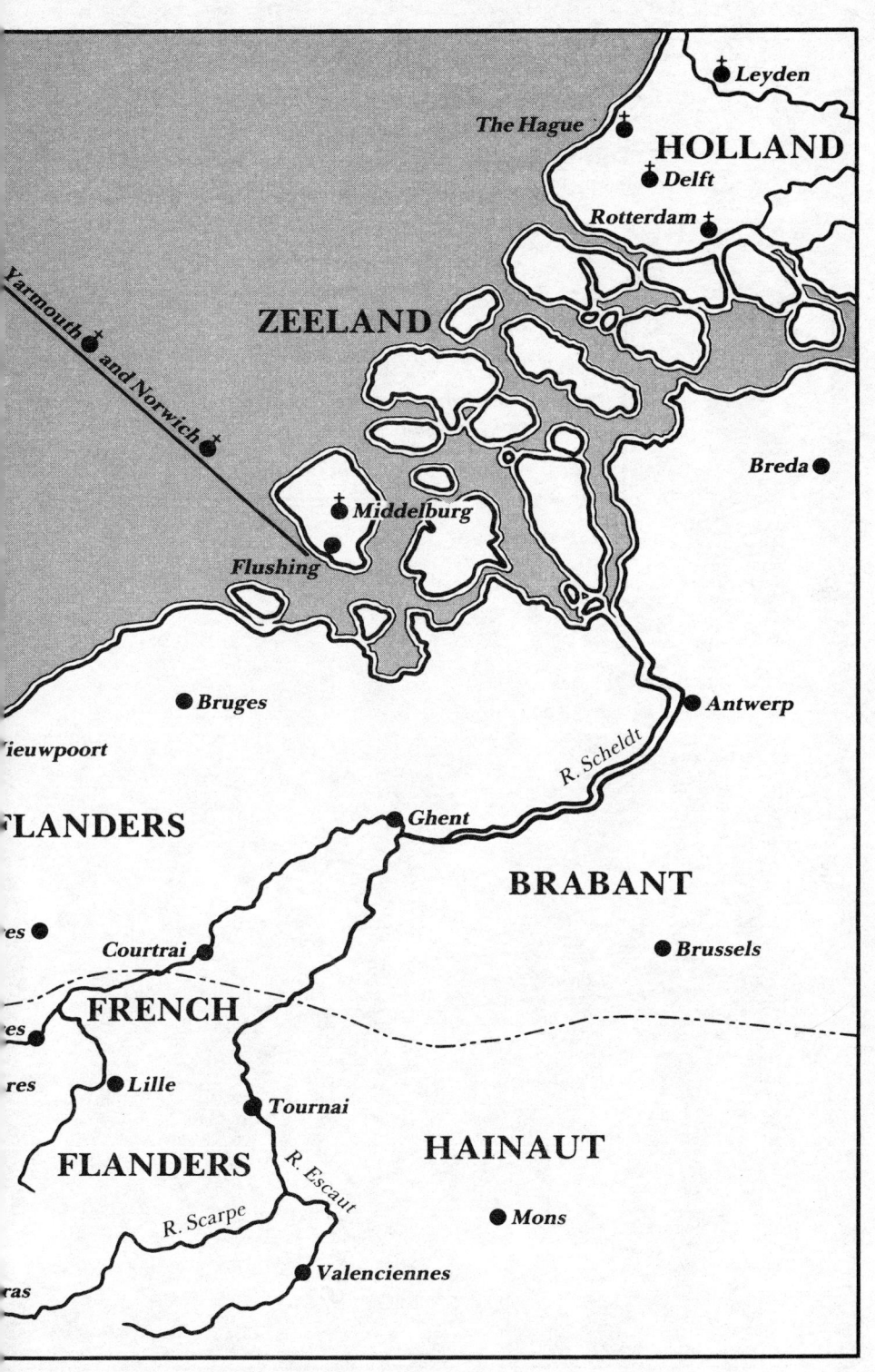

Leyden

The Hague

HOLLAND

Delft

Rotterdam

Yarmouth and Norwich

ZEELAND

Breda

Middelburg

Flushing

Bruges

Antwerp

R. Scheldt

Nieuwpoort

FLANDERS

Ghent

BRABANT

res

Courtrai

Brussels

FRENCH

res

Lille

Tournai

HAINAUT

FLANDERS

R. Escaut

R. Scarpe

Mons

ras

Valenciennes

PREFACE

The American historian C. Bridenbaugh, in his excellent book, *Vexed and Troubled Englishmen* (1976), about the country which attracted many refugees from the continent even as the American settlers left it, heads a section, "The Swarming of the English". It is a good phrase. What is it that causes groups of people to swarm, to take up sticks and remove themselves, not singly but in whole families and even whole communities? The answer seems at first sight to be obvious: surely it is a simple matter of pressure, of overpopulation, or of famine or war, or some other constraint strong enough to overcome the powerful tie to their native country? But this can hardly be the whole answer. Human beings are enormously resistent and persistent, and able to endure and survive any amount of adversity, as our own dismal century shows; individual family histories indicate that a permanent migration, as distinct from a temporary move in search of work and security, is fairly unusual, except at times of general post. For hundreds of thousands of families the sixteenth and seventeenth centuries were such a period of swarming, of mass migration that colonised the New World in Siberia and in the Americas.

This book is primarily an attempt to honour the memory of those families from Flanders who took part in the swarmings which created the modern world, and settled in England. There is no general account in English of the mass migrations from Flanders, though as my brief bibliography makes evident, the work of Geoffrey Parker in particular illuminates the story of the Dutch revolt and gives due weight to the aims and preoccupations of the Spanish rulers of the Netherlands. A great deal has been written about the Reformation in Germany and in France, where the emperor and the king had to make concessions to powerful Lutheran and Calvinist influences; for them, as for the United Provinces, it is the long struggle on nearly equal terms which lends attraction and interest to the story. In Flanders the issue was decided much more quickly and people soon forgot the brief flowering and almost total extirpation of Protestantism in that part of the Netherlands which remained under Habsburg rule. It therefore gives a family historian a sense of discovery to pick up the almost-vanished traces of the migrations, and a good deal of complicated and obscure history is made much more immediate as a result. I am left with a feeling of great respect for the people of the Netherlands, north and south, who survived in conditions quite as bad as those during the wars of our century. They prospered during the rare spells of peace, and brought the benefits of their thrift, industry, family cohesion and culture to many places in the Old World and the New. They made a contribution out of all proportion to their numbers to the great revolution in thought which made their centuries the first of the modern world. To those of them who were my ancestors this book is respectfully dedicated.

March 1984   JOHN PETERS

Prologue

Dutch, Walloons, Flemings, Irishmen and Scots,
Vaudois and Valtolins, and Huguenots,
In Good Queen Bess's charitable reign
Supplied us with three hundred thousand men.
Religion, God we thank thee, sent them hither,
Priests, Protestants, the Devil and all together.

Daniel Defoe,
The True-born Englishman

On Friday, 11 September 1635 William Jones, Clerk of the Passage at Dover, was noting down the names of the latest batch of arrivals from Calais to send to the Privy Council in London. It was not normal to take so much trouble, at least in England, but the times were uneasy. France and Spain were once again at war and the usual refugees had begun to arrive. They came from the frontier region between France and the Spanish Netherlands. Old men remembered how Flanders and Artois, the Boulonnais and the Calaisis had been overrun by rival armies in the 1580s and 1590s, when the king of France had helped the Dutch rebels to resist Spain, and the king of Spain had supported the Catholic League to make life difficult for France. This time the outlook was even less promising: there was a widely-known agreement between France and the Dutch to divide the southern Netherlands between them once the Spanish army was defeated. Therefore, people of the border provinces were again on the move, anxious to get away before the two royal armies started the next round of their long contest.

Four months earlier Luke Pepper the mayor and the five jurats of Dover had sent an urgent message to the Lord Warden of the Cinque Ports.

> Rt Honble. Our humble duty and service to your Lordship remembered. It may please your Lordship to be certified that on Saturday last and yesterday there were landed at this port and town from Calais in France near one hundred men, women and children, French and Dutch, all Protestants, some of them

bringing with them their goods and household stuff, whose dwellings were in or near Calais, but have lands and tenements in Flanders, and fly hither for security of the same in respect of the war likely to be betwixt France and Spain (as they say). Some few of them have here hired houses and lodgings for themselves, wives and families by our privities, and requested our certificate thereof and of the day of their arrival, which we granted them upon request of some neighbours to whom they are well known, but denied the like to others until your Lordship's directions be had therein, which we humbly pray for our further proceedings. We understand that the others who were here landed intended to disperse themselves in this kingdom, and that divers others of that country are resolved also shortly to come over for the cause aforesaid. And even so craving pardon for this our boldness, we humbly take leave and rest ever

> Your Lordship's at commandment
> The Mayor and Jurats of Dover.

Dover, 13 die Maii 1635.

The Lord Warden wasted no time. There had been two massive inflows of refugees from Flanders in the past seventy years, and he knew that they would need to be moved on quickly from the Channel ports before they began to overburden the local supplies, not to mention pose a threat to security. He passed the mayor's message to the Privy Council, received their instructions on the following Monday, 18 May, and passed these back to Dover, endorsed, "For his Majesty's special service. Haste, haste, post haste." The instructions were what the mayor had expected. The new arrivals were to be allowed to land, but not to take up residence in the ports: they must go inland, and a register was to be kept of their names and occupations and forwarded from time to time to the Privy Council.

So William Jones, as immigration officer, was kept busy. The first register which he sent to the Privy Council for May and June is lost; but we have his second list of "the names of such Walloons and Strangers that hath been landed here at Dover since I gave up my first noate in June last 1635 to dwell in England". Nineteen refugees landed in July, among them a Monsieur de New and family:

> From Callis 18 July. Moser Danewe and his wife and mother and three children and a mayde servant – to dwell at Canterbury.

William Jones had a healthy contempt for French styles and names, but at least "Moser Danewe" indicated a gentleman; during the same month of July some 900 Walloon artisans arrived at various English ports. When the boat from Calais arrived at Dover on 11 September and the passengers made their way ashore, sixteen men lined up in front of the desk and Jones took down their names as seemed best to him . . .

> Mycoll Du La Peire
> Wam Fromowe
> Abram De La Roye
> Abram Cosheire
> Bartholomew Favorye . . .

and so on. In the towns and villages they came from they would have been written as Michel de le Pierre, Guillaume Fremaut, Abraham de le Rue, Abraham Couchet, Berthelemé Favre; but now they underwent a stage in the process of anglicisation. Jones, having happily massacred another collection of foreign names, sent the refugees off, on foot or horseback, to join their friends and relatives already settled in the Strangers' community at Canterbury. Michel de la Pierre was my seven-times-great-grandfather.[1]

My ancestors in the male line were among the many hundreds speaking French or Flemish who left the southern provinces of the Spanish Netherlands[2] in the sixteenth and seventeenth centuries. The refugees scattered in all directions; some went to North America and founded New Amsterdam,[3] some to Germany, Prussia and further east; and some to France or to the northern provinces of the Netherlands where the revolt against Spanish rule was making headway. Many others were attracted by the comparatively tolerant Protestantism in England and soon there were small but growing settlements on this side of the North Sea and the Channel.

The main difference between the refugees from different parts of

---

[1] The French as usual have a more logical system: a grandfather is the *aieul*, his father the *bisaieul*, his father the *trisaieul*, and so on; so Michel de le Pierre, the eighth ascendant after my father, is my *octaieul*.
[2] Roughly modern Belgium and the Département du Nord in France.
[3] Franklin Delano Roosevelt (1882–1945), 32nd President of U.S., claimed descent from Claes Martenzen van Rosenvelt, one of the founders, and Philippe de Lannoy.

the Netherlands was language, and this is where it is necessary to be circumspect and draw a clear distinction early on. In England we talk easily of "Flemish weavers" and "Dutch gables", but these are vague terms; the Netherlands, in this story, means the Seventeen Provinces, which owed allegiance to Philip II of Spain on his accession in 1555 but by the time of his death in 1598 were sub-divided into the Seven (United) Provinces of the north and the Ten (Catholic) Provinces of the south. In the south the main languages were, and are, a dialect of French called Walcq and a dialect of Low German called Flemish; the speakers of Walcq and Flemish were called Walloons and Flemings. One of the features of Walcq is to turn names which we would expect to be written "de la" into "de le", for example, de le Pierre, de le Rue.

The Fleming and Walloon refugees were like oil and water; although they arrived together in the boat they quickly separated ashore. Only in the largest refugee settlements in London and Norwich were there both Flemings and Walloons; elsewhere they gravitated to different centres according to language. The chief communities were the Walloons of Canterbury and the Flemings of Colchester, and all were self-contained and self-supporting. They believed, along with those who received them, that they would not be staying for good. This hope is common among refugees: neither the French royalists who fled the Revolution in 1789 nor the Russians who emigrated in 1917 thought they would be exiled for long. Sure enough, during lulls in the troubles of the Netherlands many went home again; indeed so strong was the compulsion that a man under sentence of banishment and in danger of his life, if he were caught, would contrive to slip across the Channel to sow his patch and reap his crop. The Netherlands have had plenty of experience of rule by foreigners and of military occupation over the centuries, and the people are skilled at going on living, and living well, in spite of it.

Several thousand of the refugees preferred to stay in England where they were made welcome by successive governments, and when in due course they became naturalised they changed their names to an English equivalent.[4] Many of those who subsequently intermarried with the English also left the Calvinist Church to become good Anglicans. It was not unusual for a refugee to be baptised into one community, spend most of his life in another and die in a third: like my namesake John Peters, born Jean-Baptiste de le Pierre and baptised a Catholic in the Spanish Netherlands in 1626, who was married twice, in England and in France, by Calvinist Protestant rites, naturalised in 1663 and buried an Anglican in St Alphege's church in Canterbury in 1689; he died John Peters, MD (Leyden), owner of the Blackfriars and lord of the manor of Grove near Woodnesborough. These were enterprising men, not simply good survivors.

Because of this talent for rapid assimilation the Walloon congregations were already dwindling before the main wave of Protestant refugees arrived from France after the revocation of the Edict of Nantes in 1685. This brings me to a second important distinction. Just as people tend to confuse Flemings and Walloons, so too it is common to regard all French-speaking Protestants as Huguenots. This can be misleading, not least because no one knows what Huguenot means; and to be strictly accurate, use of the term Huguenot for French-speaking Protestant should be confined to Protestants born in France, otherwise matters already complicated become even more so. We shall see that many Walloon families from the Netherlands took refuge first in France, then in England, while some French families arrived in England by precisely the opposite route. The main thing to remember is that the Protestant refugees between 1550 and 1650 were mostly Walloons and Flemings from the Netherlands; after that they were mostly "Huguenots" from France. From 1685 onwards a French-speaking Protestant in England was more likely to be a Frenchman than a Walloon, especially after Louis XIV swallowed half of Wallonia during his long drive to push the frontier of France to the north-east.

If you go today on a Sunday afternoon to the crypt of Canterbury Cathedral, where many of my Walloon ancestors were baptised and married, you will find that there is a French Protestant service at three o'clock, including, of course, an excellent sermon, in direct succession to the Walloon services which were begun there in the middle of the sixteenth century.

---

[4] In France immigrants mostly keep their family names unaltered, apart from occasional fashions for Latinising or even anglicising, but in England there is a fairly rapid assimilation. Perhaps it is because the English refuse to twist their tongues round foreign names.

The main theme of this book is the story of what happened to a group of interrelated families of French-speaking Walloon refugees, my ancestors and their friends, during the troubles in the Ten Provinces of the southern Spanish Netherlands in the sixteenth and seventeenth centuries. It begins in the Seventeen Provinces, north and south, about the year 1500; to round it off it records briefly what became of the de le Pierre, later Peters, family in England down to 1700. It is not historical fiction: every specific incident mentioned, including family details, is supported by written evidence, and this raises a point of interest to more people than the Peters clan. My Walloon ancestors were by no means a distinguished family, certainly not by the standards of the Netherlands, and none of them features in the elaborate genealogies of well-born Belgians and Frenchmen; but the bureaucracies of the kings of France and Spain were thorough, and particularly in recording the personal details of ordinary people, who could be taxed if they stayed or whose goods could be confiscated if they were convicted of rebellion and heresy; in Spanish territory these terms were synonymous. In spite of the passage of four centuries, and even more the destructive passage of warring armies, it is possible to pick up essential traces from the records which survive.

There is a clear line from my son back to his nine-times-great-grandfather Louis de le Pierre, who married Jeanne Guiselin in Flanders about 1600. Earlier than that, only fragments of the jigsaw are still extant but unconnected for several generations, and at last the trail shops where, long since, the essential records have followed the people into dust.

The three main migrations of refugees from Flanders were, first, during the religious and political troubles of 1566–75 when the duke of Alva was Philip II's governor and captain-general in the Netherlands; the second occurred during the reconquest of the southern provinces under the duke of Parma, and in the course of Philip's intervention in the wars of religion in France in the 1580s and 1590s. The third exodus took place in the 1630s when, after a short oasis of peace, the war between France and Spain broke out again, and the stage seemed set for the final partition of the southern Netherlands. That was when Michel de le Pierre got on the boat to Dover.

PART I

Protestants and Outlaws

1500–75

CHAPTER 1

———————◆◆◆———————

The Family from Flanders

Mr Peter De La Pierre, a foreigner, who came over to practice Physic in
this kingdom.

Topographer (1790)

This is the book my father meant to write. He was the deputy
medical superintendent of the largest lunatic asylum in the London
area, behind the protective railings of which I passed a happy
childhood. When he joined the London County Council service
soon after the First World War, because that was the only work to
be had for a newly demobilised young doctor without hope of a
practice, the mental health field was a quiet area of medicine. It
seemed to be assumed, on some homoeopathic principle, that
provided the medical staff was suitably eccentric they should get
along well enough with the patients; certainly ·my father had
congenial colleagues and a peaceful life. Then came the 1930s and
everything started to go wrong. A stream of refugees poured out of
Germany and then Austria, including many a psychiatrist who took
service with the LCC; Freudians, Jungians and Adlerians, they
pursued their continental vendettas over the morning coffee in the
medical officers' mess, and the peace of the asylum was gone. The
world outside proceeded rapidly in the same direction. The government began to formulate ever more alarming forecasts of the likely
course of a new war, which my father recorded in the journal he
kept for thirty years: one day the hospital was told to prepare to
take its share of the 60,000 casualties to be expected from the first
air raids on London, and preparations were duly made.

I suspect that it was the intrusion of the outside world that
helped to quicken my father's interest in family history, because it is
an excellent way of taking your mind off the present. It is also an

insidious occupation which steadily demands more and more of your free time. The first attacks, as recorded in his journal, were comparatively mild.

> Tuesday, 24 January 1933. Memo. Grannie Shaw's brother (or was it her uncle?) was a well known amateur balloonist in his time. His name was Hill. He was also interested in canaries, and was a judge at the canary show at Crystal Palace for a good many years.

From the canary-fancier my father soon proceeded to more prestigious members of his mother's clan, or rather sept, since the Shaws were a sept of the Clan Macintosh and therefore a promising line to pursue. The Shaw family generally was more distinguished than the Peters: the sort of people who would appear in *Who's Who* or even, very occasionally, in the *Dictionary of National Biography*. The trouble was that there were so many of them. Each generation made a point of having large families, and thanks to clean living and high thinking they survived in large numbers: my paternal grandmother's father, Robert Shaw, had twelve children between 1856 and 1872, and my grandmother was the youngest of the five girls, whose ages when I knew them ranged well up into the eighties. The result was a pretty impenetrable thicket of cousins in which it was easy to get lost, and at last, after an unsuccessful search in Clerkenwell churchyard for a missing but crucial Shaw, my father called it a day. He had learnt the first rule of family history: one ancestor named Ciprian Rondeau Bunce (there was such a person, as we shall see) is worth a dozen called John Robinson or Robert Shaw.

My father had better luck with the second rule, which is to badger your elderly surviving relatives for reminiscences. The pillar-box in the village was filled with outgoing questionnaires, and the letter-box at home began to fill with the replies. He also sallied out to consult the usual archives. In those days family history was not the popular sport it has become. Today, especially in the summer, there is such a crowd of enthusiasts hunting for births, marriages and deaths among the huge ledgers at St Catherine's House, straining their eyes over the census returns in Portugal Street, browsing through wills in Somerset House and Chancery Lane, and pestering vicars and county archivists, that it is easy to get trampled in the rush. In my father's day it was more sedate, and when he first presented himself at Somerset House on Friday, 12 October 1934 he wore a new pair of shoes and was armed with a letter of introduction from a suitably respectable friend. Quite soon he was noting in his journal:

> Already the correspondence with the Heralds' College, custo-
> dians of parish registers, the Genealogical Society, librarians,
> Somerset House and family sources half-fill a fair sized fools-
> cap filing folio.

That does not sound much, but I still have the filing folio, with some of its original contents, and it is rather large. It is hardly surprising that my father felt the need for some expert help, otherwise the Peters hunt like the Shaw hunt would end up in the cemetery. On 27 April 1935 he held a family council at the Home Farm at Betteshanger in Kent with his father Frank, his brother Douglas (the farmer), and his cousin John Peters from Deal. They discussed the heap of information he had collected. The upshot was that the brothers drove into Canterbury to consult a professional antiquary and researcher called Frank Tyler; and that turned out to be the first of several strokes of luck which put them on the trail to Flanders.

Many of the letters which eventually came to me in my father's box file were from Mr Tyler, and it is clear that he was the sort of man who has given the study of local and family history a good name in England. Perhaps it is something to do with the national preference for fact over speculation. When a man sets out to hunt down his ancestors he starts by assembling basic facts, and however far and wide he goes and however deep he digs he will still be dealing in facts: there is never enough topsoil, so to speak, to encourage the sprouting of abstract theories. (It is very hard to write Whig family history, or Marxist family history.) Mr Tyler sifted through the material produced by my father and with a brisk professional eye quickly spotted the essentials.

One point in particular intrigued him: my father's great-uncle Ben, a veteran born in 1800, was remembered to have bored the family with the recollection that a Peters had married a Barling and lived in a house called Dadmans at Lynsted in Kent. The reason why this had stuck in Great-Uncle Ben's memory was that the Barlings were a respected old Kentish family, and Dadmans was the big house of its village; whereas the Peters family in Uncle Ben's time were appearing in the census returns as ostlers and auctioneers' clerks. Mr Tyler had a healthy respect for family memories, knowing them to be often more revealing (and perhaps more accurate too) than certificates transcribed from barely legible registers. The reference to Barlings and Dadmans suggested a way through the blank spaces around the early 1700s that tend to obstruct research into many a family's history.

Mr Tyler had on his shelves, along with Hasted and Lambarde and Gosling and all the other works of reference essential to a Kentish antiquarian, the bound volumes of the *Topographer* for the years 1789–91. The *Topographer*, as the sub-titles of my father's copy helpfully explains, contains "A Variety of Original Articles illustrative of the Local History and Antiquities of England"; and particularly in the

> History and Description of Ancient and Eminent Seats and Styles of Architecture; in the Preservation of curious Monumental Inscriptions; in the Genealogies and Anecdotes of Famous Families; in Disquisitions upon remarkable Tenures, and in Delineations of the Face of Countries.

This splendid work, so characteristic of the decent age that produced it, was written by the sort of amateur antiquarian who knew what would be of interest to those of the same kidney, and as indicated it is as full of useful information about places and families as a Christmas pudding is full of fruit. It is therefore a source of possible aiming-marks for a family historian: "skyhooks", in the language of an architect friend, which one is always warned to avoid in matters of genealogy. Mr Tyler had more sense. He drew my father's attention to page 116 of volume II of the *Topographer*, in the middle of an article about the Blackfriars priory in Canterbury, where it is recorded that on 29 November 1658 a certain Robert Hoveden Esq. had sold the Blackfriars estate to

> Mr Peter De La Pierre, a foreigner, who came over to practice Physic in this kingdom, of his eminent skill in which profession several testimonies now remain in his family. Previous to this purchase he and his eldest son John born at Gorne in Flanders had been naturalized . . .

and their name by naturalisation was Peters. Mr Tyler therefore proposed to my father the sporting possibility that an East Kent family called Peters, which had been based in Kent in the 1750s if Great-Uncle Ben was right, had some connection with the de la Pierres of Canterbury a century before; which connection he undertook to prove or to disprove, and my father was delighted to engage him in the search.

For two years and more they worked away, my father in London and Mr Tyler around Kent, and the progress of the search is laid out in their frequent letters to one another. Proving Great-Uncle Ben's story was the easiest part: less than a month after the conference in Canterbury Mr Tyler had made a first cast in the diocesan records, and hooked the marriage of Peter Peters of Canterbury and Elizabeth Barling of Lynsted in 1738; the baptisms of their children Sarah and Peter in 1740 and 1745; the burial of Peter the elder in 1756, and of Elizabeth in 1763. It then remained to see if there was a direct connection downwards from Peter Peters of Dadmans to John Peters of Sittingbourne (my father's grandfather), and upwards between Peter Peters of Dadmans and Peter de la Pierre of Canterbury. Each gap was about a century wide, say three generations each way: a nice puzzle for a diligent man.

The line downwards from Peter to John Peters was fixed quite quickly, in spite of a family move to Bedfordshire and back, thanks to family memory and family Bibles, census returns, civil and parish registers, but especially a useful intestacy as a result of which the lawyers had amused themselves for some time distributing a rather small amount of property among a rather large number of relatives. John's father was another John Peters; his father was a Peter Peters, who lived at Lucerne Street; and he was the son of Peter Peters and Elizabeth Barling.

Proving the line upwards to Peter de la Pierre was harder work, not surprisingly. Many an English genealogy comes to an end in the early eighteenth century as the accidents of time make holes in records and the evidence becomes ever harder to find. There was no record of Peter of Dadmans's birth at Canterbury so there was nothing for it but to make a comprehensive search of the Kent parish registers. It was no laughing matter in the days before the Mormon Computer File Index: there were over 400 parishes in Kent in the seventeenth and eighteenth centuries – only

Norfolk and Yorkshire were better endowed – but Mr Tyler set his teeth, started with the parishes near Lynsted and spiralled outwards. It was a long and tedious search, as his letters to my father indicated.

> 30 November 1935. These short dark days make searching at the Bishop's Transcripts difficult and at times impossible; as you are no doubt aware there is no artificial light or heat in the Canterbury Transcripts room.

> 2 January 1936. I am by no means weary of the search but very weary of the weather.

Then at last he struck oil.

> 21 February 1936. This morning I was looking at the early transcripts of Ripple near Deal and as usual when I have a box of transcripts down, I cast my eye over some of the years in the period under observation looking for Peters: and fortunately I came across the entry of Peter Peters, son of Edward and Mary, baptised 18 August 1714. . . . The baptism . . . is two years out on the marriage licence but I do not think this is of great importance because the licences very often do not state the correct age; and in this case, as Peter Peters was marrying Elizabeth Barling an heiress who was 20 years of age it is quite likely that he wished to appear nearer her age.

Later on, my father found the explanation for the puzzling fact that Peter Peters was baptised at Ripple, but in 1936 he was busy supplementing Mr Tyler's efforts with his own researches; and the remaining gap between Edward Peters and Peter de la Pierre proved easier to fill, because the hunt returned to Canterbury, and in particular, to the registers of the Walloon or Strangers' church of that city.

It may seem odd that the records of a Nonconformist church – the Walloons of Canterbury were Calvinists – should be more helpful than those of the Church of England. The fact is that the parish records in the Canterbury diocese, with one exception, are all missing between 1649 and 1651 because of the Civil War, the Commonwealth, and deliberate destruction by Levellers who sought to eliminate proofs of titles and successions; this sometimes makes it quite difficult for men of Kent to trace back a pedigree in direct and provable line to Tudor times. But the Walloon records survive, though even those have a gap caused by an internal quarrel.

Nonconformity in religion does not necessarily mean careful record-keeping (my wife's many Baptist and Wesleyan ancestors are infuriatingly hard to trace); but the Walloons were French-speaking Protestants and had been brought up with a reverence for the written word and the habit of record-keeping within the community of Strangers.[1] During this period the Anglican clergy were in considerable disarray from Archbishop Laud's purges of the 1630s, the Civil War and the "Vicar of Bray" period, until the end of the century. The Canterbury Walloon records are particularly voluminous, and as Pierre de la Pierre was an elder of the church the registers proved to contain many references to his friends and relations.

It was therefore thanks to the help of Pastor Jean Barnabas at the French church at Canterbury that my father eventually placed Edward Peters. He was indeed the son of a Pierre de la Pierre but not, as it turned out, the Pierre of the Blackfriars. Edward's father Pierre first appears in Canterbury in 1665 when he witnessed a baptism and is described in the register as "holandoy", a Dutchman. That was because he was the son of Michel de la Pierre, the one who landed at Dover in 1635 and later, it transpired, betook himself to Middelburg in Zeeland; and Michel was the brother of the other Pierre de la Pierre, the physician of the Blackfriars. This final link was provided by Pierre the physician's will, proved in 1668 and still in mint condition among the Canterbury Consistory Court records, which my father found and copied in triumph. Besides the tell-tale legacy of £25 to the young Pierre, "my brother Michael's son", the elder Pierre's will was sealed with a fine coat of arms; my father hastened to consult the College of Arms, to see when the coat was registered and to get official approval from the Heralds for his and Mr Tyler's researches.

He had already made the acquaintance of Mr Kerr, Rouge Croix at the college, with whom he had gone through the material for constructing a pedigree of "the family of Delapierre or Peters of Canterbury", and the final details were collected by the summer of 1936.

---

[1] "Strangers" means not only "foreigners" but also those who were admitted, exceptionally, to live in the city of Canterbury although they came originally from outside its walls.

Wednesday, 1 July 1936. To the College of Arms in Queen Victoria Street to consult with Mr Kerr the Rouge Croix Pursuivant as arranged. . . . In his room seated side by side at a large table I showed him some of the exhibits . . . I am to send him all the evidence and he will analyse it and put it into shape.

6 July 1936. After another late sitting last night I was at last able to send off to Rouge Croix the documents concerning the pedigree. . . . Tomorrow morning Mr Kerr should have in his hands the result of Mr Tyler's researches, the abstracts of wills and documents and some covering letters, the certificates of births marriages and deaths, extracts from Hasted and the publications of the Huguenot Society, census returns, the correspondence that passed concerning Peter's intestacy, guidebooks and maps and newspaper cuttings, rubbings from tombstones and my own comments, and the flyleaf from the family Bible.

Practically submerged under documents, the examiners of the College of Arms were bound to agree that the Peters family of London was indeed descended from Michel, brother of Pierre de la Pierre of Canterbury; but they were quite definite, alas, that no coat of arms such as Pierre had used to seal his will was registered at the college. Very well, said my father, kindly register it now; but it took much longer than he expected before the process was complete.

Monday, 19 October 1936. Have received from Mr Tyler an impression of the seal on Pierre De La Pierre's will. . . . Also heard from Rouge Croix that he considers the pedigree has been established, and it is now ready to be submitted to the authorities for official registration.

There is a gap of over a year before

Tuesday, 4 January 1938. Today heard from Rouge Croix that the pedigree will be placed before the Chapter of the College tomorrow.

It seems that during 1937 the coronation kept Rouge Croix so busy that he had to neglect even the important business of the de la Pierre arms; and as the international outlook became gloomier, so my father became more impatient. But he now had his own copy of the volumes of the *Topographer* with which to pass the time. The four calf-bound volumes cost him three guineas. Soon he was happy finding sky-hooks of his own.

In fact, they only just beat Hitler to it in the end.

> Tuesday, 31 May 1938. Am particularly anxious to get the pedigree established in case a sudden cataclysm destroys all traces.

> Saturday, 30 July 1938. This morning arrived a letter from Rouge Croix to say that at last the pedigree was registered and complete. Also a peremptory demand from the Inland Revenue for Income Tax – 5s in the £!

The precious documents, beautifully engrossed on vellum and stowed in scarlet pouches, were put into a separate deed-box which my father proposed should be thrown out of the window in case of fire; then, a little more practically, documents and deed-box were stowed in a fireproof safe in the dining room, to the derisive comments of my mother. As things turned out, it was not such a foolish precaution after all. In 1940 the helpful Rouge Croix was killed. On Tuesday, 29 July of that year my father recorded a narrow squeak.

> Called at St Mary Axe to have photostat copies made of the Patent of Arms but found the premises had been wrecked by a bomb, and a demolition squad at work clearing away the debris.

About two years later, while we were all asleep in the spacious Victorian cellar in which we used to spend air raid nights, a stray German bomber in difficulties jettisoned its entire load at the end of the garden. Down came all the ceilings, and in came all the windows. The safe in the dining room, like all the rest of the house, was buried in plaster and glass; from it in due course the pedigree was triumphantly recovered safe and sound.

I was sent away to boarding school in 1939 and during my schooldays I was made aware from time to time of the state of play of my father's further researches. The war might have put a temporary stop to the hunt for ancestors on the other side of the Channel but there was still plenty to follow up at home. Large envelopes would arrive for me which turned out, alas, not to contain the *Wizard* or the *Beano* but an interesting line of research suggesting that the Peters family of Kent was closely connected with the ancient kings of Wales. Feeling in my turn the claims of family piety, I would do my best to remember some of the more obvious landmarks; but I would still cause my father pain from time to time by confusing Flemings with Walloons, or Walloons with Huguenots, or one Peter Peters with another. I soothed any twinge of conscience by promising myself that when my father had at last completed his researches, I would be able to read the story straight through without picking it up seriatim; but in family history the moment when you can say, "There, that's complete," never comes. My father spent a short but happy retirement going on with the hunt, but though he compiled a great deal of material, he never put it all together; and when he died his study was full of documents and papers.

Piety, again, caused me to keep the bundles of family history from the flames of the bonfire as I tidied up after my father's death; my wife observed their arrival in our attic with silent gloom. Her presentiment was sound. Another two years or more went by, and then I too fell a victim to the family history virus. By profession I am the sort of civil servant who used to be called an "Admiralty civilian", liable to serve anywhere at home or abroad, ashore or afloat (and indeed I have visited many exotic seaports, and been seasick in every type of craft known in the Royal Navy); but as the Admiralty withdrew its tentacles from bases all round the world the scope for postings narrowed, and in the mid-1970s I found myself loaned to serve as a temporary diplomat in the British Delegation at the NATO headquarters in Brussels. That was when I remembered seeing among the papers that the Peters family of Canterbury had arrived in a hurry from Gorne in Flanders, where they were called de le Pierre. I thought it would be interesting, and undemanding, to identify the place where they came from while I was on the spot.

I made a start by looking again at my father's researches, which stopped short at Michel de la Pierre, my seven-times-great-grandfather, who crossed the Channel in the year 1635. On 1 November the same year Michel's brother Pierre de la Pierre and his wife Susanne Chiroutre[2] had a daughter Marie baptised in the crypt at Canterbury Cathedral, where the Walloons held their services. On 4 January 1637 a child called Susanne de la Pierre was buried at All Saints, Canterbury, and later that year they buried another

[2] I propose to follow the style of the Walloon records and identify wives by their maiden names.

child; so they probably had at least three children, including the eldest son John, born at Gorne in Flanders, when they came to England. There was also a reference to a François de la Pierre, "son of the late Pierre", who would be of the same vintage as Pierre. Pierre's maternal grandfather was probably called Guiselin or de Guiselin, because a portrait of "great-grandfather Gislin" hung in the gallery at the Blackfriars at the end of the seventeenth century, and there were Guiselin as well as Chiroutre relations in the community at Canterbury.

There seemed, then, to be several promising leads. I was looking for two brothers called Pierre and Michel de la Pierre who came from Gorne in Flanders, whose mother's family name was Guiselin. Pierre had a son John born at Gorne; and he was a doctor, and a Protestant.

Looked at a second time this did not seem so much to go on after all. Had I abandoned the search then, I would have saved myself a lot of time and trouble – and lost much amusement and satisfaction. The first Belgian expert to whom I applied for advice made it clear, politely but firmly, that the lack of information and the obscurity of my origins made it useless to continue the search; this naturally made me determined to prove him wrong.

But how to set about it? The amount that the average Englishman like me knows about the history of the Spanish Netherlands is fairly limited, and I could not readily have said which of the Seventeen Provinces became the Seven. The Army of Flanders and the Spanish Road, the coming of Alva and the Council of Blood, Heiligerlee and Jemmingem: all these were closed books to me. There was nothing for it but to begin at the beginning and teach myself something about Flanders, where the de la Pierre[3] family came from.

[3]From this point I propose to spell the family name de la Pierre in England and de le Pierre on the Continent, according to the usage of the time.

CHAPTER 2

Flanders in The Golden Age

During that convention the people of many nations, French and Picards, Flemings, Burgundians, Germans, men of Hainaut and Brabant, Liège and Holland and Zeeland – all lived together as if they had all been natives of a single kingdom.

"Journal of the Peace of Arras"
by Antoine de la Taverne Monk of St Vaast (1435)

I speak French to my wife, Italian to my mistress and German to my horse.

Emperor Charles V
(whose mother-tongue was Flemish) (1500–58)

No one knows the origin of the name Flanders so anyone is free to explain it. I suspect that like many other place-names it is very old and may derive from the *vla*-root which means "flat" in most European tongues. Even though the name has been at times applied to very large tracts of land as far south as the river Authie in France, which runs into the Channel south of Boulogne, for most of its history Flanders implies the flat land between the river Scheldt, the hills of Artois and the cold grey waters of the North Sea. This setting shaped the character of the hard-working people who built the county of Flanders out of the mud, and created a fertile countryside and a concentration of prosperous towns and cities to rival the Italian republics of the Renaissance. The fifteenth and early sixteenth centuries are to the Low Countries, especially Flanders and Brabant, what the Elizabethan period is in English history, and the seventeenth century to France; it was remembered as a golden age throughout the disasters of the next 150 years, and it seemed a good starting point for my self-education.

If I began around the year 1500 and moved forward, paying

particular attention to the sort of events and documents which might be of value to a family historian, I might possibly meet the de la Pierre family coming back (so to speak) from 1635. It would be too much to expect to identify direct ancestors so early but I might learn something useful about the sort of people they were. National characteristics do not change very much over the centuries: their origins may be complex but the outward signs are plainly visible. The most important of these are landscape and language.

Most of us have a clear idea of the landscape from the painters of Flanders, especially the Breughels, who depicted the little towns, villages and the countryside with a combination of detail and insight that no photographer could match. It is a place of vast open skies, veils of moisture in the air, slow moving streams and long lines of trees; the constantly-changing pattern of weather and light and the greens, browns and greys of a water-country. In geological terms all of this region was laid down during the Tertiary period, when the chalk layers which formed at the bottom of the sea were overlaid by sand and clay. In the Quaternary period the rivers flowing out of the Artois watershed, especially the Aa, the Lys and the Scheldt[1] with their tributaries, cut channels which filled with fertile soil. The line of the coast was liable to shift and to flood, and the river mouths changed shape or even closed up altogether under the force of violent storms: so Bruges, whose canals and dykes are mentioned by Dante, which had been the greatest city in north-west Europe, with bankers and brokers from Lombardy and Tuscany, traders from England and France, Spain and Germany, a large fleet and the first wet-dock in Europe, was ruined by one great storm in 1405 which closed the Zwijn but opened up the Scheldt. Such dangers and difficulties were worth combating; the fertile river margins were reclaimed and then the heaths and marshes, and converted into abundant fields, especially by Cistercian monks in the twelfth and thirteenth centuries; they established their houses in one barren spot after another, improved the land and settled their

[1] Rivers which flow from France change their names from French to Dutch as they cross the language frontier: the Lys becomes the Leie, the Scheldt starts as the Escaut. The same applies to the names of cities and towns, like Bruges, which is called Brugge by its inhabitants.

lay brothers on new farms; they cut ditches and canals, created polders along the coast, and began to clear the surrounding forest. One result of this system was a new class of free peasants, not feudal serfs, settled on the reclaimed land; a development which may explain why Belgians tend to share with the English an awkward and contrary attitude to authority which depresses their governments but pleases and encourages their friends.

It is impossible to get very far in describing the landscape of Flanders without coming up against the very marked characteristics of the people who made it. Tight-fisted, humorous, stubborn, courageous, independent and very private, the character of the people of Flanders is revealed very clearly in every portrait painting from the fifteenth century onwards. However refined and delicate the clothes and jewels, the wearer is obviously someone who loves driving a hard bargain whether in business, diplomacy or the marriage-contract. The founder of the county when it emerged from the confusion of the Viking raids of the ninth century was a fine example of the type. His name was Baldwin Iron Arm and he kidnapped Judith, daughter of Charles the Bald of France. Excommunicated by the shocked bishops of France, Baldwin went to Rome to blackmail the pope, threatening to join the Norsemen and lend them a hand in pillaging what churches and monasteries were still intact. The pope, concluding sensibly that Baldwin was the sort of person it was better to have on your side (and preferably far away), arranged for him to be restored to respectability, and appointed him King Charles's man in the northern marches, to protect them from the Norsemen he had threatened to join. From that day to this the people of Flanders have never been overscrupulous in pursuit of the advancement of their private and family affairs; and Flanders began to be organised as a county in the marshlands around the present towns of Ghent, Bruges and St Omer, to act in general in support of (but by no means necessarily subject to) the kings of France.

From its beginnings Flanders lay athwart the ancient frontier of the Roman Empire, and of the line between the Romance and Germanic languages which is, with the landscape, the most important characteristic of the county. The "language frontier" has marked a major political divide ever since the last days of the Roman Empire. Between the breaking up of the empire and the stabilising of a new frontier between the Frankish kingdoms and the Saxons, the line moved, but only a little, towards the north. Today it runs from the northern tip of France at Dunkirk to the southern tip of Holland at Maastricht. This language frontier is as clear and sharp on the ground, and on the map, as any international frontier. If you drive or cycle or walk across it, you pass in a few hundred yards from a village with a French name and French-speaking people to one with a Flemish name whose people speak Flemish and write in Dutch. The Saxon place-names on the Flemish side are as easily distinguishable as those of English towns and villages: they end in *berg* (hill), *dal* or *dael* (dale, valley), *beek* (beck, stream), *poel* (pool), *brock* (brook), *bos* (wood), *ghern* or *heim* (home, dwelling). Like the Anglo-Saxons in England, the Franks, and the Saxons who came after them in Flanders, had a word for strangers, "walla" or babbler. In Britain the Celtic strangers were pushed into Wales and Cornwall, in Flanders the Celtic predecessors of the Franks came to be called "Walloons". The main determining characteristic was, and is, language; anyone in Flanders who spoke French (Picard or Walcq) was a Walloon, and anyone who spoke the Flemish dialect of Low German was a Fleming.

It has to be admitted that Flemish is not a beautiful sound to a well-spoken Dutchman; and Walcq is likewise sneered at by the Frenchmen to the south. Here is an example of Walcq in a description of the county from De Smet's *Recueil des Chroniques de Flandres*.

> *La Comtée de Flandres est divisée en deulx par la rivière de Liz, car tout ce qui est dechà de Liz du costi de noort est nommé Flandres Flamingant, et tout ce qui est delà le Liz et vers le zuut est nommé Gallicant depuis Menin. . . . Flandres Gallicant sont les chastelz, villes et chastelleneries de Lille, de Douay et Orchies où on parl langage Walcq.*

The de la Pierre family of Canterbury were certainly Walloon and so they came, it seemed, from "Flandres Gallicant", and as I proceeded with the search I became familiar with the *langage Walcq*. It has a tendency, as shown above, to turn "c" into "ch" so that a doctor is a *medechin*, and a letter may start off:

> *Eschrist par Jacque Desrumaulx, l'ongimme*
> *jour du moy de Nobvembre l'an XV^{c}Soixante et 1X.*

(Written by Jacques Desrumaux, the eleventh day of the month of November in the year 1569.)

One soon gets used to it. It may take longer for a visitor to appreciate that the division between the languages runs through the whole of Belgian life today, as it did in the past, and you must be very sure of your company before you raise the subject of Fleming or Walloon; indeed a stranger is well advised never to raise it at all. However, the criticisms of outsiders, and especially of neighbours to the north and south, result in an instant rallying of the ranks. I therefore discovered that whereas family history may be a comparatively uncomplicated pursuit of facts, the religious and political history of Flanders is something quite different.

From the point of view of politics and religion Flanders, that flat and dull-looking region, has long been one of the earthquake belts of Europe. Besides the language frontier running from west to east and imposing its tensions, there is also a north-south divide between the French and German spheres of influence which dates from the time of Charlemagne's heirs. It is hardly surprising therefore that the history of Flanders is one of constant manoeuvres by outsiders seeking to dominate the region. So when Europe began to take shape in the thirteenth century and settled into the large political units whose alliances and wars were to create the modern world – France, the Empire, Castile and Aragon, Portugal, England – the Low Countries remained separate, and unstable. This is the reason why the name Flanders so often conjures up an image of mud and blood; and it explains why Flanders has sent so many emigrants in every direction. In Brussels, my German colleague was a general from a Prussian family which had produced many military men: I found that his ancestors had set out eastwards from one small town in Flanders at about the same time as mine left in the opposite direction from another.

However the very fact of outside pressures has always helped the inhabitants of Flanders to stick together: the plain truth is that they dislike the people of the neighbouring states even more than they dislike each other. This underlying cohesion is easily overlooked by outsiders. People tend to speak as if Belgium and the Netherlands today are comparatively new nations, dating as they do from 1830 and 1581; yet even their present frontiers are older than those of most countries in the modern world – certainly older than those of the UK, the USA, France, the Federal Republic of Germany, the USSR.

After Baldwin Iron Arm, the counts of Flanders called themselves *Marchios*, Marcher Lords, and though they were nominally the king of France's men they saw that their interest lay in changing sides adroitly from time to time, so as to take advantage of the balance of power. As a result they were often allied to England, and always closely connected with English affairs. Thus (in family history terms) Baldwin Iron Arm's bride was not only a daughter of the king of France but also the widow of the Anglo-Saxon king, Ethelwulf of Wessex; his son married a daughter of Alfred the Great; and Baldwin V of Flanders was the father-in-law of William the Conqueror.

In the Middle Ages the cloth industry of Flanders made growing use of English wool as well as home-grown flax, until by 1300 Ghent was the biggest producer of cloth in western Europe; the English industry expanded with the help of Flemish weavers, and more and more English cloth (rather than English raw materials) was imported into the Netherlands during the two centuries after the Black Death. The cloth industry and the cloth trade brought great prosperity to both countries; in Flanders it also brought most of the social features of the industrial revolution centuries before the steam engine was invented. From the early Middle Ages there was a marked difference between the country towns of northern France, which lived on and for the surrounding country, and the towns of Flanders where there was an "urban proletariat" making textiles for export. These "industrial" towns were very large indeed by contemporary standards. In the 1300s only Paris north of the Alps had a bigger population than Ghent's 60,000; Bruges had 35,000, which was not far short of the population of London after the Black Death. The Flanders towns worked like factories, with the church clock marking the hours of work and the master providing premises and wool for the weavers: the rules of work were strict, apparently based on a system borrowed from Byzantium. So highly organised was the business that enterprising people began to establish new towns, free from the constraints of the "bosses and the unions" (*réunions de métier*) of the old. Out in the countryside labour costs were low and there was land to buy, free from restrictions; this was the origin of such places as Armentières, and of the new textile industries established by the counts of Flanders in the little towns along the language frontier on the river Lys.

The export trade was equally highly organised. Arras exported cloth to Italy, St Omer to England, Ghent to the empire; and English merchants travelled through Wissant, Thérouanne, Arras and Rheims on their way to the rich markets of the south. Great bourgeois families established themselves, like the Lanstier and the Hucquedieu in Arras and the Markiet in Douai; they spent a good deal of their time on the road, so as to turn over their capital in trade, in caravans of giant wagons that carried cloth all the way to Lombardy and beyond. Today on the motorways along the Rhine one sees the juggernauts from every country in Europe still engaged in the same pursuit of prosperity; the rivers and canals are crowded with giant barges ploughing up from Rotterdam, successors of the craft which thronged the waterways of the Middle Ages.

Gradually, for all their wealth and desire for independence, the towns and little states of the Netherlands were forced into the system of larger European units. In 1384 Philip the Bold the duke of Burgundy, uncle of the king Charles VI of France, inherited the county of Flanders; during the next century, he and his descendants by purchase or marriage added Namur, Hainaut, Holland, Zeeland, Brabant, Limburg and Luxembourg to the Burgundian lands. The Grand Council and the States-General were established; the Netherlands were ruled from Brussels. When Charles duke of Burgundy married Margaret of York, a sister of Edward IV of England, the re-establishment of the Anglo-Burgundian alliance was celebrated at Bruges in 1468 with a party so splendid that even the locals remembered. (They had high standards of comparison. When Duke Philip the Good gave a banquet at Lille in 1454, there were "pantomimes" between the courses and an enormous pasty opened to reveal an orchestra of 28 players. Cecil B de Mille seldom attempted so much.) But Charles resembled his Yorkist relatives too much. Like them, he could not resist display and unnecessary gambles; he threw away first his silver bath-tub, then his life in wholly unnecessary battles. When the Swiss and the men of Lorraine killed him outside the walls of Nancy on 5 January 1477 all his possessions went to his only child Mary. Naturally the would-be husbands flocked around. One was the dauphin of France, another was Adolf duke of Gelderland the "local boy", but it was the third suitor Maximilian of Austria, son of the emperor, who won the hand of the princess and married her at Bruges in August 1477. So the Habsburgs beat the Valois to the prize, and when Maximilian's grandson Charles was born in 1500 he was heir to Spain and the Holy Roman Empire as well as the Netherlands.

Charles, later the Emperor Charles V or "Charles Quint", was born in Flanders, at Ghent, and Flemish was his mother tongue; and like a true man of Flanders he did not rest content with his inheritance, huge as it was, but went on accumulating more. He added Friesland, Groningen, Utrecht and Gelderland to his possessions in the Netherlands, until by 1548 he was able to unite them with a common supreme court, a common States-General, and a central government at Brussels. The result was the Seventeen Provinces[2] whose brief union seemed to set the seal on the golden age of Burgundy.

I suspect that the people who lived during those exciting times tended not to see things from the same exalted point of view as their rulers. The wars and excitements that brought power and glory to the king or the emperor was usually bad news for his subjects, and certainly the subjects of Charles V had plenty to contend with. Perhaps because of this, some tended to look back with nostalgia on the great days of Burgundy as a time when the many nationalities living in the crowded cities and countryside of the Low Countries were peaceful and prosperous. The monk of St Vaast who wrote the "Journal of the Peace of Arras", whose words are quoted at the head of this chapter, noted how the dukes of Burgundy had given unity to people whose subsequent history was one of continual warfare and contention. The Burgundian territories were as diffuse and their inhabitants as diverse as those of the Austro-Hungarian empire, and no one was quite sure how to describe the Low Countries and the people living in them. The most usual term for the country was "*les pays d'embas*", later "*les Pays-bas*". As for the people, the Italians called them "*Fiamminghi*", Flemings.

[2] The Seven (Northern) Provinces were Holland, Friesland, Groningen, Drente, Overijsel, Gueldre, Utrecht. The Ten (Southern) Provinces were Brabant, Limburg, Flanders, Hainaut, Luxembourg, Artois, "French Flanders", Namur, Tournai and Mechelen. The national emblem was a lion holding a sword and a sheaf of 17 arrows representing the provinces.

The Germans called them "*Niederländer*", the English "Netherlanders". The French called them "*Bourguignons*", Burgundians, which in typical French dismissive style was the term applied to the "Imperialists" in general; and indeed the army of Flanders of the following centuries fought under the red St Andrew's cross of Burgundy.

What did the people call themselves? Before Charles V's reforms they were inhabitants of a fine-sounding collection of little states: the duchies of Burgundy, Lotharingia, Brabant, Limburg, Luxembourg, Gueldre; the counties of Flanders, Artois, Hainaut, Holland, Zeeland, Namur and Zutphen; the marquisate of the Holy Roman Empire; the seigneuries of Frisia, Utrecht, Overijsse, Groningen, Faulquemont, Daelhem, Selins, Maastricht and Mechelen: indeed it was a considerable feat of local government reform when these ancient and picturesque units were reduced to the Seventeen Provinces. However, it is dukes and counts and marquises who think in terms of duchies, counties and marquisates. The people thought of themselves as inhabitants either of a town – the great Erasmus, one of the most important men in Europe, was "Erasmus of Rotterdam" – or of a province, or rather of a *pays*.

It was, and is, common in Flanders, as it is in France, to apply local names to regions which derive their particular character from some physical or other peculiarity. There are nine such units, or *pays*, in Flanders between the Lys and the Scheldt, most of them dating back to the origins of the county in the tenth century. Baroeil, Tournaisis and Escrebieu are the *pays* round Lille, Tournai and Douai respectively; Ferrain refers to the hills between the rivers Deule and Lys; Carembault the plateau between the Lys and La Bassée; Mélantois the chalk uplands between Lille and Tournai; Pévèle is the basin between Mélantois and the Scarpe; Ostrevant the dry sandy *pays* between the Scarpe and the Scheldt, and Gohelle the part between Pévèle and the chalk hills of Artois. Just over the border in Artois is the Pays de l'Alleu between the Lys and its tributary the Lawe; and further downstream and north of the Lys is the Pays de Weppe. Of these names, the Pays de l'Alleu crops up most frequently in this story, and deserves some explanation. It sounds as if it has something to do with alluvium, and indeed the *pays* is very low-lying and waterlogged; but the name is derived from the Latin *elymosina* and is a feudal term meaning free of dues.

An *alleu* (called in Flemish *vrije erve* or *vrije grond*) is land which did not belong to a superior authority, so that when the free-holder died it could be bequeathed unimpaired to his direct or collateral heirs. Such incentives were usually designed to encourage settlement.

By the time that I had collected such basic information on the lie of the land and the state of Flanders at the start of the sixteenth century, I was beginning to feel distinctly uneasy about the possibility of tracing the origins of the de la Pierre family. That is usual when total ignorance gives way to partial knowledge: the more you go on, the more you realise how much you do not know, indeed cannot possibly know. The trouble with looking for ancestors in Flanders is that there were so many people there. If the de la Pierre family came from the countryside the chance of finding them seemed about as remote as the prospects of the fat smiling babies in Breughel's "Massacre of the Innocents". If they came from a town, it looked even worse. For example, it had seemed worth trying out the hypothesis that "Gorne in Flanders" where the de la Pierres came from was Ghent, supposing that the English clerk had misheard a Walloon pronunciation, as Ghent is called "Gand" by Walloons; but the difficulty in identifying individual citizens is immense.

Ghent in 1500, built on twenty-three islands at the junction of the Lys and the Scheldt, had over two hundred bridges, and over 100,000 inhabitants. Such towns contained many fine and beautiful buildings; they were also desperately dirty, crowded and smelly, so much so that even their inhabitants noticed it. It was not until near the end of the sixteenth century that the linen-bleachers were ordered to use separate "stinkerds" in which to dump their dye, so as not to pollute the water which had to be used by other industries as well as by people. The cotton-printers dumped their inks and dyes into the canals. There were paper mills, breweries, distilleries, chandleries, soap-works, brick-works, madder-ovens, tanneries (which used whale-oil and were called "*stinkmolen*"), all working away and polluting the air and the water. Things have not changed all that much: as you drive down the auto-route today, your nose tells you that you are getting near Ghent as soon as it begins to sniff the horrible smells from the chemical works on the outskirts.

In between the towns (which were almost continuous in places) every patch and parcel of land was intensively cultivated to provide food for the urban masses; the work was attractive and profitable for smallholders with large families, just as it still is today. It was done on the "Chinese system"; besides the night soil of the towns and the dung from the cattle-byres, pigeon droppings and ash were dug into the soil, and fallow was unheard of. Cereals (wheat, rye, barley, oats) and greens (colza, cabbage), vegetables and legumes (beans, clover, vetches) and root crops (turnips, carrots, beetroots); later potatoes and tobacco from the New World; all were intensively cultivated. Cattle and piglets were raised for the town markets. In their free time, surely strictly limited, the farmer and his family and farmhands occupied themselves with weaving for the men, spinning for the women. All told, it was a scene of industry so amazing that I was almost inclined to disbelieve it; and it caused as much amazement and admiration then among visiting strangers as the Irish navvies who showed the world how to build railways in the 1840s and 1850s.

It is also a scene which is rather daunting to the family historian trying to identify an ancestor. How can one possibly identify, out of those teeming towns and villages of Flanders, one small family that set out for England in 1635?

CHAPTER 3

The Reformation in Flanders under Charles V

1520–55

> If princes command anything contrary to God, this is not to be obeyed. . . . If they command anything arising out of the public interest, this must be obeyed. . . . If any of their commands are tyrannical, here too the magistrate is to be suffered for charity's sake in all cases where change is impossible without public commotion and sedition.
>
> The humanist Philip Melancthon, 1521

> Father Martin Luther of the order of St Augustine, supporter of old and damned heresies and inventor of new ones.
>
> from the Second Proclamation by Charles V against heretics, 1521

> 23 February 1545 – Marie De Le Pierre – Buried alive.
>
> Archives of the city of Tournai

The first way to narrow down the search, in any old-fashioned detective story, is to consider motive. Why would a family take the enormous step of moving from its home town or village or farm and crossing the Channel to England?

There are several possible motives, some of which could work in combination. In particular, the need to find a livelihood for a family and the need to escape from war have compelled people throughout history to move from one place to another; in the sixteenth and seventeenth centuries a third and more powerful motive still was added: religion. The Reformation divided and polarised the states of Europe for the best part of these two centuries, beginning with

31

persecution and internal repressions, then proceeding to civil war, and war between nations; war brought pillage, famine and plague. Many families were thrown into turmoil by these events, and moved at least for a while to a safer town or province. The families who decided to make a permanent move to another country, even to cross the Channel or the Atlantic, were often seeking freedom of religion as well as safety. Knowing that the de la Pierre family in England attended the Walloon church it seemed worthwhile assuming that a hunt among the Protestants of Flanders would narrow the search considerably; by the end of the sixteenth century Protestants were very rare birds in the southern provinces of the Netherlands.

The Walloon church had been very helpful in my father's search because the records of births, marriages and deaths contained more details and had survived better than the Anglican parish registers of the period. With any luck their religious beliefs would equally help to identify people in the Netherlands. The persecution of heretics started sooner there and claimed more victims than anywhere else in Europe, and the cases were fairly well documented in the State Papers; that much I knew, and that over the border in France the wars of religion had been particularly bloodthirsty; but I felt that without more details of the course of the Reformation in Flanders and Artois it would be a matter of searching blindfold. The first thing to do was to find some general introduction to the Reformation in the southern provinces of the Netherlands, from the time of the emperor Charles V.

It was easier said than done. In the middle of the sixteenth century there were perhaps 100,000 Protestants in the Netherlands, mainly in Flanders, Brabant, Hainaut and Artois; by the end of the century there was, officially, none: those who had refused to conform were dead, in prison, or refugees in foreign lands. The Walloon refugees abroad mostly became naturalised in the countries to which they had fled, and those who still clung to their language and customs were swamped by the many thousands of Protestants who left France at the revocation of the Edict of Nantes in 1685. Today, while there are a number of surviving French Protestant churches which mark the site of former Walloon settlements, for instance, at Canterbury, only a tiny handful of Walloon churches are left, mostly in the modern kingdom of the Netherlands; and to unearth the story of the early days of the reform in the southern provinces is not easy. Certainly there are very many books about the Reformation, the Dutch revolt, and other aspects of a period which has always fascinated historians;[1] but the reform that was snuffed out, the revolt that failed, have not found a place in any English account so far as I could discover.

As Geoffrey Parker puts it:

> The problem of overabundant source material on the Dutch Revolt only exists . . . for those able to read the languages of all the governments involved in the struggle Spanish, Dutch, English, French and German. For the English reader the situation with regard to sources is enormously simplified: there is scarcely anything left.

If that is the case for the interesting story of the Dutch revolt, it is even more so for the story of the Walloon rebellion. The most instructive of the moderns[2] are concerned with the main action: the political, social and economic developments as Spain and the Turks, Spain and France, Spain and the Dutch rebels gained or lost ground in their constant struggle for the upper hand. They are less concerned with the fortunes (usually misfortunes) of the people of the border provinces in between the main antagonists. Similarly, historians of the Reformation, like G. R. Elton, and of the Protestant exiles like Agnew, tend to deal with the success stories, Calvinism in France and Switzerland, Lutheranism in Germany, the more distinguished French and German Protestants, rather than with the masses of Walloon refugees most of whom were practically destitute and few of them men of distinction. If I wanted a brisk summary of what happened to the Protestants of Wallonia under Charles V, I would have to compile it myself, mainly from the Belgian studies and documents.

Luckily I was in the right place to make a start, because the Bibliothèque Albert Premier in Brussels is a first-class library full of material about the history of the southern provinces, including many sets of documents published by the excellent Belgian Royal Historical Commission; from these it was possible first to grasp the

[1] A comprehensive list of books and articles on the Dutch revolt runs to over 300 titles.

[2] Braudel for the general scene, Geoffrey Parker for Spain and the Netherlands, Robin Briggs for early modern France.

outlines of the growth and suppression of Protestantism in the Netherlands, and then to identify the sort of documents which might be of some value for identifying individual Protestant families.

The repression of heretics in the Netherlands had begun even before the famous confrontation between Charles V and Martin Luther at Worms in April 1521; and it was more severe than in any other country, not excluding Spain. In September 1520 Charles V received the Papal Nuncio at Antwerp and immediately afterwards issued the first of a series of "placards" or proclamations against heresy. The text of the first placard is lost but it probably dealt with suppressing heretical books rather than people, because in October the Nuncio, Jerome Alexander, caused a number of books to be burnt in public, and the following March a second placard was issued against heretical writings. After April 1521 Luther, who acknowledged his writings but refused to recant, got away to Wartburg, where he settled down to translate the Bible into German, but there was no safe conduct for his followers. The Edict of Worms announcing the final outcome of this meeting denounced the Lutheran heresy and demanded that all princes should suppress it. Charles moved swiftly. Like his fellow monarchs Henry VIII in England, François I in France and Leo X in Rome, he was not disposed to waste time which could be better spent (in war, for example) arguing the toss with dreary heretics. He issued a third placard applying these instructions throughout the former Burgundian territory: all magistrates were to prosecute the followers of "Father Martin Luther of the order of Saint Augustine, supporter of old and damned heresies and inventor of new ones", under pain of death and confiscation of goods. Later, a placard issued on 14 October 1529 and another on 7 October 1531 made death the penalty for all offences connected with heresy. Full-scale persecution began.

Slowly, in spite of repression and against all reasonable expectation, the new ideas made headway, spreading into France and Switzerland, and even into the provinces of the Netherlands. Admittedly the first signs in the Netherlands were not particularly heroic. One of Luther's first followers was the prior of Antwerp, and in 1521 he preached against indulgences. His name was Jacques Proost, and he came from Ypres. Proost was arrested, and promptly recanted; released, he "reformed" again, but sensibly took himself off at once to Bremen and safety. Those who followed him were made of sterner stuff and so were their persecutors. In 1522 François van der Hulst, a layman, was made Grand Inquisitor in Flanders, Brabant, Holland, Zeeland, Hainaut and Artois, charged with seeking out all individuals "infected with the venom of heresy". Van der Hulst had full powers of arrest, investigation and punishment, and he soon began to hunt out heretics. The first executions came in 1523: on 1 July of that year Jean Voes, Henri van Esschen and Lambert Thoren, ex-Augustinians like Luther, were burnt in the Grand' Place in Brussels, the first Protestant martyrs in the world. On 26 July the first folios of the first translation of the New Testament into Dutch began to come off the presses of Adrien van Bergen. The Reformation of the Netherlands was under way.

The next years of the early Reformation have been described as a time of "magnificent anarchy", and certainly there was plenty of variety in the Netherlands: Lutherans, Anabaptists, followers of Martin Bucer of Strasbourg and of Zwingli at Zürich, Joris Cassander of Bruges, and others; the government called them Lutherans, Anabaptists or Sectaries and van der Hulst the Inquisitor did his best to suppress them whatever they were. He soon made himself so unpopular that he had to lie low for a while. On 21 February 1524 the governor-general wrote to the emperor:

> Because of the harsh conduct of Mr van der Hulst in his role as Inquisitor, all your subjects in the Netherlands, and particularly those in Flanders, Holland and Antwerp, have taken a great dislike to him (*ont conçu un grand regret contre lui*), to the point where he dares not show himself in these provinces nor at Antwerp.

All the same the suppression of heresy went on. In 1529 Charles decreed that heretics who repented should be beheaded not burnt; women, as a humane gesture, were simply to be buried alive. Many hundreds of people were to be executed in the Netherlands (though only a select few are counted as Protestant martyrs) and tens of thousands more were to be imprisoned or banished, or to flee into exile for safety; until the last victim, an unfortunate servant girl called Annelise van den Hove, was buried alive in the Grand' Place in Brussels on 15 July 1591. Her death caused such a revulsion of feeling that the death penalty was used no more in the southern provinces for matters of religion.

What is most important is to note the very different methods of tackling Protestantism which were adopted in France and Germany on the one hand, and in England and the Netherlands on the other. In the first two countries, king and emperor were forced to make concessions to powerful subjects: in the second two, no concessions were thought necessary, or granted. Thus when Charles V allowed freedom of worship in Germany in 1532 he expressly forbade it in the Netherlands; while in England Henry VIII's reforms were to lead to the establishment of authorised worship and the suppression of the old religion, which his son Edward VI developed, his daughter Mary reversed, and after her Elizabeth again followed. Concessions were made where they could not be avoided, otherwise every ruler agreed that if he had the power to impose uniformity it was his duty to do so, to spare the mass of his subjects the horrors of civil war. No one who studies what happened in France and Germany in the sixteenth and seventeenth centuries as a result of the concessions made to powerful Protestant subjects can very well argue that Charles was wrong to aim at the complete suppression of heresy in the Netherlands. What is more, he very nearly succeeded.

The 1530s saw two important developments for French-speaking Protestants. In 1533 a twenty-four-year old student of theology and the law called Jean Calvin, younger son of a notary from Noyon in Picardy, underwent a sudden religious conversion which convinced him that he was under God's orders to proclaim the truth; then in October 1534 some unknown reformers plastered the walls of Paris and other French cities, and even the king's own bedroom at Amboise, with posters denouncing the Catholic doctrines of the mass and the Eucharist. These were in a sense placards, but the reverse of Charles's sort. In the ensuing clamp-down by the authorities Calvin found it prudent to take flight, and his travels brought him to Ferrara, to Strasbourg, to Basle where in 1536 he published his *Institution of the Christian Religion*; and later in the same year to Geneva to guide the reform there. The *Ecclesiastical Ordinances* was published in November 1541, and from them were derived the characteristics of all the later Calvinist churches.

Calvin the Reformer soon replaced Luther the Protestant (to use the old distinction) as the leading figure of the Reformation in western Europe outside Germany and Scandinavia. In the Netherlands the new ideas spread from the south rather than the east, and so it came about that first the Walloons and then the Flemish and Dutch Protestants formed Calvinist rather than Lutheran congregations. This made things more difficult for the authorities. The first persecutions had generally dealt with the unfortunate Anabaptists, who were regarded as fair game wherever they appeared, since their idea of religion had no more place in it for pastors or elders or deacons than for priests; the Calvinists were much harder to tackle. As G. R. Elton explains it,

> Under the pressure of persecution and resistance the Calvinists grew in self-reliance and contempt for all others; by no means sectarians in intent, they nevertheless acquired the sectarian's unshakable endurance in the face of adversity, an endurance born of their conviction that they were the Lord's elect. And the Calvinist system of Church government enabled them to translate this spirit into action. Based on the individual congregation with its tight order, its elective principles, and its active mixture of lay and clerical participation, Calvinist groups were extraordinarily difficult to root out and sometimes even difficult to detect.

Was it possible that one of these "individual congregations" was the spiritual home of the de la Pierre family; and if so, which one? My thoughts turned towards the archives at Tournai, a very important city of French Flanders and a noted centre of Protestantism from the earliest days. Charles V had added Tournai to his possessions by conquest in 1521, though by long tradition it was loyal to the kings of France; indeed, Childeric had died and Clovis had been born there, so Tournai could claim to be the birthplace of the French royal line. In the middle of the sixteenth century, as we shall see, Tournai became a stronghold of Protestantism in the southern provinces, and at one stage held out for two months against the Spanish captain-general. Moreover there was some evidence from the Walloon registers at Canterbury to link the name de la Pierre with Tournai. For example, Peronne de la Pierre, born at Tournai, the widow of Harmon le Febvre, married Jan Lienard at Canterbury on 30 November 1595; and Arnout de la Pierre the son of Pierre, born at Tournai, was in London at the end of the century. I knew of no direct connection between these early refugees and the de la Pierre family of 1635; but Tournai might not be a bad place to look for the origins of the family on the other side of the Channel.

There are no surviving records of Protestant baptisms and marriages at Tournai; but there are, from the earliest years of the reform, records of Protestant deaths. Heretics were criminals, and their crimes, trials and executions were recorded in documents which have survived in considerable numbers, either in the central records of the governor-general in Brussels or in the municipal archives of the larger towns. The records at Tournai are particularly useful, especially the *Régistres aux Comptes Généraux* and the *Régistres de la Loi*. For example, on 13 July 1528 Henri of Westphalia was executed: he was an Augustinian and so belonged to the first generation of reformers. During the 1530s there were no executions for heresy, but a number of lesser sentences were imposed, prison, fines, pilgrimages, public penances. Then came the 1540s which was a decade of persecution throughout the Netherlands. On 16 July 1541 Jean Deprez from Peruwelz was executed at Tournai, and on 14 June 1542 Dominique le Gilon met the same end. In the spring of 1545 there came a whole string of executions.

The chief actor in the events of spring 1545 was Pierre Brully, a famous Protestant minister from Mercy-le-Haut. His is a fascinating story, and typical of a Protestant pastor in those hair-raising times. A very early convert to Calvinism, he arrived from Strasbourg in 1537 to preach the word of the Lord in French Flanders, Hainaut and Artois. He looked after the small and hidden Calvinist communities of Valenciennes, Tournai, Arras and Lille, and encouraged them with edifying tales of the rule of the godly in Geneva: psalm-singing by the congregation, strict rules for marriage,[3] the Eucharist under both kinds, and other features of the new Calvinist revolution. Brully survived for a while in his dangerous ministry but in 1544 the emperor and the king of France made peace so as to be able to turn their attention to the extirpation of heresy in their dominions, for which purpose they agreed that each would extradite any heretic who took refuge in the other's

[3] Until the conclusion of the Council of Trent in 1563 the Catholic Church's arrangements for marriage were fairly free and easy. Provided there was full and mutual consent between the parties and the union was consummated, that was good enough for the Church.

realms: frontier-hopping was a common method of keeping one jump ahead of the law. The hunt was up and Brully was cornered at Tournai; but hidden by friends he decided to emulate St Paul and have himself lowered over the town wall by night. At first all went well, but then, alas, the scriptural pattern was broken: a clumsy friend leant over the parapet with a last message and dislodged a stone which fell on Brully, breaking his thigh. The sound of his groans attracted the watch and he was caught and hauled off to prison. A number of his disciples soon followed him.

Trials and condemnations followed the inevitable course. At the end of January 1545 two (or possibly three) of Brully's followers were executed, Arnould Estaluffret and Pieter Myoche (it may be that "Pieter Myoche" was Arnould's alias) on 30 January; Jean de Barbigant the next day. On 5 February Roland de Grimaupont followed them to the scaffold; and on 19 February Pierre Brully himself was burnt, ending his life as an "obstinate heretic" and setting the sort of example to his flock which was expected of a Protestant minister in the heroic age of the reform. The final scene was on 23 February, when a husband and wife were executed. Jacques de la Tombe, a tailor from Roubaix, was beheaded, and his wife was buried alive. Her name was Marie, or Marion, de la Pierre.

It was rather exciting to find this record, sad as it was, of Marie de le Pierre and her husband Jacques de la Tombe. It did not prove, of course, that a Protestant family called de la Pierre was likely to have come from Tournai, but in my game of Hunt the Slipper it certainly counted as "warm" rather than "cold". Even Agnew, the historian of French Protestant exiles whose standards of genealogy were austere, allowed that the Ogiers of Canterbury were probably of the same clan as Robert Ougier, executed with his wife and two sons at Lille in March 1557, and that the prolific Caron family in London and Canterbury were of the same family as Antoine Karon, burnt as a heretic at Cambrai in 1561. Indeed my hopes were raised still further by the name of the very next Protestant to be executed at Tournai: Quentin Theiffry of Ath, who died on Christmas eve 1546 along with Jean Lecomte of Arras. I knew that Elizabeth Barling was descended from several Walloon refugee families, including a certain William Thieffries, a spice-merchant living at Tournai in the parish of St Piat, and married to Helene Bousin; he was condemned for heresy and imprisoned in the cells at Notre Dame church, but managed to escape to England. It would be very respectable as well as satisfying to be able to prove a link between the de le Pierre and Theiffry sufferers of the 1540s and my Peters and Barling ancestors two hundred years later.

Respectable, but difficult, though not for the first reason that springs to mind, namely that an execution is likely to mark a fairly definite full stop in a family line. Families in the sixteenth century tended to be large, and although there were one or two cases, mainly involving Anabaptists, where an entire family died on the scaffold, this was exceptional even by contemporary standards. Mostly the dead were survived by widows, children, brothers and sisters, cousins, uncles and aunts; many of them perhaps in sympathy with their opinions though they managed to avoid their fate, usually by hasty emigration. A family name in a list of the condemned can serve as a useful pointer; if a person of that surname from that place at that time was convicted of heresy, then a family of Protestants found in England or one of the other countries of refuge about the same time might well be related more or less closely. The difficulty is to prove the link, because the records surviving from the 1540s onwards are much more patchy on the continent than in England, where we have been spoiled by freedom from invasion and the survival of parish records in a surprisingly complete state.[4] The former Burgundian territory and the northernmost provinces of France were not so fortunate, and it is harder to come by evidence concerning the ordinary citizens. In order to appreciate the difficulties, and the possibilities, it is necessary for someone hunting a Walloon ancestor on the continent to know something about the main types of record available.

Take France first: after the campaigns of Louis XIV during the seventeenth century most of Walloon Flanders was finally absorbed into French territory and now forms part of the Département du Nord, so its archives are found among the Archives du Nord at Lille. For the family historian the basic documents form what is called the

---

[4]Henry VIII ordered parish registers to be kept, starting in 1538, and several hundred parishes (out of 11,000 all told) have records surviving from that time. There are also rich stores of earlier manorial and court records, tax returns and other sources of information.

état civil. The *état* of a person, in French law, is his status as regards the enjoyment and exercise of his rights, his *droits privés*. In the Middle Ages, and subsequently, it was the clergy who recorded the facts about the *état* of their parishioners which are of most interest to their descendants. Then in 1406 Henry the Bearded, bishop of Nantes, ordered his diocesan clergy to keep a record of baptisms with the names of godfather and godmother; his concern, and the constant preoccupation of the parish clergy, was to ensure that in the small and interbreeding communities of the *pays* marriage within the forbidden degrees of kindred was avoided.

In August 1539, soon after Henry VIII's decree in England, François I by the ordinance of Villers-Cotterets ordered all the parish priests of France to record baptisms and burials, and to send the registers every year to the local *bailli* or *sénéschal*; he was probably less concerned with the marriage of cousins than with the collection of facts and figures needed for comprehensive and thorough tax-collection. In the rest of Christendom it was not until the conclusion of the Council of Trent in 1563 that the Catholic clergy were ordered to keep records of baptisms and marriages. In this as in other respects the Church was reacting to the example set by Protestants. In 1559 the first national synod of the French Reformed Church was held (in secret) in Paris, and it was decided there that each Protestant community should keep a register of baptisms and marriages.

Such were the principles: the practice was not always perfect, and wars and disasters, thefts and losses, human error and negligence, have taken their toll through the centuries. In France and Belgium as a general rule the parish registers began earlier in the larger towns than in the villages, and the first surviving registers usually date from towards the end of the sixteenth century. There are exceptions: if you happen to come from the town of Givry (Saône et Loire) you will find registers going all the way back to 1334, thanks to a long line of diligent priests; for Roz-Landrieux (Île et Villaine) there are records for the period 1451–1528; but these cases are rare. In Belgium the oldest-known registers are those of the parish of St Gudule at Brussels, for the period 25 May 1482 to 2 September 1497; fighting and fire have ravaged the records in what is now Belgium even more than those of Northern France, and you are very lucky to find any registers going further back than 1565.

This will help to explain my pleasure in finding the reference to Marie de le Pierre in the records at Tournai, and even though I could find no other record of her existence it seemed worthwhile to go on looking for traces in the neighbourhood of that city. I knew that Pierre de la Pierre had come from "Gorne in Flanders": was there a place of that name, or something like it, in the Tournaisis, the *pays* of which Tournai is the focus?

In trying to answer this question I came across some more of the difficulties which lie in wait for ancestor-hunters in Belgium. It is hard to find a good modern map of a Belgian province, such as one needs to search the countryside by car. This is surprising, considering that some of the greatest cosmographers including the great Mercator himself were men of Flanders, and that the superb maps of the southern provinces made in 1771–8 at the order of the Comte de Ferraris are some of the finest examples of their sort. For modern Belgium the available road maps are a sad come-down for those used to the Ordnance Survey; and I pored for a long time over the province of Hainaut (where Tournai is) without finding anywhere called anything like Gorne. I was no more successful with the much better French maps of the frontier region; good as they are for motorists and military engineers, the maps of Michelin and the Institut Géographique National are not in the same class as the old one-inch Ordnance Survey for the purposes of an amateur topographer and family historian.

It is not only the poor quality of the maps which hinders research in French Flanders and Artois: the physical structure itself which the maps record has been simply rubbed out in the course of centuries of warfare, especially in the wide swathes of ground where the front lines of the Great War of 1914–18 moved slowly backwards and forwards across the landscape, with thousands of tons of high explosive obliterating every landmark and then churning up the land itself until there was nothing left to recognise. In England when you walk in the countryside, the landscape follows the lines built into it by hundreds of generations of farmers from the Neolithic age onwards; in country districts, at least, the estate maps of the seventeenth century, accurately surveyed, can be overlaid on the Ordnance Survey and every feature, even every field-name, checks and correlates; even in towns and suburbs the underlying structure can be traced a long way into the past. By contrast in large areas of northern France the huge open fields and the ugly country villages are quite likely to date from the 1920s, like the ribbon development in an English suburb. Any hopes I had of getting a line on the whereabouts of Gorne by quartering the countryside with a good map soon had to be given up; although in the end, one of Mercator's maps provided a vital clue.

CHAPTER 4

The Protestant Recovery
in Flanders
1556–66

Heresy grows here in proportion to the situation in our neighbours' lands.

> Margaret of Parma to Philip II,
> May 1561

We assure you, Sire, that in your Netherlands there are more than 100,000 men holding and following the religion . . . and none of them is proposing rebellion, nor has anyone heard them say a word which tends in that direction.

> Guy de Brès to Philip II,
> *Confession of Faith* (1561)

Madam my good sister: the great and varied matters of business which have come upon me for several months past have caused my long delay in replying to several letters which you have written me.

> Philip II to Margaret of Parma,
> 17 October 1565

By 1550 Charles V had practically eradicated the Protestants of the Netherlands, or at least all overt traces of them. He had also completed the equally hard task of unifying and sorting out the miscellany of small local units which he inherited in the Burgundian Netherlands. The Augsburg Transactions of 1548 freed the Seventeen Provinces from imperial legislation and jurisdiction, and by the "Pragmatic Sanction" of 1549 each province undertook to obey the same ruler after the emperor's death. In that year Charles's son and heir-apparent Philip made a grand tour of the Netherlands. His father was a man of Flanders by birth but Philip was now leaving

Spain for the first time in his life. Philip and his party arrived in Brussels on 1 April 1549 where they were received by Charles himself, and from Brussels they set out on a royal progress through the Seventeen Provinces.

In the large and splendid party were Charles V and his son Philip; Philip's aunt Mary of Hungary, regent of the Netherlands; the duke of Alva and other Spanish advisers; and many nobles of the Netherlands including the prince of Orange and the counts of Egmont and of Hornes. The members of this party were to bring about between them the destruction of much of the Netherlands, and the permanent division of the Seventeen Provinces; they were also to set off the first great wave of emigration from Flanders.

The search for the de la Pierre family through religion, which had begun so promisingly, looked as if it was running out of clues. In the ten years after the death of Marie de le Pierre in 1545 there were only nine executions for heresy at Tournai; in several years there was none at all. When the royal procession passed through the border provinces in 1549, along the river Lys on the way to Lille through the region where the "new opinions" had first taken root, it was undisturbed by any signs of heresy: the single execution at Tournai that year was left tactfully until 26 October, by which time Philip's party was well on its way into the northern provinces. Yet twelve years later there were reckoned to be 100,000 Protestants or more in the Netherlands, most of them in the south in Flanders, Artois, Hainaut and Brabant. After the troubles broke out in the later 1560s nearly 200 heretics were executed at Tournai, 92 of them in the single year of 1568.

What had happened? Why were there no Protestants in 1550 and 100,000 in 1561? And was the de la Pierre family a part of the new crop?

The explanation of the disappearance of heretics is the logical one: the Inquisition dealt with those who were prominent, the rest took cover. In 1550, the year in which Calvin was first condemned in one of Charles V's placards, a man called Titelman became full-time Inquisitor in the Netherlands, and for the next twenty years set an example which his Spanish colleagues might envy. Philip himself once remarked that the Inquisition in the Netherlands was even more pitiless than the Spanish, and he was in a position to know. The Inquisitor had the right to question anyone, arrest anyone, have suspects committed for trial anywhere, and Titelman made full use of his powers: with only three or four assistants, says Geoffrey Parker, "He rode ceaselessly all over his territory in search of his prey, lying in wait for hours in a suspected area, plotting with informers, following up anonymous tips, making arrests at dead of night or in thunderstorms in order to avoid ugly scenes, interrogating and condemning." Between 1550 and 1566 Titelman is said to have tried 1,600 cases in Flanders alone, which works out on average at a hundred a year or one every three working days; this seems scarcely credible, yet there is no doubt about the fear and hatred Titelman aroused by his activities, just as his predecessor van der Hulst had done before him.

Naturally Titelman did not work alone: the town authorities took action if necessary when a notorious heretic could be apprehended. Take for example the sad end of Josse Tkint at Courtrai in 1553. He was an Anabaptist; the town archives record the bill for capturing, examining and executing him.

	£	s	d
To Jehan Van Der Beke (sub-bailly), Adrien Van Der Buercht and other sergeants for arresting Josse Tkint . . .		16	0
For the messenger sent to Ghent to fetch the *officier criminel* . . .		10	0
To Maitre Mathys Du Mond (the *officier criminel*) for his work including three days idle . . .	3	15	0
For another messenger sent to Ghent . . .		10	0
For four more days idle, including one when he was waiting for other business, at 15 *patars* a day . . .	3	0	0
For cords, nails, powder, candles, gloves and other necessities . . .		8	0
To Jacques Scherlym the town carpenter – for building the scaffold . . .		10	0
for ten stands (?*chappys*) round the scaffold . . .		15	0
for a fence of four rails to keep the crowd in order . . .		5	0
To Mas Van Den Abeele "*nayeur*" who delivered all the wood . . .	3	1	3
For bringing the wood to the front of the Town Hall . . .		2	3

	£	s	d
For (*estrais*) paid to Jehan Nyffelle . . .		10	0
For irons, chains, pitchforks etc. . . .		15	0
For the last meal ("banket") of the sufferer and his confessor, with *vin ordinaire* . . .		12	0
To Brother Josse Nerynck for doing his duty and examining the conscience of the said sufferer . . .		12	0
Because the said sufferer was a townsman of Courtrai and there was a great crowd every time he was brought out of prison . . . so that the *bailli* had to send his servants and sergeants to keep good order on the day of the execution . . .	3	0	0
To the Procureur for doing his duty to help the sufferer defend himself . . .		12	0
For the meals ("banket") of the *messagers de la loi* and their time spent . . .	9	0	0

And at last

	£	s	d
To Maitre Mathys Du Mond for executing by fire Josse Tkint . . .	5	0	0
For carting the cinders and other rubbish from the front of the Town Hall to the River Lys . . .		6	0

All of this amounts to the tidy sum, for 1553, of £33 19s 6d[1] for the execution of one obstinate heretic. Marguerite Yourcenar, in *Archives du Nord*, notes that beheading a heretic cost the authorities of Bailleul £10 0s 10d, whereas a bonfire cost £19 13s; little more than half what Courtrai spent on Josse Tkint, but the treasurer at Bailleul was so mean he even refused to pay for the torch used by the executioner, on the grounds that he could have used some glowing coals from a fire.

Several things struck me in reading this extract from the Courtrai town treasurer's accounts. How expensive lawyers were (and are) compared to useful people like carpenters and *nayeurs*; the clergy did not do badly either, even though there was only *vin ordinaire* for the condemned man's hearty breakfast; and how it

---

[1] It is pleasantly familiar for anyone brought up before decimal currency to see accounts drawn up in *£sd*, the unit of money measure throughout western Europe in the old days. In Flanders 12 *deniers* (*d*) made one *sou* or *sol* (*s*) and 20 *sous* or *sols* made one *livre* (*£*) or *franc*. A *patar* was a *sou* with the head of St Peter on the reverse.

must have grieved the burghers to pay so much to the *officier criminel* and his lackeys for time they spent doing nothing. ("What's so unusual about that?" they would have said.)[2] Most of all, there is a definite air of reluctance, even of sympathy for the victim, a local man tried and executed by an outsider from Ghent in spite of the opposition of the townspeople.

To go through so much – the disturbances among the citizens, the trouble and fuss, to say nothing of the grisly scene of the execution itself – and then be faced with a heavy bill at the end of it, must have been a strong deterrent to zeal in persecuting heretics; and indeed the agents of the government were increasingly hindered by local action in the Netherlands as well as in France. Thus Bruges excluded the Inquisition, and in 1564 actually arrested two of Titelman's henchmen who broke the law. In the end despite his efforts the number of Calvinist communities in the Netherlands grew. From a score or so (it was said) in 1561 there were possibly several hundred by 1566, of which over one hundred were in Flanders. Even the Anabaptists revived in small cells, led from 1556 to 1582 by Lenaert Bouwents.

Charles V abdicated in the spring of 1556 in favour of his son, and Philip II of Spain came into his full inheritance. And what was the Most Catholic King doing all this time? More interesting things than hunting heretics. The reform was one problem which seemed to have been solved. The Calvinist communities of the first generation, like the Anabaptists, had been broken up and mostly eliminated. The few that were left were better organised and more determined but were confined to the frontier regions of the south, closest to France and to French influence. In particular there was still a Protestant nucleus along the river Lys, in the villages of the Pays de l'Alleu and in Merville, Armentières and Commines; also at Tournai. If only Charles had completed the task of eliminating heresy and if only Philip had not been distracted by events in Spain and the Mediterranean during the first years of his reign, a great many things would have happened differently during the second

[2] Nor is it unusual in England today: "One fifth of the total cost of criminal legal aid in magistrates' courts, about £9.5m, is spent on 'waiting time' which means doing precisely nothing at all." Lord Hailsham, the Lord Chancellor, speaking on 15 October 1982.

half of the sixteenth century. Instead, war and revolution, famine and plague descended on the prosperous Netherlands, and the people of Flanders were scattered in every direction.

It did not happen all at once. For the ten years during which the Protestants were able to recover their breath, Philip had urgent business to attend to. He had inherited from Charles V a fantastic accumulation of dynastic booty, the richest parts of the New World as well as the Old; his territories in Spain and in Italy were quite as important to him as the Netherlands and more vulnerable to attack. It is hardly surprising that with so much to do he soon tired of the querulous north. There was plenty going on elsewhere which offered honour, expense and distraction.

Philip's chief rival, like his father's, was the king of France. The latest in the succession of wars between the kingdoms had started in 1551. France with her usual pragmatism in foreign affairs had allied herself to the Protestants in Germany (though Protestants were formally proscribed in France) and to the Ottoman Sultan (though the Turks were formally the enemies of Christendom). The wars dragged on in Africa, in Flanders, in Italy, and the kings competed to see who would go bankrupt first. The Netherlanders, always tender in their wallets, complained that they had borne the brunt of payments for the wars in Naples, Milan and Navarre; it was not strictly true – the taxpayers of Castile normally had the privilege of contributing the most to sustain the ambitions of the kings of Spain – but central taxation had soared under Charles V, and Philip in his bankrupt state was open to pressure from anyone who had money to send. When the States-General of the Netherlands eventually agreed to bail him out with a massive loan it was on condition that they collected and distributed the money themselves, to make sure that none of it was sent abroad. It was just enough cash to help Philip bring the war with France to a reasonably successful conclusion by the treaty of Câteau-Cambrésis, a town on the border between France and Flanders, in April 1559.

The other main reason besides bankruptcy which impelled both Philip II and Henri II to make peace was the need to tackle the surprising growth of Protestantism in their domains, which by then could no longer be ignored. In France the 1550s witnessed the steady growth of Huguenot influence, and the same influence was felt in the French-speaking parts of the Netherlands; and the last spasms of the war between the two kingdoms created a stronghold for the Protestants in the north. Each side managed to snatch a final victory. The Spanish army under Egmont routed the French at Gravelines on 13 July 1558; but the French had already scored a double win over two old foes, the English and the Spanish, by seizing Calais on 1 January of the same year. The story of the taking of Calais from its English garrison after more than two hundred years of occupation, and under the nose of England's Spanish allies, had always given much satisfaction to Frenchmen and indeed it was a fine exploit in its own right. Queen Mary of England, with her customary lack of judgment, had married Philip of Spain in 1554. Calais was her last possession on the mainland of Europe; the territory included the town and the hinterland for a few miles around it, and the English had made use of this sally-port on the continent to intervene in mainland affairs.

The French plan to remove this irritant was, for a sixteenth century operation, well prepared. During one of the truces in the war the French statesman Gaspard de Coligny had sent an agent, M. de Briquemaut, in disguise to reconnoitre Calais; he brought back a report on the weak points in the defences, and Coligny plotted the attack for Henri II. The truce ended in January 1557, and in June Queen Mary dutifully declared war on France in support of her husband. The campaign opened in the usual rather messy fashion of the times: the Spanish army besieged Coligny in St Quentin, and defeated a French relief force under Montmorency, but then in effect went on strike because it had received no pay. The duc de Guise, recalled from Italy, proceeded to turn the tables by laying siege to Calais, but there was a problem: according to the story,[3] the secret plan of attack was in Coligny's possession and he was now a prisoner of the Spanish, so his wife had to take advantage of a visit to recover the plan from her husband and pass it on to Guise. Whether the story was embroidered or not, the plan worked without a hitch.

The problem facing the French after they had reduced the forts and villages of the hinterland was that the town of Calais was

---

[3]Pierre de Bourdeille, seigneur de Brantôme, recorded this among other tales without supplying a source when a fall from his horse forced him to become a lay abbot and writer of doubtful reputation.

almost entirely surrounded by water and marshes. The sea came up to the walls in places and a river fed the moats where it did not; the only approach was by a causeway well protected by forts. When the water level rose, as it did in winter, the natural protection was even greater. The English thought it safe in these conditions to reduce the garrison, relying on prompt reinforcements in case of need either from Dover or from the Spanish forces on the mainland.

They reckoned without Guise's energy. In only three days he took the three forts – Sainte Agathe, Nieullay and Rijsbank – that commanded the causeway. Then, with bundles of faggots to stand on and hurdles to protect them from view, his sappers cut a channel in the bank between the moat and the sea, which duly emptied the water from the moat at low tide; naturally it still filled up again every time the tide came in. Guise therefore planted fifteen large siege cannon in the bed of the moat at low tide, and fastened them down with grapnels. At high tide they were covered by the sea; as the water went down the gunners went into the moat, manned, cleaned and fired their pieces (standing in water and mud and under heavy fire from the ramparts of the town) until at last they opened a breach in the walls. That evening, even though the tide was coming in, Guise led the assault on the breach; he and his men, several hundred arquebusiers and gentlemen volunteers, had to wade waist deep in the rising, freezing cold water. It was a terrible risk to take, but the assault succeeded, and the citadel was captured, which still left the English in possession of the lower town. Guise left his men in the citadel and went back across the moat, this time with water up to his neck, to collect help. While the high tide prevented immediate reinforcements for the French, the English governor Lord Wentworth brought his own cannon up against the gate of the citadel and launched several attacks during the night, but all of them were beaten off by the French assault-party. In the morning, like a sensible man, Wentworth gave up. All the inhabitants of Calais, French and English, were allowed *"vie sauve et libre sortie"*, and by the time the English reinforcements arrived from Dover, they were too late. It had taken Guise only eight days from the start of the siege to capture Calais.

The reason for describing this exploit is not just that it makes a good story, and one of the better episodes in the life of the rather unpleasant duc de Guise, but because it provided such important help for the Protestant cause in the surrounding regions. In 1347 when Edward III had taken Calais for England he offered houses, lands and privileges to any who would settle in the town; by 1558 the population was part English and part French. Once again the winning side planted settlers in the *pays reconquis*. The Calaisis was divided into twenty-four cantons or parishes, including Calais itself and the small towns of Guînes and Marcq, and people displaced by the war from the frontier regions began to arrive in large numbers, many of them Protestants; there they joined Protestant soldiers of the French army who had decided to stay in Calais under the colonel-general of the infantry, d'Andelot, who was Coligny's brother and Calvinist. Houses and lands were distributed in 1561; one of the boundaries was fixed by firing a round from a cannon loaded half with French powder and half with English, and the shot landed at a spot where there had been a brewery in "the time of the English". By this time the government in Paris was becoming alarmed by the growing strength of the Protestants, and ordered searches to be made for Calvinists in Calais, but the hunt was half-hearted and the Protestants who were found were soon released. The first war of religion in France began soon afterwards in 1562; it ended the next year, and the Edict of Amboise conceded general liberty of conscience. Protestants were now allowed for the first time public worship in certain towns; a Protestant temple was opened at Marcq in the Calaisis near the frontier with the Netherlands, and many more Protestant families from Artois and Flanders were attracted to the place. From that time onwards, the temple and community at Marcq, and another temple built not far away at Guînes, were centres for Protestants throughout the region, and the success and respectability of Calvinism in France encouraged the communities on either side of the frontier. On 2 January 1567 naturalisation was granted to strangers arriving in Calais from Flanders and Artois, as well as to many English who had decided to stay there.

So by the time that France and Spain made peace in 1559 there was plenty for both kings to attend to in their own dominions. Even in Spain, Protestant cells were discovered. It was believed by the Protestants after Câteau-Cambrésis that besides the formal treaty there was a secret pact between Philip II and Henri II to extirpate heresy. It was certainly proposed by the Spanish negotiators, and the story goes that Henri said as much to William of Orange during a stag-hunt in the Bois de Vincennes while the treaty negotiations were in progress; and that King Henri and the duke of Alva, Philip's ambassador, had discussed the systematic suppression of Protestantism in every country where Spanish troops could be used. But oddly enough they could not be used in the Netherlands.

As soon as the treaty of Câteau-Cambrésis was signed Philip began to issue orders for an offensive against the Turkish stronghold at Tripoli; he himself set off home to Spain to take charge of the war and the suppression of heresy there. He left Brussels on 5 July 1559 and took ship at Flushing on 24 August, and never came back to the Netherlands. For the next six years, until the Turks were forced to withdraw defeated from their great siege of Malta, Philip's attention was fixed on the Mediterranean. The Spanish troops who had fought in the French wars and then remained to garrison the frontier fortresses of Flanders and Artois were also needed elsewhere. In the spring of 1560 the Tripoli expedition ended in disaster, and 10,000 of Philip's troops including his best Spanish veterans were lost. He was reluctant, even so, to withdraw the 3,000 men from the frontier towns of the southern provinces, but the States-General turned the screw: they would release no money to pay the troops' wages, and Philip had to give way. On 10 January 1561 the Spaniards embarked in troop-ships at Zeeland and sailed for the Mediterranean, leaving the frontier forts held by Walloon garrisons in the pay of the States. The way was open for the free passage of men and ideas from the Protestant regions of France.

There were probably two main reasons for the growth of Protestantism in Flanders in this period, besides the influence of affairs in France. One was the fact that officials like the Inquisitor Titelman created a reaction in favour of the persecuted; and there was also the greater attractiveness of the new ideas, and the new men who preached them, in the years before the Catholic Church reorganised and rallied herself to resist. As Robin Briggs points out, writing about France, there came a time when the policy of forcibly suppressing heretics became counter-productive: "Persecution made martyrs, whose faith impressed onlookers: this was particularly true in a society which placed considerable emphasis on a man's behaviour at the moment of death." The same applied over the border; one suspects too that in this as in other respects, the natural disinclination of a man of Flanders to lose money to the government had a fairly powerful influence. Even today a Belgian regards it as his duty to himself and his family to ensure that the central government gets as little cash as possible out of his pocket; people in the fifteenth century were used to unpleasant public spectacles and no one would have dreamed of questioning a ruler's right and duty to suppress activities which could endanger the fabric of society, but citizens objected strongly to losing money, especially to people as unpleasant as Titelman and his kind. Heresy was classed as treason, a "Federal Offence", and after 1549 the goods of a condemned heretic were confiscated; the towns and provinces (who normally tried their own criminal cases) were liable to lose the proceeds if a government agent carried out the trial of a local citizen in some other place.

The other main element in the growth of Protestant influence in the north was the hard work and good example of the new ministers of religion, trained in Geneva and other centres and sent out in growing numbers to the mission fields. The first generation of pastors had mainly come from the regular clergy, especially Luther's own Augustinians. Calvin produced ministers of a new model, deliberately recruited and trained to out-match the old-style Catholic clergy both socially and intellectually. Even today you are likely to hear a more stimulating and rigorous sermon from a French Protestant pastor than from the Catholic curé: in the days before the Jesuits and the reforming popes had set the Catholic Church in better shape to resist its opponents, the contrast must have been marked indeed. The ministers needed all their training and moral stamina; they lived hectic lives and ended them all too often on the scaffold, like Brully at Tournai. Another who deserves an honoured memory is Guy de Brès, the man who provided the Walloon Protestants with their manifesto, the *Confession of Faith*. De Brès had led the usual wandering life of a minister of the reform. Born in Walloon Flanders in 1524, he became a Protestant as a young man, and in 1550 went to England to escape the placards of the emperor. There he remained for three years during the reign of Edward VI, but when Mary came to the English throne he had to move again and went first to Lille, then to Frankfurt, and then to Geneva. In 1559 he returned to Flanders and worked under the code-name "Jerome", mainly at Tournai, Lille and Valenciennes.

He had many narrow escapes. In 1562 a fire at a house in Tournai revealed his hiding-place; luckily for him he was away from home, but his books, letters and manuscript notes were burnt. He had already published his chief claim to fame, the *Confession of Faith*, for the members of the Walloon Protestant congregation, the so-called "*Confessio Belgica*" printed in 1561. De Brès's version was modelled on the Confession agreed at the first national synod of French Protestants in Paris in 1559. Both Confessions begin with the passage from I Peter iii.15, "Be always ready with your defence whenever you are called to account for the hope that is in you"; in the French of the day, "*Soyez toujours appareillez à respondre à chacun qui vous demande raison de l'espérance qui est en vous*", and deal in turn with God, Sin, Grace, Jesus Christ, the Sacraments, the "Magistracy"; there are Thirty-seven Articles in the Walloon version (compared to Forty Articles in the French; or to the Thirty-nine Articles of the Church of England). De Brès's Confession was formally addressed to Philip II and designed (with more hope than policy) to persuade him that his Protestant people were as good and loyal subjects as the Catholics. The title-page says that it was "made by common accord by the faithful who live in the Netherlands, who wish to live according to the pure Gospel of Our Lord Jesus Christ". De Brès reckoned their number at over 100,000; and it kept on growing.

From 1562 the Calvinist Walloons referred to themselves as "reformed" and their communities (still careful to keep their heads down) as *Les Églises sous la Croix*. Each church had a code name: "Vine" at Antwerp, "Sword" at Ghent, "Palm" at Tournai, "Rose" at Lille; they met secretly at night to hear the preaching of someone like Brully or de Brès, then as time went by they began to meet more openly by day. Public singing of the psalms (*chanteries*) began at Tournai in 1561, and open-air services with a sermon (*presches*) followed in 1562. By 1563 great assemblies called *grands presches* were attracting hundreds of people: on Saturday, 26 May of that year there was an assembly in the forest of Berchem outside Antwerp, followed a month later by another in a clearing at Bergerhout.

All this was intensely worrying and irritating for the government in Brussels and particularly for the governor-general appointed by Philip in 1559 when he left Brussels for Spain. This was his half-sister Margaret of Parma, the child of Charles V and a Flemish maid-servant; a blood relation made a safer regent than an outsider when it was a matter of looking after the family's property. Even though she was a woman of Flanders by both her parents Margaret was not at home there, and found it difficult either to stomach what she considered the insolence of the local nobles, or to curb it. She had been brought up by a tough pair of aunts, Margaret of Austria (the previous regent) and Mary of Hungary; but she was fonder of complaining than of taking charge and in any case Philip insisted that she should consult him about any matter of importance and take no decisions on her own. To head her team of advisers he had appointed an unpopular man, Antoine Perrenot, who became Cardinal Granvelle. The opposition to Granvelle was led by two nobles, the count of Egmont, who had earned himself great credit by defeating the French army at Gravelines in 1558, and the count of Hornes, who was related to the Montmorencys of France, and for ten years had been captain of King Philip's bodyguard; within a short time Egmont and Hornes and their supporters were able to remove Granvelle at a time when Philip was preoccupied with another Mediterranean crisis. Granvelle left Brussels on 13 March 1564; and Margaret of Parma was left to work alone with the nobles. But it was not long before the governing factions had to unite in the face of two clearly growing crises: economic problems made worse by bad harvests, and the greatly increased strength of Protestantism.

By then the *grands presches* could not be ignored. We have accounts of these secret gatherings. A pulpit would be erected in the open air; women and children stood nearest, the men with their hats off behind them. An elder would open the proceedings with a prayer and a reading, then a psalm was said or sung in French or Flemish; the French from the metrical version by Marot. The preacher would then deliver his sermon, the high spot of the occasion possibly lasting a couple of hours, after which there would be another psalm, and so home again. Rather like a modern pop festival, the gatherings were social as well as religious events, and lasted sometimes for two days; marriages were celebrated at them, and children baptised. Alas, no registers of these have survived, if indeed any were kept.

Such large-scale assemblies could not go unnoticed by the local authorities, especially as the Catholic Church had at last tightened up the formalities of its own observance. In December 1563 Pope Pius IV confirmed the decrees of the Council of Trent, which had been proposed eighteen years earlier: they were at once published and given the force of law in the Netherlands. In every parish a list was to be drawn up of the inhabitants, their servants and relatives, and their attendance at mass, their baptisms and marriages were duly noted. In principle, therefore, 1564 should mark the start of a series of valuable parish records for the family historian looking for traces in the Netherlands; sadly, as in the case of the French records kept from 1539, the ravages of war and accident have left more holes than fabric. For example, at Valenciennes, with Tournai the main centre of French-speaking Protestants, there were six parishes before the French Revolution: of these the earliest records are those of St Nicholas dating from 1567, St Géry from 1580, and St Jacques from 1597; the records of the other three parishes, St Vast-en-Ville, Notre-Dame-la-Grande and Notre-Dame-de-la-Chaussée, start at the beginning of the seventeenth century, and even then there are large gaps.[4]

An ancestor-hunt is therefore in difficulties during the early years of Philip II's reign in the Netherlands. The Catholic parish registers are scanty and full of gaps. The Calvinist churches have left no records from this period. Surprisingly there are Anabaptist records because Lenaert Bouwents managed to keep a register of his baptisms, but the de la Pierres do not feature in it. (Just as well, perhaps, or the whole family might have fallen victims to the Inquisition, like the family of Jan de Zwarte at Hondschoote, eighteen of whom were executed between 1558 and 1567.) By 1564 the persecution of Calvinists in Flanders had practically ceased and the law was no longer effective. The government in Brussels realised that they must either make a new effort to enforce the law, or else change it.

The new parish records must have revealed to them for the first time the full extent of the growth of Protestantism. Even if a magistrate turned a blind eye, the parish priest could hardly fail to note that many members of his nominal flock were attending other

---

[4] The records that survive are not as revealing as one would like; in the sixteenth century the mother's name is rarely shown in baptisms, the parents' names are not included for marriages, and the record of death gives only the dead person's name.

people's services somewhere in the woods. Not all magistrates wanted to turn a blind eye. On Saturday, 14 June 1565 there was a *grand presche* outside Ghent and the *bailli* Cornelius Croes decided, unwisely, to interrupt it: he was quickly chased away. A few days later, a placard was issued formally forbidding such gatherings. The Protestants reacted by going to the assemblies fully armed and forming ramparts of wagons round the crowd, like American pioneers. It was not long before people started to go in procession from one assembly to the next, with flags flying and drums beating.

This was the fatal transition from secret, or at least concealed, religious assemblies to open defiance of the civil authority. No ruler could afford to let such things go unchecked. In France it was precisely the "coming out" of the Protestants into the open which was decisive; in the confused, short reign of François II, the son of Henri II, the Huguenots defied the royal council by holding open-air services in full view outside many towns, including Paris; and their first national synod had met the month after peace was signed with Spain. All at once it was time for men to declare themselves on one side or the other, and the result was the outbreak of civil war in 1562. It was the example of the French, and no doubt the presence of many refugees from the French wars, which directed the civil disobedience in Flanders; but the king of Spain was not a boy of fifteen like François II, and thanks to the victory of Malta he was no longer preoccupied elsewhere. The cat had been away long enough, and the mice had become careless.

By now, there was a very large number of mice. On 4 September 1561 the Council of Flanders wrote to the governor that to repress heresy in the West Quarter

> would be very difficult and complicated, having regard to the great multitudes and infinite number of those infected with heresy in the said Quarter, or who have offended against the placards by holding conventicles or otherwise; so that to prosecute and execute those transgressors with the rigour of the law it would be necessary to shed a terrible amount of blood (*faudroit user d'une terrible effusion de sang*) which would mean not only the depopulation and destruction of the said Quarter but also many other problems.

Even before the *grands presches* the Inquisitor Titelman had grumbled that the number of Protestants kept on growing in spite of all his efforts. There was continual contact and mutual support between the Protestants of Flanders, England and northern France. In Tournai by 1566 there were more Protestants than Catholics. On Wednesday, 9 January 1566 Margaret of Parma wrote to Philip from Brussels complaining that she had very little support from the provincial governors, who (like the Council of Flanders) said that they could not agree to suppress heresy if it meant burning fifty or sixty thousand people. Philip's advisers were more sanguine. Fray Lorenço de Villavicencio, one of Philip's secret agents in the Netherlands, assured him that a couple of thousand executions would be enough to cow the dissenters, and reminded him of splendid examples: King David, who slew all his enemies without sparing men, women or children; Moses, who had killed 3,000 men of Israel in a single day; best of all, the anonymous angel who had put to death 60,000 of God's enemies in one night. Surely if one angel could do it, the provincial authorities could manage?

Open-air assemblies were all very well in the summer time, but winter in Flanders is not conducive to such activities. The winter of 1564/5 had been phenomenally cold, with icebergs in the North Sea and in the river Maas; we know how it looked in Flanders thanks to Breughel's "Hunters in the Snow", which started the fashion for winter scenes by him and other Flemish artists; it was followed by a bad harvest, so that at Ghent (said the archives) "there arrived in this town about 300 destitute people from the region of Armentières who, it is to be feared, are infected with heresy". The number of Protestants was now so large that men began to ask why they should not be allowed public exercise of their religion as in France and Germany; the city of Antwerp, remembering what a powerful lever money had been in the past, offered Philip three million florins for a licence to secure religious liberty and build churches. To Margaret, this was one more example of the insufferable insolence of the people of Flanders; and this time, in the winter of 1565, Philip did not need the cash as badly as he had done in 1558.

The scene was set for the Troubles to begin. Philip was preoccupied during 1565, first with the threat and then the reality of the Turkish siege of Malta, but he kept the nobles in Brussels quiet by seeming to be ready to relax the rules against heretics, while in fact preparing to enforce them. He had no intention of compromising with heresy, and he laid plans with his usual care for the suppression of rebellion in the Netherlands. On Monday, 12 August 1566 he was able to write to Don Luis de Requesens, his ambassador to the pope, saying that he had decided to use force. He knew well that this could involve the destruction of the Netherlands:

> ... in which case I wish to be the one to carry out my intentions, and neither the peril I run, nor the ruin of these Provinces, could prevent me from accomplishing what a Christian and God-fearing prince is bound to do for his holy duty, the maintenance of the Catholic faith and the authority and honour of the Holy See.

Before Philip's letter had time to reach Rome, the "ruin of these Provinces" had begun.

CHAPTER 5

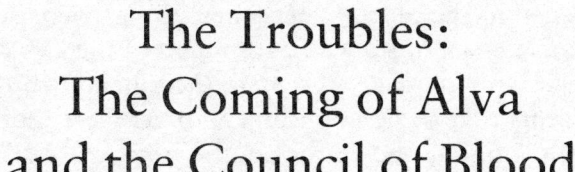

The Troubles:
The Coming of Alva
and the Council of Blood
1566–75

They used to chant the psalms in French there in the manner of the Calvinists; because a number of townspeople, rich and influential thanks to industry and commerce, had imbibed the venom of the new opinions through their dealings with foreigners.

> Cardinal Granvelle,
> on the French influence in Wallonia

And God, who is just and zealous to protect His honour, by inscrutable ways and means has since then taken a cruel revenge for all that; because all the places where these things happened were for the most part taken, looted, destroyed and sacked by war, pillage, plague and disaster.

> Renon de France,
> *Histoire des Troubles des Pays-bas*

On Thursday, 15 August 1566, when the faithful should have celebrated the Feast of the Assumption, gangs of armed men with hammers, axes and picks went into the churches in the towns and villages on the border between Flanders and Artois, and set to work methodically to remove all the graven images in them. Statues were torn down, carvings were smashed and furnishings pillaged. At Estaires, Richebourg, La Gorgue, Laventie, Menin, Metteren, Vieille Chapelle, Givenchy and Langies they left a trail of vandalism. In the next few days more than four hundred churches were ruined: on Tuesday, 20 August Antwerp Cathedral itself was sacked.[1] It was a disastrous act of rebellion. Innumerable master-pieces were lost; more to the point, such deliberate law-breaking was a challenge which the government could not decline, and in the result it ruined Flanders and Artois. Renon de France, writing at the start of the next century as governor of Artois after the restoration of total orthodoxy in the southern provinces, recorded with relish what happened to the places where these things were done: *prins, pillez, detruictz et saccagéz* was the epitaph of the Lys valley.

No one was really sure who were the villains who started it, though it seems that some Englishmen, or refugees returned from England, lent a hand, and in the southern provinces there was a small hard core of iconoclasts (paid apparently by Calvinist consistories) who set the example. What was not in doubt was the large measure of support, or at least non-intervention, among the citizens. The town guard at Middelburg told the magistrates, "We will not fight for church, pope and monks"; at Antwerp they watched the image-breakers going from door to door, but did nothing. Margaret of Parma sent urgent letters to Philip on 17 and 18 August with the news, repeating that he must choose either to send an army to restore his authority in the Netherlands, or to abandon them; Granvelle in Rome had already told him how everyone in Italy expected that if the Netherlands went, Milan and Naples would go too. There could be little doubt which course he would follow. When the news from the Netherlands arrived, he is said to have given way to an uncharacteristic display of rage: he tore his beard and vowed, "It will cost them dear! It will cost them dear! I swear it on the soul of my father!" He was as good as his word.

Later on, Cardinal Granvelle held that it was the French in-fluence in Wallonia in the early 1560s, greatly increased by the arrival of Huguenot refugees from the wars of religion in France, which had spread "the venom of the new opinions" in the towns of southern Flanders. Margaret in Brussels was also sure that it was the *nouvelles opinions* which were to blame for the outrage and she at

---

[1] Bruges escaped the general destruction because the *bailli* and *eschevins* arranged for the main entrance to the church to be locked and guarded while the statues, pictures and altars, and even the organs, were smuggled out into hiding. In the same way the people of Canterbury later saved the cathedral from Roundhead vandals; they might sympathise with their views, but saw no reason why local treasures should be pillaged by outsiders.

once hired troops from Germany to reinforce the royal authority in the disturbed areas. In fact, Philip had sent orders to this effect at the end of July. The only regular troops left in the country since the departure of the Spanish regiments in 1561 were the Walloon garrisons of ten fortresses on the French frontier, and their loyalty along with their religious beliefs was doubtful. Many of the Germans were Lutherans, but at least they were not Calvinists, and Margaret thought they would be reliable enough for restoring order in a foreign country. In vain did the local Protestants, seeing disaster coming, deny responsibility for the vandalism. One preacher with more scholarship than tact pointed out that it was Achab, who introduced the worship of idols, and not Elias who denounced them, who was responsible for the misfortunes of Israel. The nobles, already deep in Margaret's black books as a result of their independence (when they brought one set of demands to her, said an onlooker, "she was so angry she thought she would burst") were suspect too, and had to take vigorous action to disprove any suggestion of complicity. William of Orange, ordered by Margaret to restore order in Antwerp, did so promptly and effectively, and hanged three image-breakers caught in the act. Only ten days after the Feast of the Assumption a proclamation was issued from Brussels on Sunday 25 August.

> By the King to the Governor of Lille. Whereas various seditious and rebellious sectaries have risen and pillaged, sacked, destroyed and burnt many churches and monasteries in our Netherlands: We very expressly forbid all and any to pillage any churches, cloisters, monasteries or other houses of God, or to help others to do so, or to take anything away . . . on pain of hanging and confiscation of property . . . declaring them sacrilegious, public robbers, enemies of God, of us, and of the world, whom we allow everyone to kill, not only with impunity, but with honour, as one does a common enemy of the fatherland and the public good (*grassateur publique*). . . . We order all lords, judges and burgesses to put a stop to them, under pain of being punished themselves . . . and we forbid any one to carry arms (except in the exercise of his duty) in a public gathering, on pain of death.

In the event, once Margaret and the nobles started acting together, and the burgesses had time to reflect on the consequences of rebellion, order was restored so promptly that it was almost unnecessary for Philip to intervene at all. The Protestant pastors hastily left the towns of Flanders, spurred on by the news that the Protestant town of Valenciennes had been taken by government troops; Guy de Brès was captured, and on 31 May 1567 he was hanged; also executed were Peregrine de la Grange (also a gentleman and a minister), Michel Herlin and his son Michel, and Jean Mahieu.

In other towns in Wallonia image-breakers were tried and sentenced. The summaries of evidence show how the tacit tolerance of Protestantism during the early 1560s had led to the growth of reformed congregations, and eventually to the practice of carrying arms to defend them. There is evidence that Protestant temples were established in several towns along the Lys, at Merville, Armentières, and Commines, where ministers trained in Geneva, London or Heidelberg came to serve them. Here is an example of the trial of an *eschevin* from Merville.

> Antoine Delbecque . . . first *eschevin* of Merville-sur-le-Lys in the year of the Troubles 1566 charged with having attended the *presches* of the new pretended religion since they began, when people went to them carrying weapons; and on St Laurence's Day (10 August) at the village of Richebourg being armed with a sword; and when the *presches* were tolerated, having required and exhorted others to attend them; and speaking every day with the principal sectaries of Merville, in whose company he was seen the day after the day of the Assumption of Our Lady in the same church, breaking images, altars, the repository, candelabra and other ornaments; and having taken the child of a certain Charles Cambreling to the temple; and in the fashion of the said new religion, and on the urging of the Minister of La Gorgue, having brought and signed the "concept" of the said sectaries to find three million gold florins to buy freedom of religion. . . . Delbecque was sentenced to be beheaded (or hanged if he remained obstinate) at Brussels on 9 July 1568.

So there was a minister at La Gorgue (a little way down the river Lys from Merville) but not as far as we know a temple; but if the woods were too risky or too uncomfortable, the Protestants did not scruple to use the parish church if they could. Indeed, one possible reason for image-breaking was to "purify" a church so that it could properly be used for Protestant services. That is what happened at Sailly, the next village to La Gorgue:

Christopher Traisnel of Sailly-sur-le-Lys ... charged with having by his own authority enrolled the inhabitants (in trained bands) and called the roll; and being in the church at Sailly during the image-breaking and not preventing it; and allowing his son Antoine to preach in the church the next Sunday after the Assumption. ... Traisnel was beheaded at Brussels on 21 June 1570.

Clearly the middle part of the Lys valley was a hot-bed of Protestantism, particularly in the small area of the Pays de l'Alleu, every one of the towns and villages of which appears in the accounts of the tribunal. But most of all to appear were the twin towns of La Gorgue and Estaires: we have seen the minister of La Gorgue and some of his flock; and at Estaires too the new religion was flourishing, and the Protestants were armed:

The brothers Charles and Jehan Brixis . . . charged with attending *presches*, going most seditiously armed with an arquebus and drums in the company of a large troop of people to help those in Estaires who are great sectaries and where the new religion has been in full swing (*entièrement exercée*). . . .

and

Charles (Del) Becque . . . charged with attending the *presches* of the new religion in this town of Estaires during the recent Troubles . . . and in other towns round about, during the tolerance of such things (*la tolleran dicelles*) and afterwards; sometimes carrying sword and pistol and obeying the orders of Jehan (Des) Rumaualt and other principal rebels and traitors before Christmas 1566. . . .

The "tolerance of such things" was now over, especially the tolerance of carrying arms, and the government troops had no difficulty in rounding up such armed bands as offered any trouble. Typical of the scattered engagements which took place was the so-called "battle of Lannoy" when one of the Protestant ministers from the Pays de l'Alleu, a man called Corneille de Lezenne, set off with some of his parishioners on a forlorn hope to try to help their fellow-Protestants besieged in Valenciennes. They joined some other rebel companies and managed in the end to muster thirteen standards and a score or so of cavalry. There were only a few former professional soldiers among them, the rest were shopkeepers, workmen and peasants. When they ran into the government troops at

Lannoy, the result was a foregone conclusion: the rebels were scattered in all directions and those who did not get away were killed on the spot or captured and executed later, including Antoine de Lespienne, a young bachelor and fruit-seller from La Gorgue, Jehan le Plat from Bondues, Hugh and Jacques de le Dicque and Fleurus Fremaut from Wasquehal, all of them hanged at Lille on 10 April 1568.

By the end of 1566 armed rebellion in the south had been suppressed, and in February 1567 Margaret ordered the demolition of many Protestant temples, including no fewer than five (three Calvinist and two Lutheran) in Antwerp. On 27 April a special courier arrived at Philip's court with a message from Margaret to say that she had now restored order, and it would be better not to send Spanish troops to the Netherlands since that would only hinder a settlement. Margaret's envoy, Gaspar de Robles, actually persuaded Philip to allow the Council of State to debate the matter, and the Council was evenly divided – but Philip had the casting vote and Philip had already decided what he would do. On the same day that Gaspar de Robles arrived at court, the duke of Alva left Spain to take command in Italy of the veteran army which was intended to restore Philip's full authority in the Netherlands.

The story of the Army of Flanders and how it came to the Netherlands up the "Spanish Road" from Italy is a remarkable one, well recounted by Geoffrey Parker, but it belongs more to the story of the Eighty Years War and the Dutch Revolt than to that of the Protestant refugees. The Army's march from Italy to Brussels was an amazing feat of organisation, comparable to the equipping of the Armada itself, and only Spain in her great century was capable of it. Even to the Spaniards the difficulties were immense, and the Spanish Road became a byword: *Poner una pica en Flandes* (to put a pikeman into Flanders) was a saying for doing things the hard way. To collect an army of veteran troops in northern Italy, replace them there with recruits from Spain, and bring them up across the Alps and along the borders of the empire, along a route surveyed by engineers, opened up by pioneers, and stocked with supplies by the commissariat – all this was something rival kings could only marvel at, and envy. Everyone in Europe knew what was up; there were even stories that the Protestants of Switzerland were busy infecting the Spanish Road with plague. The difficulties to be overcome, and the massive preparations which had to be made, demonstrate that Philip was committed to the armed conquest of the rebels in the Netherlands well in advance of the message from Margaret saying that she had already achieved it. Like Kaiser Wilhelm in August 1914, Philip was hardly able to stop the consequences of his own mobilisation. In any case, he did not particularly want to do so: still less did the man he had appointed as his captain-general have any doubts in the matter.

Don Fernando Alvarez de Toledo, duke of Alva, captain-general of king Philip in the Netherlands from 1567 to 1573, earned himself the execration of the Protestants of Europe and the hearty dislike of the king's subjects by the brutality of his suppression of the "new opinions" and the overbearing arrogance of his style of government; but he was a very effective soldier at a time when the Spaniards were teaching the world how to use military force. He joined his army in Italy on 31 May 1567: 10,000 men including one regiment of Germans, but mainly Spanish veteran infantry. On 18 June he set off from Asti on the long march to the north. Even though it was midsummer the weather was very bad, with snow in the mountains, and there was a constant danger of Protestant ambush (if not of Protestant biological warfare) so that the column had to proceed with caution. Nevertheless they reached Lorraine on 24 July and the next day celebrated their national day, the feast of Santiago; they crossed the frontier of the Netherlands near Thionville on 3 August, and arrived in Namur on Assumption day, the first anniversary of the outbreak of the troubles. The last stage of the journey was leisurely; Alva rode into Brussels on 22 August.[2]

From the moment of his arrival Alva made Margaret's position very difficult if not impossible. She had not wanted him to come; she was humiliated by his arrival, and by the way the nobles flocked to attend on him. He ordered the immediate demobilisation of the troops she had raised to restore order, and insisted on garrisoning his own men in loyal towns like Brussels rather than other places which had openly rebelled. The *tercio* or regiment of Naples, nineteen companies strong, marched into Ghent on 30 August in

[2] Alva's march was good going, but later Spanish commanders improved on it. The shortest time taken to march the 700 miles up the Spanish Road from Italy to the Netherlands was 32 days, by Figueroa with 5,000 men in February/March 1578.

ranks of five, followed by large numbers of prostitutes and camp followers; the Spanish troops caused more scandal than admiration wherever they went. Worst of all, the duke was determined to establish a special court to try cases of treason, and on 5 September a decree was issued creating the "Council of Troubles". On 9 September Hornes and Egmont, Margaret's Counsellors, were arrested by Spanish troops and their papers seized. This was the last straw for Margaret who saw that she could no longer stay as regent. She created Alva governor-general and left for Italy on 30 December, abandoning the Netherlands to its new ruler. It would make a fair tract for feminists to consider, that when the quarrel between Protestant and Catholic reached fighting-point, it was the women regents of France and the Netherlands, Catherine de Medici and Margaret of Parma, who did their best to bring about a moderate settlement, and that both were defeated by the folly of men. So much the worse for both countries. France was to be distracted by civil war until the end of the century; in the Netherlands Alva set to work through the Council of Troubles to root out and destroy a sizeable proportion of the population, starting in the southern provinces.

We know a great deal about the work of the Council of Troubles because it was well-served by its bureaucrats and their papers still exist in great profusion – so great that most of them have never been published. In Brussels, thanks to the work of the Royal Historical Commission, I have been able to browse through edited volumes of papers, including the notes made by the civil servants as they prepared themselves for their huge task. The register of the *procès-verbaux* (a phrase familiar to all readers of Simenon) starts off with the sessions held in October 1567:

> Register of the decrees or resolutions taken in Council in the presence of Monseigneur the Duke of Alva etc . . . of which the Secretary Johan de Vlierden kept the record when he served the said Council. And first, the same day (7 October) it was agreed to proceed to list the possessions of all those who had fled or were in hiding as a result of the late Troubles. . . .

The Council of Troubles (or Council of Blood as it was soon known by the people) was composed mainly of Spaniards, and Alva was usually chairman; his deputy was Jean de Vargas, a man who made himself notorious by the saying, "All the Netherlanders deserve to die, the heretics because they pillaged the churches and the Catholics for not preventing them." Heresy meant showing any reserve about the doctrine and practice of the Church as recently prescribed by the Council of Trent; treason included complaining about the Inquisition or the placards. The council sat for seven, eight or nine hours a day; it appointed commissioners who went on assize throughout the Seventeen Provinces, trying and condemning all those suspected of active or passive complicity in breaking the law. The first commissioner, Anthonin van Gryspere, was appointed on 3 September 1567; the last one, Pierre des Mares, on 15 November 1575. The Pays de l'Alleu was a very early target; Estaires and La Gorgue are first cited in the records of the council in January 1568, and commissioners were appointed to l'Alleu (Charles de la Buissière) and to Tournai (Jehan Gombault) on the same day, 3 February 1568. Later that month King Philip gave it as his own view that the whole of the Netherlands should be regarded as infected with heresy. Alva set to work with a will to root it out.

Philip had given Alva secret instructions which ended by advising him to imitate Julius Caesar "who wanted to conquer more by clemency than by harshness". Alva does not seem to have read his instructions to the end. Later he boasted at table that he had personally sentenced 18,000 people and the figure is probably not much exaggerated; but most of the verdicts were delivered in the absence of the people charged, and most of the sentences never carried out. Very soon people learnt that if they were summoned to appear before the council it was best to run for it, even though all their goods were confiscated and their families ruined. At Ghent 150 people were summoned: of the eighteen who actually appeared in court, six were beheaded and twelve hanged. It was hardly an encouragement to submit oneself to the due processes of law. We can get a fair idea of how the council worked from the following extract from a report by the secretary, giving a summary of business from January to April 1568.

> The XXIII of the said month (January) there were summoned by the officers (*huissiers*) of the Grand Council at 11 o'clock before mid-day at the sound of the trumpet the Prince of Orange, the Counts of Hoogestrate, Culembourg, and van den Berghem, Louis of Nassau and Henry to appear before His Excellency to purge their crimes.

(Needless to say, the summons went unanswered.)

> The same day a writ was served against three inhabitants of
> Merville, against whom (when they failed to appear) an ad-
> journment was granted. The last day of January, another writ
> against 23 from La Gorgue; the same day, writ served against
> 36 inhabitants of Estaires; the XVI of March, a third default
> against those from Messines whose case was previously
> adjourned ... the same against those of La Gorgue and
> Steenvorde.... Likewise against those from Merville. The
> XX of March XXXV prisoners held in divers towns and
> quarters on accounts of the Troubles ... will be judged and
> executed by the supreme penalty at the places where they have
> been held.

As the trials went on, the paper piled up. Pierre Hauwys, the
huissier of the council, kept an account of the stationery used by the
busy clerks. In a single month the bill came to £8 14s including –

Une rime de papier	–	11	lb	VIs
Ung pot d'encre	–			VIs
Ung sac de Cavenas	–			VIIs VId
Une livre de filet à				
cacheter lettres	–			XIIs
Une carton de plumes à				
escripre	–			IIIs

The surviving files contain the names of over 12,000 people
condemned for complicity in the troubles; in 1,105 cases a sentence
of death or banishment is recorded; for the rest, the assumption
must be that they got away before the magistrate's men arrived.
This List of the Condemned, as it is called, is therefore a document
of prime importance for a family historian, because it records the
names and homes of individuals who almost certainly fled from the
Netherlands to take refuge in other countries. It enables us to make
an analysis of the chief centres of Protestantism in the southern
provinces; for example, the density of the convicted Protestants
reveals clearly where there were temples and ministers around
which the congregations were based. At the main centres, like
Tournai, hundreds were condemned; and along the river Lys there
were several concentrations, such as that in the Pays de l'Alleu.

The details of the trials, where these survive, not only give names
and dates but also a glimpse of the state of the towns of Flanders and

Artois in the mid-sixteenth century and the sort of people who were involved in the Protestant revival and revolt. They were by no means a collection of fanatics or ruffians; if the bands of iconoclasts were led by a few determined rebels, they seem to have set off a popular movement which soon attracted support in the towns, up to and including the town councillors themselves. Here are a few examples of the sort of hard cases that clearly denote the ringleaders of the first outbreaks of image-breaking.

> Jacques De Bruyne . . . charged with being an image-breaker who had lived many years according to the new religion . . . condemned to be hanged and his goods confiscated to the profit of his Majesty . . . sentence given in the town of Brussels the last day of March 1568.

> Jehan Van Verne . . . charged with having followed the *presches* and newfangled doings (*nouvellitez*) of the sectaries in public and in secret, and with having joined that religion and taken part in the Calvinist eucharist . . . and having been found in the company of image-breakers and pillagers in the church of Quesnoy. . . . Hanged at Lille 9 April 1568.

> Arnould Des Nulescamps . . . charged with having often attended the *presches* of the sectarian ministers. . . . Hanged at Tournai 14 April 1568.

> Piert Fiefvet . . . charged with attending the *presches* of the sectarian ministers armed with a stick to help defend them, and having been found at an illicit assembly at the said Hollain where Jehan Cautre preached the word and exhorted (the congregation) until nightfall in the Calvinist fashion; moreover on St Bartholomew's day of the said year 1566, having been found with many hooligans and pillagers (*mechans garnement et saccageurs*) of his parish church of Hollain, and then helped by means of a rope attached to the crucifix to break the foot of the cross; and having been found at the village of La Celle, where they were celebrating the eucharist in the style of Geneva. . . . Beheaded 29 September 1568.

Jacques De Bruyne, who had "lived many years according to the new religion", may have been one of the first generation of Protestants; and the other cases illustrate how openly the placards were being flouted. It is ironic that it is the records of their misdemeanours that gives us not only the most information but also the most insight into the way people became involved in Protestantism even at the risk of being convicted as rebels and heretics; rather as the documents of the Inquisition gave the historian Le Roy Ladurie the story of the Cathars in the village of Montaillou in the fourteenth century, so the registers of the Council of Troubles and the accounts of the officers of justice cast unexpected light on the doings of individual people in the villages along the Lys valley in the middle of the sixteenth century. The Spanish empire was known for its bureaucracy: Philip himself, a brilliant bureaucrat, could deal with several hundred pieces of business in a single day, and he left behind in the castle of Simancas a memorial in the shape of thirty million documents; though the people of Flanders no doubt had rude things to say about it, the family historian can only bless the industry which filed away so much treasure.

There are large gaps in the documents all the same. Sometimes all the papers of a single archive were destroyed at once, like those at Brussels which were destroyed by a French bombardment in 1695, or the papers at the castle of Vilvoorde (where many executions took place) which also went up in flames. Some records were lost by neglect, or because the parchment was used again and the original message was lost; and sometimes there were specific orders to destroy the records. Thus when the people of the Netherlands grew sick of perpetual trouble and the Pacification of Ghent brought a truce for a while, the States-General sent an order to the Provost of Valenciennes on 23 April 1578 telling him to burn, in the presence of two or three magistrates,

> such papers as criminal trials, whether the culprit was executed or was banished and has now returned; and any information, reports, charges and secret accusations and similar papers and records resulting from the said Troubles . . . which papers cannot serve any purpose in future except as reminders and odious reproaches of these past events.

So the papers from Valenciennes are largely lost; but they survive from many other places, and most of all there are the Lists of the Condemned. In Tournai, the de le Pierre family were in trouble again. Four names from the family are listed, out of several hundred entries for the chief Protestant city of the southern provinces: Gervoys de le Pierre, Simon de le Pierre, Pierre de le Pierre and one woman, Catherine de le Pierre the wife of Jehan de le Pree. Pierre de le Pierre had an alias, *Cra Cul* which means "Big End" (or something even less complimentary). There is no record of what became of these de le Pierres, who probably left Tournai in a hurry. While I could make no firm connection, they were one generation nearer than Marie (executed at Tournai in 1545). The first de la Pierres recorded in Canterbury include Peronne de la Pierre from Tournai who married a second husband on 30 November 1595; and in London Arnoult de la Pierre from Tournai, son of Pierre who died before 1604, married Bache van de Perre on 30 December 1606. All coincidences perhaps, but at last it was beginning to look possible to suggest quite plausible links between Flanders and England for the first generation of refugees.

All this time I was still trying to pinpoint exactly where my de la Pierre ancestors came from. The Lists of the Condemned show a heavy concentration of convictions in the little towns along the river Lys; these were the places to which the first Protestant refugees had come from France after 1562, and were the scene of the first outbreaks of iconoclasm in 1566. Estaires heads the list with 89 names; La Gorgue and Laventie contribute 42 and 37 names respectively; there are 14 from Lestrem, 11 from Fleurbaix, 9 from l'Alleu, 8 from Merville, 8 from Sailly and 2 from Erquinghem: in all, the names of 200 men and 20 women convicted in the small area of the Pays de l'Alleu. Bearing in mind that these were small places, the proportion of the population haled before the magistrates was very large. At La Gorgue, for instance, the taxation lists of 1469 show sixty households; the prosecution and conviction a century later of forty-two people (two of whom were executed) from over thirty different families must represent a pretty heavy cull.

I have mentioned the possible connection between the de le Pierres condemned at Tournai, and the de la Pierres among the Walloon congregations at Canterbury and London a generation later. One difficulty about confirming such links is that respectable people tended later on to conceal the fact that relatives of theirs had been convicted of civil disorders, if not worse. Marguerite Yourcenar, telling the story of her family in *Archives du Nord*, recalls how she too had combed through the Lists of the Condemned and the people banished in the time of the troubles, and found names belonging to practically every family in the region, including some bearing the surname of her own ancestors; but if they were indeed her distant relatives, their names had been carefully expunged from the family history.[3] Some went to England and disappeared from view; those who stayed behind were probably on the side of law and order, indignant when parish priests were murdered and English Protestants landed on the dunes to help the church-wreckers and the local rebels hiding in the woods. All the same I felt that the de le Pierres of Tournai who were condemned during the troubles may very well have been connected with Marie de le Pierre, executed in 1545. Besides the local connection the records show that Protestantism survived in the same families from the early days of persecution, due to the relative tolerance of Margaret of Parma's regency. Take, for example, the following case tried in Brussels in 1568.

> Nicholas Salengre . . . charged with attending the first *presche* at Laventie on the feast of St James and St Christopher and all the succeeding ones, and making his wife and children attend; and having been present in the church at Laventie at the time of the image-breaking without opposing it even though he was *eschevin* on the contrary being seen to laugh when a young girl threw or dropped certain images to the ground; and taking the keys of the church from the warden and giving them to Mahieu Bezaert a sectary; and saying that they should break the bells of the church and turn them into cannon; and when Mahieu Crocheroy, the *eschevin* of l'Alleu objected that as an *eschevin* he (Salengre) should not have allowed to be sold in the market at Laventie books attacking the sacrifice of the Mass, having told Mahieu Crocheroy that it was a mortal sin to say his rosary and worship the Virgin Mary and that it was a bad deed to go to Mass . . . and having signed the subscription list for buying the liberty of religion, and contributed 20 or 40 *patars*; and showing to Sr François Caron, chaplain of the parish of Laventie, in the house of Jehan de Wastepaste an altar stone coming from the said church of Laventie in which had been set in wood certain relics of saints and saying to him that here were the witchcraft and magic (*l'enchanterie et sorcellerie*) that he and priests like him used in saying Mass; having said that if there was anything owing to him (Caron) for his services to the church, then he should come to them (the Protestants) and they would pay him tithes from the proceeds of the sale of chalices, ornaments and vestments from the said church; and having

---

[3] Her real name is Marguerite-Jeanne-Ghislaine Cleenewerck de Crayencour; her mother was a De Cartier de Marchienne, and her ancestors were *baillis* and *greffiers* in French Flanders in the fifteenth century.

spent 25 years infected with the forbidden sectarian virus. . . .
Was condemned to be beheaded at Brussels on 21 June 1568.
(Salengre was in fact burnt on 25 June for remaining obstinate
in his heresy.)

This record is interesting for a number of reasons. It shows how a
Protestant had survived and persisted in his convictions for twenty-
five years, in spite of the placards, and was even a member of the
town council; how there were plenty of other Protestants in the
place, including children; and how the Protestants were able to talk
on level terms with the curé and the *bien-pensants* of Laventie, until
at last the magistrates arrived and non-conformists were removed
from the scene. The mention of Jehan de Wastepaste is another
example of several members of the same family being in trouble:
Philippe and Pierre Wastepaste are on the List of the Condemned at
La Gorgue, charged with trying to raise subscriptions for the fund to
secure freedom of religion in Flanders. As for the spread of Protestantism through the classes, two facts are intriguing: between
1520 and 1566 twenty-three street-singers were tried for heresy in
Flanders; during the assizes after the troubles two of those convicted in the Pays de l'Alleu, Jehan Duhem at Laventie and Jehan de
Warennes at Frelinghem, are shown as *seigneurs*, that is, lords of the
manor.

The year 1568 saw not only the peak of the repression in the
southern provinces but also the opening shots in what was to prove
the Eighty Years War for the independence of the north. At Tournai
there were 13 executions in 1567, 92 in 1568, 53 in 1569 and 19 in
1570: those were the ones that did not get away.

On Sunday, 23 May 1568 Louis of Nassau, brother of William
of Orange who had fled to the north, won an engagement against
government troops at Heiligerlee, but his brother Adolphe was
killed, and Alva's riposte was swift and deadly: he arrived with his
main army in a few days, caught the rebels at Jemmingem and
destroyed them, and Louis himself barely escaped from the disaster.
In Brussels, on three days at the beginning of June, Egmont, Hornes
and twenty-two other nobles were executed: the crowd was hostile
to the government, pressed round the scaffold booing loudly, and
dipped their handerchiefs in the dead men's blood. Alva was not
worried. He demolished the house of the count of Culembourg,
where the nobles had met in November 1565 to form a solemn

league to secure the abolition of the Inquisition and the moderation of the laws against heresy. On the site he had a column erected, with an inscription which ran:

> In the reign of Philip II the Most Catholic King of Spain, Don Ferdinand Alvarez de Toledo, Duke of Alva, Governor of the Netherlands, had the house which used to stand here demolished, because of the conspiracies hatched in it against the Roman Catholic Church and against His Majesty, 1568.

By the end of 1568 there was little left for Alva's troops to do in the south. Such armed rebellion as had been attempted by the Protestants had been suppressed with very little difficulty, and the temples were demolished like the count of Culembourg's house. In October 1568 Pierre Hazard, the minister of the temple at Commines, was burnt in the market place at Lille: the following month Corneille de Lezenne was hanged there. He had got away from the "battle of Lannoy", but was captured at Jemmingem serving as a chaplain in the rebel army of Louis of Nassau, and this time he did not escape.

There were still a few more ambushes and skirmishes before Alva restored complete control in the south. On 2 April 1568 the provost of the Marshals of Artois, who had been ordered to pursue and arrest sectaries accused of pillage and murder, paused to stop the night at the house of Jehan Caulier at Lestrem, along with sixteen of his men; that midnight they were attacked and killed by the local Protestants led by two sons of François de Lescluse, who had been condemned at La Gorgue and executed, and his property confiscated. Later the same year the people of the town attacked the *bailli* and the curé of La Gorgue while they were travelling on the road to La Gorgue from Béthune: both men were badly wounded and died soon afterwards. However, such small-scale violence was soon suppressed, and Flanders was pacified. Alva had another monument erected to himself at Antwerp: a statue cast in bronze from rebel cannon captured at Jemmingem, with the inscription:

> To Ferdinand Alvarez de Toledo, Duke of Alva, Governor of the Netherlands under Philip II, for having extinguished sedition, punished rebellion, re-established religion, assured justice and strengthened peace, the most faithful Minister of the best of Kings, this monument is erected.

The remaining Protestant pastors fled or were caught, the underground committees were broken up; consistories had to be held in the strictest secrecy. The only refuge left was in a dense forest on the border between Flanders and Hainaut: today the village of Hoorbeke Sainte Marie is one of the very few in Belgium where Protestantism has survived since the Reformation. Even the records were scattered, and most of them disappeared; the only reason why we know the story of Corneille de Lezenne is that in 1857 Charles Louis Frossard an amateur historian found some manuscript registers "in such an advanced state of decay that in a few years they would have been illegible" and wrote some notes on the history of the Reformed Church at Lille during the period of the Spanish rule. By 1568 that history had practically come to an end. Unless you were very brave, or unable to move, the best course for Protestants was to leave Flanders for one of the churches abroad, and wait there for better times to come – if ever they did.

PART II

The
Great Migrations
1560–1635

CHAPTER 6

The First Exodus from Flanders
1560–75

> There is great uncertainty about the number of our people who have fled from here on account of religion. They estimate that there are 18,000 to 20,000 in London, Sandwich and the places near by.
>
> Letter from Christopher Dassonville,
> 24 April 1563

> The mother of Mahieu de le Pierre has asked me to ask you to commend her to him and to his wife; she had heard that his wife was very ill, and in child birth.
>
> Letter to Guillaume le Roy,
> a refugee in England,
> from his daughter in Flanders,
> 20 February 1570

In July 1568, at the height of the executions, Tournai was deserted. In many streets, it was said, only half a dozen people were to be found; according to the bishop's pronotary, half of the entire population had disappeared "by flight, execution or banishment". The other former centres of Protestantism in Flanders were in a similar plight; Lille for example was reckoned to have lost one-third of its population by the time that Alva left the Netherlands in 1573. It was naturally assumed by people at the time that it was religion, or rather the suppression of heresy, that was the reason for this first great migration from Flanders, and that it was the coming of Alva with his army which turned the stream of refugees into a flood; but in fact the mass movement of people was well under way long before the Spanish regiments crossed the frontier in the summer of 1567, and economic as well as religious pressures were at work. Otherwise it is hard to see why, during the comparative tolerance of

Margaret of Parma's fairly popular regency, so many people from the southern provinces found it necessary to cross the French frontier into the Calaisis and the Boulonnais, while others went over the Channel into England.

Christopher Dassonville, who kept the banished Granvelle informed about the state of affairs in the Netherlands, wrote to him on 15 January 1565, in the middle of the harsh winter depicted in Breughel's "Hunters in the Snow".

> The country is so depopulated (he said) one sees daily people from the country going to England with their families and the tools of their trade; already London, Sandwich and the parts near by are so full (of refugees) they say the number exceeds 30,000.

Two years earlier Dassonville had estimated the number of refugees in England "on account of religion" at 18,000 to 20,000, and even if his estimates are exaggerated there was clearly a steady increase in migration during the early 1560s; and the reference in the second letter to men taking with them their families and the tools of their trade is revealing: this was a true emigration, not a temporary seeking of shelter. Far too many skilled hands were leaving the southern provinces and as the news of Alva's preparations caused the flow of refugees to increase, Margaret in Brussels did her best to stop it. On Monday, 7 July 1567, some weeks before Alva's arrival, she sent orders to the magistrates all along the coast, at Dunkirk, Nieupoort, Gravelines, Middelburg, Flushing and Armijden:

> Many of my subjects are passing to England (through your ports) with my goods. Enquiries are to be made and if they say they go for business, let them pass but without their goods and tools. If they are going to change their domicile, then arrest them.

In spite of these instructions, the coming of Alva in August 1567 soon made things worse. On 8 September Margaret sent an indignant letter to Philip:

> Great numbers of people with their goods and manufactures have fled to foreign lands, either because of the oppression of these unwelcome guests (that is, the Spanish regiments) or because they despair of pardon, or through dread of miseries to come.

It is worth noting how Margaret seems to be taking the side of the people against the Spaniards; much as she disliked the nobles (who probably did not let her forget that her Flemish mother Johanna van der Gheest was the daughter of a weaver) she was a native of Flanders herself and could appreciate both the fear the Spanish troops aroused and the damage their presence was doing to the economy of the province. She put the number of fugitives as high as 100,000, probably to impress Philip with the seriousness of affairs, perhaps in a deliberate echo of the number of Protestants claimed in de Brès's Confession; the number may have been exaggerated, but it seems clear enough that during this period tens of thousands of refugees fled into the northern provinces, eastward into Germany, and west into France and England. The latter were not much impeded by Margaret's orders to the magistrates in the Channel ports because there was an easy way to avoid them. It lay along the waterways into France.

By 1567 the balance of power between Catholic and Protestant in France was too even for the authorities to close the northern frontier to Protestant refugees from the Netherlands. Thus, de Gourdon the governor of Calais was under no instructions to arrest refugees from King Philip's dominions; as for de Morvillers the governor of Boulogne, he was himself a Protestant and had caused the images to be removed from the town churches. Refugees from Flanders were therefore able to settle in the Calaisis and the Boulonnais and practise the Protestant religion at one of the new temples; or they could take ship from Calais to England.

For the people of Flanders in the sixteenth and seventeenth centuries (and for a long time before and afterwards) the best way to travel was by water. The roads were bad and often waterlogged; the rivers, streams and canals went everywhere and travel by boat was quick and easy. The river valleys were thickly populated and it was by water that goods and people travelled.[1] The Lys and the Scheldt were the main routes of Flanders; using them, their tributaries and the network of artificial waterways, it was possible to reach any part of the province, or to cross over into France by boat or barge. Thus people from Armentières and round about would regularly go to

---

[1] When Wenceslaus Hollar accompanied Thomas Howard, earl of Arundel, on his mission to the Austrian emperor in 1636, the party travelled in a flotilla of barges along the Rhine, the Main and the Danube.

Calais to market. That meant crossing a frontier and a couple of days travelling, but it was a perfectly practicable journey with goods to carry, and it was made frequently enough to provide cover for the escape of refugees from Flanders, or for their return. Others who preferred to try their luck in the Boulonnais would travel as far as possible up the Lys, then over the watershed which formed the frontier between the territories of the kings of France and Spain; the towns just over the border, Maninghem, Clainleu, Cormont-en-Boulonnais, are names which occur often in the stories of the refugees.

So it happened that in spite of the attempt of the authorities to stem the flood, the refugees continued to leave Flanders in thousands as life under Alva's rule became harder for those who stayed. In 1571 another of Granvelle's correspondents, Maximilian Morillon the vicar-general of the diocese of Mechelen, wrote to tell him that even the moneylenders had run out of funds; everything which could be pawned was already pledged and the beggars were to be numbered in hundreds in some of the towns and villages. Such was the result, deliberately sought and achieved, of Philip's policy of repression in what had been the most prosperous part of his dominions, if not in Europe; for all his qualities he was as great a disaster to his subjects in the Netherlands as Louis XIV would prove to Frenchmen in the next century. Many of the refugees returned as soon as Alva had gone and more peaceful conditions were restored, but Granvelle reckoned in 1575 that something like 6,000 "Belges" had emigrated permanently to England, and that, for once in a way, was probably a modest estimate. Indeed between 1560 and 1575 there had been a mass movement of people in which single families, groups of families and even whole communities had left the Netherlands to seek safety abroad.

We have witnessed similar migrations in the twentieth century and can realise what was involved. Flanders herself has been afflicted twice in our time, in 1914 and in 1940, and a description of what happened on the second of these occasions may give us some idea of what happened in the sixteenth century. In May 1940, as the defence of France was collapsing, Pierre Mendès-France watched the refugees from the north pouring through his town of Louviers, and later described it. First came the fast cars of the rich, then the older cars, then the cyclists.

Last of all came the heavy wagons of the peasants from Flanders; they advanced slowly, laden with the sick and the aged; strings of these wagons, stretching for a mile or more, would represent the evacuation of an entire village, with its mayor, its priest, the old schoolmaster, the policeman. It was a colossal uprooting.

The refugees of the sixteenth century had to be more circumspect than this. They would have travelled singly or in small groups and taken only what they could carry, but over a period of years there was a similar massive movement of population; and the same social distinctions as in 1940 probably applied. The well-to-do, better informed and better equipped, would tend to move first, followed by a mass of humbler folk, many of whom had to leave their families behind until there was a chance to return home, or to get them out of the country as well.

Despite the confusion of the times, this period of the first great exodus from Flanders provides new and valuable sources of information for the family historian. The surviving registers of the Walloon communities in England start in the 1560s; they can provide, if one is very lucky, the sort of information which makes it possible to identify individuals and families. In London, the influx of foreigners prompted the authorities to keep a check on the new arrivals, and lists of strangers began to be compiled in various wards of the city of London. Most important of all, from the point of view of gaining some insight into the life of the refugees and the way the emigration affected families, it is from this period that we begin to see private papers surviving in the form of letters and wills. These sources are often fragmentary but out of them one can begin to build up sections of the jigsaw. Using a combination of these records it is possible to trace, from the time of the first exodus onwards, the movement of various related families who left the Netherlands for England.

This does not sound a particularly striking proposition, but to those who know the history of the refugees it is a bold claim to make. Agnew, a careful historian whose work on the French-speaking Protestant exiles is one of the foundations of all such studies, did not believe that it could be done. At the beginning of his historical introduction, telling about the movement of the refugees from northern France and the Netherlands, he says:

A history tracing this exodus hither and thither might be compiled; but the materials for refugee biography at the earlier date (1567) are non-existent, at least when the theme is limited to persons whose destination was England. We cannot single out any remarkable sufferers and portray their sufferings in their native Flanders, and then proceed to exhibit them in England as refugees and citizens of an adopted country, whose lives have survived in the memories of their fellow countrymen.

But we can. It is quite true, as Agnew points out, that the surviving registers of most of the largest Strangers' churches do not begin until nearly a generation after the first refugees arrived: in Canterbury, July 1581; Norwich, June 1595; London (Threadneedle Street), January 1600. There is one register which dates from the start of the refuge, that of the Walloon church at Southampton, but Agnew dismisses this on the grounds that "the earliest names are of no celebrity". Perhaps it is because one of these earliest names is that of a certain Mahieu de le Pierre that I have not felt inclined to take as proven that we cannot "trace this exodus hither and thither".

There are certainly cases in which a continuous line can be traced. Agnew himself tells the story of two such families. Laurent des Bouveries, born in 1542, was the younger son of the lord of the chateau of Bouvines, which still stands at Sainghin-en-Mélantois near Lille. The father was a strict Catholic, and he noticed (this was in the 1560s) that his younger son often played truant from mass. In the end, suspecting that Laurent was talking too much to his heretic tenants, he told him that if he did not appear at mass the following Sunday he would have him examined by the Inquisition. Even if Laurent was not already a Protestant, the prospect of being hauled up in front of the tribunal was enough to convince him that he should make himself scarce; he fled to Frankfurt-on-Main, where he ended up on the doorstep of another Protestant refugee who had settled at Frankfurt and started a silk factory. According to the story the old man said to Laurent, "I see by the whiteness of your hands that you have not been used to hard work, but stay with me and keep the accounts and supervise the workmen." He did stay, and in proper storybook style, married his benefactor's niece, Barbara van den Hove, whose own family (to judge by the name) were also refugees from Flanders. In due course, when Queen Elizabeth invited continental Protestants to come to England, Laurent (with his brothers Jean and Antoine) was among those who accepted. They came first to Sandwich in 1567; the next year Laurent and Barbara moved to Canterbury; they had five sons and three daughters before Barbara died in October 1591; Laurent married again, and survived until November 1610.

In Canterbury at the same time was another refugee family whose coming had been far less sedate. Jean de la Forterie and his wife came from Lille in Flanders. In 1567 they left home in such a hurry that their son Nicholas was actually born "on shipboard as they came". This Nicholas when he grew up married Anne, the daughter of William Thessies, or Thieffries, a Protestant spice merchant from Tournai, and moved to London where he too became a merchant; Nicholas and Anne had three sons before he died in about 1590; she survived him. Peter, the third son of Nicholas and Anne de la Fortrye (by now the name was anglicised) married Leah the youngest child of Laurent and Barbara des Bouveries; and one of their daughters was called Leah after her mother.

By this time the reader may be wondering if the list of Bouveries and Fortryes is going on for ever, but we have reached the point of the story. Young Leah Fortrye was the great-grandmother of Elizabeth Barling of Lynsted in Kent; and Elizabeth Barling was my four-times-great-grandmother; and so I, like a lot of other people, am descended from Laurent des Bouveries who ran away to Frankfurt in the 1560s, and from Nicholas de la Forterie who was born in the middle of the Channel in 1567.

What this means is that by about the time of the first exodus, roughly the years around the troubles of the 1560s, we begin to have enough material to make family trees and even to catch glimpses of the individuals concerned. It is personal details which are the life and soul of family history; while it is essential to have dates and places for births, marriages and deaths, it is pretty dull to have nothing more, and any extra facts which can be gleaned are precious. A surprisingly wide range of material can be gathered, even from the sixteenth century, to make up a brief biography of an ancestor. One of the richest sources of personal details are letters passing between members of the family, particularly between correspondents in different countries with a good deal of urgent news to impart.

It may not seem very likely that such documents will have survived from four hundred years and more ago, especially from a time of great danger and confusion like the troubles in the Netherlands, but it is always worth keeping a sharp look-out. One day in the Bibliothèque Albert Premier in Brussels, while I was browsing through the proceedings of the Royal Historical Commission, I made a discovery.

Before I say what the discovery was, it is ironic to reflect for a moment on the selectivity of written records: how it is often the careful collections which are lost, and the unexpected scraps which survive. Any researcher, professional or amateur, has to reckon with the random culling of his sources by the accidents of history; the gaps appear more and more frequently as one moves back into the past, until the period is reached where there is nothing but blank space. (For a family historian it is the first gap that spells the end of a sure line of ascent.) For historians working in the north of France, or in the provinces of the Netherlands, it is war which has done most damage to the archives, which to begin with were extremely rich. Over the centuries the painstaking officials of the kings of France and Spain built up massive stacks of records, especially in the Seventeen Provinces: the Spanish word for red tape *balduque* is a corruption of the name of the town of s'Hertogenbosch (Bois le Duc in French) because even to Spaniards the Netherlands seemed to be a bureaucrat's paradise. For someone hunting ancestors from the southern provinces two archives in particular would be most useful: the records of the present Département of the Pas de Calais, which were housed in the Hotel de Ville at Arras, and the municipal records at Middelburg in Zeeland. Unfortunately they are no longer available. On 5 July 1915 the German artillery outside Arras laid down a barrage which destroyed the cathedral and the Palais St Vaast; the departmental archives, the municipal library, the museum all went up in flames. In May 1940 the Germans attacked the Netherlands, and the bombs destroyed the centre of the old town of Middelburg; the municipal records from the founding of the republic and all the church registers were lost. Since this sort of thing has gone on through the centuries, one might reasonably assume that the disasters of war are always bad for historians and that it is not worth hoping to find much left about families from the "cockpit of Europe". One would be wrong.

At eight o'clock one Sunday morning, 26 February 1570, outside the frontier fort of Henuin, a party of travellers from Flanders was crossing a spit of land between two waterways, to take Jean Rouzée's boat for Calais from St Omer. Two of the passengers, a Walloon called Henri Fléel, and a boy called Jean Desmadry who was travelling with him, were arrested by a soldier from the fort named Jehan Goetrauwe and taken in for questioning. Fléel was formally charged with being *de la nouvelle religion*, did not deny it, and was searched: inside the tops of his boots, and in the false bottom of a basket he was carrying, under cheeses, *confitures* and onions, were found nearly eighty letters. As soon as they were read it was apparent that the letters were on their way to refugees in England from their families in Flanders, and that Fléel was a regular courier; one of the letters, from Marie de le Ruelle, revealed that she was the mother of the boy with Fléel. She wrote to her husband Jean Desmadry, who had been banished in 1568:

> Lille, 8 February 1570. This is to let you know that I received your last letter by the hand of the bearer of this, in which you told me to send my son Jean with the bearer of this. I do not know who he really is but I did not want to disobey you. . . .

Louis de Moncheau, the governor of the fort, also wanted to know who Fléel really was, and where he had got the letters from. "From Pierre du Buis" was the answer, at a place between Hondschoote and Reninghulst. (A safe reply: the places were 25 kilometres apart and "Pierre du Buis" was about as rare a name as Jean Moulin.) Where was he taking them? To give to a man at the tavern des Trois Rois in Calais. Naturally this tale did not pass muster; de Moncheau was persistent and in the end the full story came out. Henri's real name was Henri de Busnes. He had left his family at Neuve Eglise on 23 February to go to St Omer. It was the boy Jean Desmadry who had brought him the packet of letters, with 21 livres, one as a fee, to take the letters to England and the rest to be delivered with the letters to various refugees. The boy said it was "some woman" who had given him the letters, and after various other sensible answers to awkward questions, he got off;[2] de Busnes was identified as a Calvinist (he denied being an Anabaptist or a Lutheran) and was sent to Brussels as a heretic, where one suspects, though there is no further record, that he became one of Alva's victims.

And the letters? They were put into a file, labelled *En ceste fillache y at quattre-vingtz lettres trouvées en la possession de Henri Fléel à St Omer*, and put away in the archives at Brussels. There they stayed intact for nearly four hundred years, until they were edited by Mr Verheyden, the same scholar who edited the Lists of the Condemned for the Belgian Royal Historical Commission.

It is rare to have original letters from ordinary people preserved intact from the sixteenth century. These ones were written in a greaty hurry (one at five o'clock in the morning) so as to seize the opportunity of the messenger passing by, and they are quite free of the formalities, pieties and philosophical reflections which an educated letter-writer of the period would have felt obliged to include. They are written in Walcq, often extremely fractured French: one woman, who sounds rather fun, advises the recipient, her brother, to read her letter several times because, "*J'ay puer ne le savé lyr*," and she is right, it is the devil to read:

> *Je vous prye lysiès cy due ouz troy foys . . . me volà tout mon myel de par cel que connysiés depuis saynt Jaque et Saint Chrytoffes jour. Voutre amy à tout.*

Apart from the difficulty, the letters make very rewarding reading. In the first place they give us revealing glimpses of the life of ordinary people trying to survive the troubles; in particular they illustrate how families were broken up when several members went to England while the rest stayed at home in Flanders, but with the firm intention to reunite the family in one place or the other as soon as it was safe to do so. Secondly, the letters are full of names and even addresses (a lapse in security which may have had sad consequences) so they give us the means of identifying individuals and linking refugees in England with their place of birth in the Netherlands.

[2] To judge from her letter, Jean's mother was a Calvinist, but her son told the examining magistrates that she observed Lent and regularly went to mass, and that was probably sufficient to keep her out of trouble.

One letter is from Marie Lenghon to her husband Guy Juire, who was banished from Armentières as an iconoclast on 13 April 1568.

> As for news of the *pays*, no one is making a penny, either in the countryside or in Armentières, and there is not a single weaver now in business (*eil n'ey a poein acun drapier quy drapaey maintenan*). . . . My husband, though it has pleased God to separate us one from another He has certainly not made us forget one another in our hearts. When I remember the happy past, there is not a day when my heart does not weep. I pray God who watches over us always to give us good patience. I have good hopes that things will not remain long in this state.

All the letters show the same mixture of material worries and personal feeling, though the proportions vary; not surprisingly the confiscations and especially the billeting of Spanish troops loom large. Jean Demain's brother wrote to him on 3 February 1570.

> As for news from here (*de par decha*) I don't know what to tell you, except that we are pestered (*fort tourmentez*) by Spanish soldiers worse than ever, because they decreed at the beginning of this month of February that every soldier should have each week one hour of candle-light . . . and linen, towels and napkins (*linge, nappe et serviette*) and (the right) to heat himself at his landlord's fire, which is completely unreasonable.

In spite of the presence of troops, the repression is "less savage than before" (not saying very much!) and there are several references to the chances of coming home. One man called Pierre is advised to come back to Flanders because he is no longer on the wanted list: "You could easily come by Calais, and you could travel on the boat with the people coming back from Calais market, which is on Saturday", that is, to come back the same way as the letters were going out. However the journey was still risky. Gilles Piet was banished from Tournai on 21 January 1569; his brother wrote to him a year later:

> My brother, I must warn you that we cannot return by the same route without a passport, because I have seen with my own eyes men from here who were not allowed to pass without it. . . . Do not take it in bad part if we delay, but the roads are water-logged everywhere and it is impossible for carts to get through.

This letter, incidentally, has a reference to the landlord of the Three Kings inn in Calais, which Henri Fléel also mentioned; it must have been a rendezvous for travellers on lawful occasions, and otherwise. Other letters have addresses in them, and this helps to place those which have no such information; by combining dates and places (where known) we can work out that although the letters had been written over a period of about three months, Fléel seems to have collected them in a rapid tour of the *pays* during February. The first letter in the bundle dates from November 1569. Many of the later letters were written "in haste" because Fléel only stayed in the place a day or two before moving on; being a courier was risky. Thus on Wednesday, 1 February and Thursday, 2 February 1570 he was at Valenciennes; on Friday, 3rd at Tournai, on Saturday, 4th at Ath; on Sunday, 5th at Neuve Eglise (his home) and on Wednesday, 8th at Lille; at Armentières on Friday, 10 February, at Ypres the following Wednesday and at Armentières again on Friday, 17 February. He left home at Neuve Eglise with all the letters, hidden in his boots and the basket, on Thursday, 23 February.

The reason why it was worthwhile to work out the route taken by Fléel was that it enabled me to place somewhere in the Pays de l'Alleu near Armentières the following letter from a girl called le Roy to her father Guillaume. It was written on Monday, 20 February 1570 and interested me very much for reasons which will be apparent.

> Salvation in Jesus Christ.
> My very honoured and good friend, my father, I commend myself to you with all my heart. I am very upset not to know for sure whether or not I should also commend myself to my mother. I have heard from Jean Hadoux that Jacquet Roussel had told him that my mother had left this world. He was very surprised not to have had any letter, nor have I, and I do not know what to think: I pray you, set my mind at rest. Also, however that may be (if God has permitted it) I would very much like to know how all my friends are. . . . I pray to our good God that he may comfort us all together, if there is need of it.
>
> I pray to be commended to my brother Guillaume. I heard from the mother of Mahieu de le Pierre that his wife was ill; I do not know the truth of it at all, and so we wait all the time to have news of you, whether she is dead or not; I pray you all to send me news of how everything is going. Commend us to my brother Pierre and to my sister Susanne; I thank her for the

needles she has sent me, and so does Jan Gaven. My brother
Guillaume, if we have the means, one day we will repay you
everything.

The mother of Mahieu de le Pierre has asked me to ask
you to commend her to him (Mahieu) and to his wife; she had
heard that she was very ill, and in childbirth; and she told me to
ask you to say to Mahieu her son that she is doing her best to
send him what he asked should be sent to Antwerp. . . .
Christian Sause asks earnestly to be commended to you and to
all your family: he was at my house for the festival at Ypres. [It
would take more than the troubles to stop this popular festival.] As regards your scales, I will do my best; I have sent to
Merville, and my uncle Jan Stuf has replied that he would give
no more for the whole lot including weights than £4 4s 0d; and
Christian Sause told me that he told my sister Mahiette that he
would give a gold angelot for it, but he got hold of another
when he heard he could not have it. So, I will do my best, and
will send you what turns up.

Nothing else for the present, except that God give you His
grace. In haste, this 20th of February. From your daughter, as
you know her. [In the margin] My father, I send you a pot of
cream, which my sister wanted to send you.

My uncle Jan Stuf has sent a . . . (?*cemique*) to our house: I
will send him one back when there is an opportunity. [On the
back] To be given to Guillaume le Roy.

This letter struck me as useful and exciting in a number of ways.
It listed several members of the same families at one time: Guillaume le Roy and his wife (if she was still alive) with their children
Guillaume, Pierre and Susanne in England, their daughter (the
writer) and at least one sister Mahiette left behind in the Pays de
l'Alleu; Mahieu de le Pierre and his wife (if she was still alive) and
perhaps a baby in England, while his mother was left behind to sort
out his affairs in the *pays*; le Roy's brother-in-law Jan Stuf, and his
friends Jean Hadoux, Jacquet Roussel and Christian Sause – these
names and relationships offered the prospect of being able to
identify particular families in particular places. I found that Guillaume le Roy himself came from Sailly; he had taken part in a plot to
murder the Baron d'Auxy who had been sent by the regent Margaret with another counsellor called Couronnel as commissioners
to visit the damaged churches in the Pays de l'Alleu. Le Roy was
convicted of iconoclasm at Laventie and banished on 7 December
1568; he took refuge first in Sandwich, then in 1576 moved to

Canterbury, and ended up in London where his children Ezechias and Ester were born; Samuel des Bouveries was a witness at the baptism of Ezechias's son Guillaume on 9 August 1607. There are also several mentions of a Louis Stuf (or Sturfe) from Merville in the Walloon registers at Canterbury in the 1590s.

Naturally enough, the other point which struck me about the letter to Guillaume le Roy was the mention of Mahieu de le Pierre. There is no trace of him or his wife (or a baby) at Sandwich or at Canterbury. However, the register of the Walloon church at Southampton, the earliest of those which survive, shows that on 2 January 1569 Mahieu de le Pierre and his wife Elizabeth du Maret were professed, with a number of other new arrivals, a date which would match very well with le Roy's expulsion the previous month. Clearly le Roy's daughter thought that Mahieu de le Pierre and her father were in contact with each other in 1570, but she could have been mistaken since her letter shows that there had been no news from the refugees for a while. Was it possible that the de le Pierre family from the Pays de l'Alleu was closer to my de la Pierre relatives than the family or families in Tournai? At least there was another section of jigsaw which might connect up if further pieces could only be found.

The sixth letter in the bundle is from Jeanne Castel, whose relatives were in the French church in London in 1564. Another letter from the Pays de l'Alleu was written by Philippe Caulier to Jacques de la Haye on 16 February 1570.

This writer too can be identified and given a biographical note. Suspected of heresy as far back as 1542; one of the iconoclasts of Laventie on 15 August 1566; an elder of the Calvinist community at La Gorgue and entrusted by them with the "act of accord" with Egmont and Hornes; and banished (not surprisingly) on 24 November 1565, Caulier had prudently decamped already, and the confiscation of his property raised the sum of £78 16s 6d. At his trial *in absentia* one of his neighbours stated:

> He knew he (Caulier) had left his house for some time; did not know why or where; he had come back to sow his land and reap the crop; at present he is in hiding, for fear of being caught as an outlaw and being hauled in front of some other tribunal and not the ordinary magistrates before whom he would submit himself and not go absent.

In other words, the local magistrates would be sympathetic to a local Calvinist, whereas "some other tribunal" such as Titelman would most likely have condemned him to death. Philippe must have returned to Flanders before 1570 to write this letter, probably from Armentières:

> We have heard that my cousin was about to give birth to some Englishman or Englishwoman; if it has happened, I pray the Creator to grant it increase of virtue and good morals.

Some of the letters, even at this distance in time, are very moving. Thomas Le Den wrote to his sister Jeanne on 1 February 1570:

> Know, my sister, that my mother too is in good health for the present, and she prays and we pray that you will return to us, because since the hour and the day that you left, her eyes have never been dry, she weeps all the time, praying God that you may wish to return to her and all of us. [That "you may wish" may suggest that Jeanne was the only Protestant in her family.]

Martin Plennart's wife wrote to him on 1 February 1570:

> I don't have any more news to send you for the present, except that your daughters Annette and Marie ask all the time when their father will come; your daughter Marie says that you can't come, you have something wrong with your feet. God be with you.

Jacques Bérot to his daughter Agnes:

> My daughter, I commend myself with all my heart to you and to your husband, so does your mother and your nephew and niece, not to forget your two children. . . . We were very anxious to have news of you; your two children here are very well and growing in size and beauty, and little David is a joy (*fort plaisant*). All for now, the bearer of this is leaving in a hurry. Praying God the Creator to help you in His holy grace. From Valenciennes this 11 day of February 1570. Your father Jacques Bérot. P.S. The said David commends himself to his mother, his brother and his sister, and has kissed me this morning to seal it. I have given to the bearer as his fee 5 *patars*.

Another meaty letter this, from the family point of view; it identifies the members of the Bérot family in England and those at Valenciennes in February 1570; all are in good health. A much sadder letter from Valenciennes was written by his niece to Pierre Gruels, who was banished on 15 January 1569; he too had got off lightly, having been a member of the delegation sent to Brussels to seek freedom of religion, and also an image-breaker. The letter goes:

> First is to tell you that we have no more mother for the last 4½ months, she died the 2nd of October 1569, on Sunday evening, at half past nine . . . and my mother was not at all ill when she went to bed, and an hour afterwards she died beside my father without being ill and without speaking, just at the point of death (*à l'artiecque de la mort*) she threw her arm over my father, who was quite astonished and so were all of us . . . and we are without a mother since then, and as for my uncle and my aunt, we have lost them all by plague . . . so we are at this hour 7 poor children without a mother and with a father who is a little bad-tempered (*fauceu*) as you well know. . . . In haste, this 2 February 1570 – and my sister Katelin is also without a mother – from your niece whom you know well.

This sad letter was addressed "to my uncle, Pierre Gruels, wherever he may be"; perhaps it is just as well for his peace of mind that it never reached him, there was nothing he could do about it. Presumably he was the brother of the dead woman. It sounds as if all the family, father, mother and seven children, were in the same room (and perhaps the same bed) when the poor woman died suddenly in the night; the uncle and aunt who died of the plague probably lived in another house or there would have been an even longer list of disasters to relate.

It is worth noting that Pierre Gruels's niece, and Guillaume le Roy's daughter, do not sign their names but use the formula "whom you know well", or "as you know her". The risk of the letters being intercepted was a hazard and for the same reason, no doubt, some of the letters bear no other address than the name; but some were directed to London, Southampton and Norwich, and the bearer was no doubt expected to visit each of the communities, travelling via Sandwich and Canterbury, and to make enquiries as he went. By the time of "Henri Fléel's" abortive journey there were several thousand Walloons in the churches in England, not simply tolerated but actively encouraged by the prudent Queen. It is time to cross the Channel ourselves to see how the first large wave of emigrants was getting on.

CHAPTER 7

The First Walloon Communities
in England

Glory of the virtuous followers of Jesus, elder of the revered ladies of
the Christian community, moderator of the affairs of the Nazarene
sect . . . Queen of the land of England, may her end be blissful [i.e. may
she be converted and die a Muslim].

Ottoman diplomat addressing
Elizabeth I

Agreed . . . to receive a company of Strangers to live in the liberties of
this City.

Canterbury Court of Berghmote,
15 July 1567

On 21 August 1567 – the day before Alva arrived in Brussels – Claes
van Werken wrote from Norwich to his wife in Ypres. The government in London, like that in Brussels, tried to stop private letters
going abroad and the two quoted here were impounded, but there
are no state secrets in them, only the normal Flanders preoccupations of family, money and food.

> You would never believe how friendly our people are together,
> and the English are the same and very well disposed to our
> nation. If you come here with half our property you would
> never think of going (back) to live in Flanders. Send my money
> and the three children; come at once and do not be anxious.
> When you come bring a dough-trough, because there are none
> here. . . . Buy two little dishes to make butter, all the Nether-
> landers and Flemings make their own because here it is all
> pig-fat.

Leonard Keerlinck, writing ten days later, is astonished at the
cheapness of food in England. "More can be bought at Norwich for

97

a penny than for three at Ypres. Do not bring more than is necessary to keep house, because the freight is expensive."

As the names van Werken and Keerlinck indicate, these letters were written in Dutch: Norwich was the main centre for Flemings from the north of Flanders. Like refugees at any period, people went if they could to stay with fellow-exiles from the same place, who could help to give them a start in their new country. In London among the 3,835 refugees from the southern provinces listed by the queen's officials in 1571, there are some familiar names.

> 1571. Tower Ward: St Dunstan Parish. Nicholas Fortrye of Thiel, Merchant, came to this realm iiii years past for religion; Margaret his wife, Margaret and Samuel, children; Michael his servant; and late in his house Gilam Jefrye of Thiel who came ii months past for religion; Elizabeth his wife; Elizabeth and Antonetta his children.

Nicholas was the uncle of young Nicholas "born on shipboard as they came" in 1567. At London there were Walloons and Flemings too, and the same at Southampton where Mahieu de le Pierre and his wife Elizabeth du Maret were admitted to the Eucharist in January 1569; but mostly the Walloons and Flemings went to different centres, the Flemings through Antwerp to Norwich, Yarmouth and Colchester, while the refugees from French Flanders and the Lys valley went through Calais to Sandwich and ended up, most of them, in Canterbury.

The Walloon (later French) church at Canterbury has a good claim to be the oldest Calvinist congregation in the English-speaking world. It was established in the reign of Edward VI whose godfather Thomas Cranmer, archbishop of Canterbury, offered a refuge in England to Protestant theologians and teachers from the continent. As he put it, he hoped to obtain "the assistance of learned men who, having compared their opinions together with us, may do away with all devotional controversies, and build up an entire system of doctrine," a worthy aim which has long inspired the Church of England but did not, then or later, succeed in healing the divisions in the Protestant ranks. One of those who received Cranmer's invitation was a Polish gentleman called John Alasco (or Lasco) who had ministered to a community in the Netherlands; he was Cranmer's guest for some time. Two more invitations went to Martin Bucer and Paul Fagius, preachers and professors of the reform at Strasbourg but then destitute. "Those who can no longer keep to the high sea because of the tempest take refuge in port," Cranmer told them; and that the kingdom of England would be a very safe shelter for them; let them come and be fellow-workers in the Lord's harvest. It was typical of Cranmer's decency that he sought arguments to calm the consciences of men who might well have replied that it was their duty to face the persecution at any risk to themselves.

Two Italians preceded Bucer to England, Peter Martyr Vermigli and Bernardino Ochino; Vermigli had been a professor of theology at Strasbourg, Ochino had preached at Geneva and at Basle; eventually he became a canon of Canterbury Cathedral. Most of these distinguished foreigners made their way in due course to London, Oxford or Cambridge, but two of them, Jean Utenhove and François de la Rivière,[1] spent two years ministering to the French and Walloon refugees in Canterbury, and it is from this time that we get the very first mention of the refugee church there. On 15 January 1549 Vermigli wrote to Utenhove in Canterbury:

> I rejoice greatly to hear that you have a place where you can practise your religion (*vous pouvez maintenir vos cultes dans un local*). . . . God grant that you may soon see the number of the faithful growing still more.

It sounds as if a meeting place for the refugees existed but it was not necessarily a church.

In 1550 Guy de Brès also took refuge in England; and on 24 July the same year Edward VI granted letters patent to John Lasco appointing him superintendent of the refugee churches in England. Alas, this respectability was short-lived: Mary Tudor came to the throne in 1553 and married Philip of Spain the following year. Luckily there is no need to go too deeply into the story of persecutions, executions and other sad events illustrated for generations of Englishmen by the horrific tales in Foxe's Book of Martyrs. But the immigrant Protestants were dispersed: Guy de Brès fled the country to write the Walloon Confession; and John Lasco took Edward's

---

[1] Utenhove came of a distinguished family, prominent among the Protestants of the Netherlands; a layman held in high regard by the reformers, he had fled to Cologne, but one of his brothers was killed. De la Rivière, formerly a Franciscan monk, escaped to Geneva where he met Calvin and became a minister.

patent with him to Poland, and brought it back again in the autumn of 1559. When Elizabeth succeeded to the throne on 17 November 1558 she reinstated Edward's Prayer Book, and England became safe again for Protestants; just in time for the first great influx of refugees from Flanders.

Indeed it seems a feature of the Protestant migrations that the places where persecution was harshest, and places of safe refuge, changed with remarkable rapidity. A drawing of them would look rather like an internal combustion engine, with explosions in a succession of places, and openings here and there to allow the refugees to escape. The first persecutions of Protestants in France and the Netherlands were balanced by tolerance or Protestant ascendancy in Germany and Switzerland, and then England. In 1553–8 England under Mary reverted to the Catholic side; but persecution died down in Flanders and the Protestants gained ground in France. Then, at the time of the troubles in the Netherlands and the massacre of St Bartholomew in France, England was once again a place of refuge. And so it went on throughout the century. When in 1570 the new pope finally excommunicated Elizabeth[2] persecution in England was directed mainly against Catholics.

In trying to trace the movements of Protestant families it is important to determine when, and therefore which way, they were likely to be moving. By the end of the 1560s this movement was sharply from Flanders towards England, France and the north; soon the number of Walloon refugees in Canterbury made it essential for them to find a permanent place of worship. On 15 July 1567 – when Alva's army was on the march up the Spanish Road – the Canterbury Court of Berghmote replied to a petition from the Walloons. They agreed "to receive a company of Strangers to live in the liberties of this city", Strangers meaning that the petitioners were men born outside the city boundaries. In 1568 (by which time the Council of Blood was at work and the flight from Flanders at its height) Archbishop Parker granted the Walloons the use of part of

[2] It is worth noting that Philip II persuaded the previous pope, Pius IV, not to excommunicate Elizabeth in 1561, and again in 1563, because he could not afford bad relations with her at that time; nor would Alva intervene to help the revolt of the northern earls in England in 1569. After the excommunication Philip refused to publish the Bull in his dominions.

the crypt of Canterbury Cathedral to serve them as a school as well as for the practice of their religion. The city records show that when Peter Kelsham was mayor, "the undercroft of the Cathedral was this year given by the Queen to the fugitive Walloons". It was to serve as their centre, and as a place of refuge for further migrations from the perils of the mainland, for well over a century to come.

In the dismal annals of the civil and religious hatreds of the sixteenth century, filled with the doings of ferocious monarchs, murderous churchmen and turbulent citizens, the good deed of Matthew Parker and Mayor Kelsham stands out in splendid isolation. It is hard for us to appreciate how magnanimous it was for the Anglican bishops (if not the civil authorities) to receive the Protestant refugees from the continent so kindly. The immigrants were mostly Calvinists, and it was rare indeed for sixteenth century Protestants of different persuasions to treat each other with any more charity than they showed to Catholics, or Catholics to them. In spite of this, in many places in England the Protestants from Flanders were received as friends and given churches, sometimes a share in the parish church, in which to worship; and in "the most notable instance of all in the metropolitical city itself, the consecrated crypt of the Mother Church of England Christendom was given them for their services", says the historian Cross.

In those days the entrance to the crypt was from the nave or the south transept, through the south-west door; later a doorway was made out of the Close from a window in the Black Prince's chantry. Seven bays of the west side of the crypt, from the west wall to the Lady chapel, were reserved for the Strangers. The scriptural texts in French which they painted on the northern piers were still discernible in the 1890s, and one is still extant in the chantry.

Throughout the early 1570s the Walloon community at Canterbury continued to grow as newcomers from Flanders exceeded those who departed for home. They arrived singly, or in families and other groups. In 1571 Christian de la Quenellerie, pastor of the Protestant community at Armentières, led a party to England and they probably came as a group to Canterbury. In 1574 Hector Hamon, pastor of the refugees sheltering in the coastal ports at Rye and Winchelsea, brought his small flock up to the city; and soon after there was larger influx. On 6 September 1575 Lord Cobham, Warden of the Cinque Ports, wrote to the Privy Council that the number of refugees at Sandwich exceeded the quota which had been set by the queen, and suggested that they too should move inland; the Privy Council agreed, and on 20 February 1576 the mayor of Canterbury asked for the necessary licences. The Privy Council instructed Cobham to issue 100 franchises (perhaps one per family) to move to the city of Canterbury by midsummer's day; he was to choose "not the meanest sort" but skilled weavers. On 15 March the mayor and jurats signed the articles of agreement which were the Strangers' charter thenceforth.

We should be realistic about the motives which impelled the city fathers of Canterbury to welcome the skilled Walloon weavers who, according to the articles of agreement, were to manufacture cloth "after the Flanders fashion". Canterbury in the 1570s was in a very parlous state. Its prosperity had rested on the pilgrim trade to the shrine of St Thomas, and the Reformation had abolished the shrine and the pilgrims with it. As Hasted put it, "from great opulence and reputation, multitudes of inhabitants and beautiful buildings, this city fell suddenly to extreme poverty, nakedness and decay". The new draperies helped to restore the city's fortunes, especially since retail trade of all sorts was reserved for native Englishmen, and the Crown too reaped a profit of 6s 8d duty on every "short cloth" (24 yards) which was exported. To make quite sure that the coming of the Strangers would not be a burden, the articles of agreement laid down that they were to give shelter to other refugees passing through the city, and to provide relief to their own poor. For the Strangers, however, the most important clauses of the agreement were those which granted them formal freedom of worship, and allowed them to reside in the city although they were aliens. With these two basic rights confirmed, the Walloons were able to establish themselves securely in their new home.

About the Walloon community and the Strangers' church at Canterbury we know a good deal, rather too much, one is sometimes ungratefully tempted to say. The great de Schickler, whose massive volumes I leafed through in the library of the Société de l'Histoire du Protestantisme Français in Paris one dark Sunday afternoon while thunder boomed and rain poured down on the glass roof, gave a good deal of information about it; but even he did not go as deep as Francis Cross, whose *History of the Walloon and*

Huguenot Church at Canterbury tells all that one could possibly wish to know. The pastors and elders of the Strangers' church were as fascinated by religious controversy, as sure of their own right-eousness and of the sinful blindness of everyone else, as any other Protestants of their time, and they were as fond as the others of writing pamphlets. Add to that their careful keeping of records and accounts, and there is no shortage of raw material for the historian.

> Dr Schickler's noble work [says Cross with feeling] was aware of the existence of many of the Walloon records. . . . Before commencing to write a chapter, I had examined several thousand folios of more-or-less legible manuscript contained in the archives of the City and of the Cathedral, and had read, line by line, the whole of the voluminous Act Books, Elders' and Deacons' Accounts, letters and other documents. . . .

Thanks to Cross's industry it is possible to summarise the essential points with a tithe of his labour. The refugees settled mainly in the parishes of St Alphege, St Mary Northgate, St Peter, Holy Cross, and St Mildred; and especially in the buildings and gardens of the former Blackfriars monastery, some of which are in use both secular and religious in the 1980s, just as in the days of the Walloons four hundred years ago. All of this property was acquired at the dissolution of the monasteries by the speculators John Harrington and George Burden, who at once resold it to William Ovenden, a clothmaker, who came to live in the main building. He let out the rest of the estate to the Strangers for the spinning, weaving and market gardening trades which were their main occupations. The old refectory building (still standing by the Stour river) was used as a weavers' hall and as an exchange and mart for the Walloons. Many other trades or professions besides weaving came to be represented among the refugees: a census of new arrivals from France taken at Dover early in the next century found two preachers, three physicians and surgeons, two advocates, three merchants, two "esquires", two schoolmasters, thirteen drapers, grocers, brewers and butchers, twelve mariners, eight weavers, one gardener and one buttonmaker; while in London, a census taken in 1621 found 121 different trades among the foreign settlers. Never-theless it was for their spinning and weaving that the Walloons were best known, then and afterwards, and most valued by the govern-ment. In 1573 the queen herself visited Sandwich where the refugee children gave her an exhibition of spinning, "a thing well-liked both by her Majesty and by the nobility and ladies"; the Walloons at Sandwich were weavers of woollen cloth, woolcombers, spinners and dyers, while those who came up from Rye and Winchelsea with Hector Hamon wove serge, silken taffeta and bombazines. At Canterbury itself the staple business was the manufacture of "bayes and sayes" – coarse woollen cloth – and dyeing; the finished cloth had to be passed by an official examiner who charged twopence a piece for his services. Those who practised other trades were allowed to do business provided it was kept within the Strangers' community, but not outside it – that was still the preserve of the native English.

It followed from the rules of the settlement that the Walloon community at Canterbury was an enclosed one, and inward-looking for a period of perhaps two generations, until the younger members began to look outside for excitement and for company. The language usually spoken, at least during the sixteenth century, was Walcq; and the centre of the community was the Calvinist congregation with its ministers, elders and deacons who administered all the Strangers' business both religious and secular.

We get a glimpse of them at church in the next century, from William Somner's *Antiquities of Canterbury*, published in 1640, soon after the final arrival of Pierre de la Pierre and his family at a period when the congregation, as in the early 1570s, was swollen by newcomers because of trouble on the continent.

> Let me now lead you to the Undercroft, a place fit . . . to keep in memory the subterranean temples of the Primitives, in the time of persecution. The most part thereof being spacious and lightsome, for many years hath been the Strangers' Church. A congregation of the most part of exiles, grown so great and yet daily multiplying that the place in short time is likely to prove a hive too little to contain such a swarm.

The minister during the early period was Hector Hamon until Samuel le Chevalier was appointed in 1591. They governed their flock according to the discipline which had been drawn up by John Lasco; the doctrine was that of Guy de Brès's Confession of Faith. The liturgy was appointed by the synod of the Walloon churches and provided for ordinary worship, communion, baptism and marriages; there were services twice on Sundays and at least once during the week, special services on public feasts and festivals, and catechism classes for the children. The ingredients of the services were the familiar Protestant ones: exhortation, confession, prayers, systematic reading of the Scriptures, psalms in the Marot version, and hymns; blessings for the sovereign, for pastors, for those "still wandering in ignorance" and for all sufferers from war, pestilence and famine, the poor and the sick, prisoners and exiles. The most important part of the service was the sermon, at least an hour long, when the minister expounded the Word of the Lord from the pulpit.

At the front of the congregation sat the pastor's chief helpers, the elders, "sound in the Faith, grave and prudent men of honest life, free from reproach and zealous for the glory of God", who served for two or three years at a time; helping them were the deacons, whose main job was to look after the sick and the poor. Since many of the Walloons were sick and most of them were very poor, the deacons must have been busy men. The minister, the elders and sometimes the deacons formed the Consistory, which was the chief church authority; thus on 12 July 1576 the Consistory made an order "prohibiting the going to taverns and inns", a pious hope indeed, and the records show that the most common cause of scandal was drunkenness; hardly surprising considering the wretched conditions in which many of the refugees must have been living. Of one sinner it was recorded that he "drank to excess because he was suffering from a fever, just as one cuts off a limb to save a life!" Like sensible men, the Consistory did not attempt to make the community teetotal: it was permissible to take a drink with people coming from a distance, or when discussing matters of importance, or when passing through a village while taking a walk, which covered many of the circumstances of daily life. In any case, as the French advertisements tell you to this day, "water kills, but not wine"; the water of the river Stour in Canterbury was noted even in those days for its pestilential quality, and was avoided as much as possible by sensible men, who had little wine but made up for it with beer.

The Consistory had only moral authority, and if more practical sanctions were needed it had to appeal to the civil powers. One villain was summoned three times to appear before the Consistory and refused, perhaps with some disobliging references to the Inquisition; then he was summoned to appear before the committee of twelve men selected to deal with new arrivals and miscreants, and he refused again; so he was reported to the mayor, who promptly arrested him, and ordered him to make a public confession and apology to the congregation. Such bad hats were to be found even in the company of the godly, in spite of careful vetting of applicants for admission to the church. In December 1582 it was decided to publish the rules for entry once more: no one should present himself unless he knew the Articles of Faith, the Ten Commandments, the Lord's Prayer, the Little Catechism; applicants who were ignorant and unable to establish their credentials had to wait six months so that their piety and conduct could be tested, and if past misconduct came to light the postulant might be made to wait longer, or be refused admittance altogether. All these rules and practices had the tendency to keep the Strangers a close-knit group, but the elders were careful to ensure that the community took its share of public duties. In 1577 the Walloons contributed £2 to the scouring of the city dyke; in 1592 they paid £3 to equip four armed men to go into France to help the Protestant cause; and they helped to pay for the city watch.

They were also meticulous about keeping records, as Cross found out to his cost and our benefit; and from the time when the register of baptisms and deaths begins in June 1581 we have a great deal of information about the Walloons of Canterbury and their relationships. Because so many English families have Walloon ancestry the start of the Canterbury registers in 1581 is an import-ant date for ancestor-hunters. For those trying to establish an earlier connection with families on the continent it may also mark a considerable barrier. The first large migration from Flanders, as we have seen, took place from the early 1560s, so that there is a gap of at least ten years and sometimes twenty between the record of a banishment from Flanders and the first prospect of picking up a trace in Canterbury; that means, in many cases, a gap of a gener-ation, which to a family historian can mean a complete bar to establishing a family line, unless a way across can be found. One possibility is to find other records from which to fill the gap, some of which have been illustrated earlier: for example, private papers like the letters siezed at Henuin, and registers from other Walloon churches in England as at Southampton; also the names of Walloon families recorded as living in London, or moving from Sandwich to

Canterbury. A second method, more laborious but much less dependent on pure chance, is to construct a sort of web or network of information about related families – what Marguerite Yourcenar calls a *"réseau"* – so that even if there is a hole in the net where members of one's own family should be, there are ways round the hole to a previous generation through cousins, uncles, aunts, step-parents, witnesses of births and marriage-contracts, and all the other elaborations of family structure.

Cross made an analysis of a thousand individual Walloons married in Canterbury between 1590 and 1627, and found that most of them came from within a few miles of the present Franco-Belgian border – from Armentières, Tournai, Lille, Cambrai, St Amand, Tourcoing, Valenciennes and the small townships along the Lys valley. They seem to have obeyed the dictum to go to the places where relatives and friends had preceded them, and during this period they tended to marry within the community. Good Archbishop Parker had gently rebuked the Dutch church in London for discouraging marriage to English girls, saying, "I am surprised that you should wish thus to keep yourselves apart from us. Warn (your people) to abstain from such severity and not to be too hard on the Queen's subjects." In particular, those families with a little more distinction or money than the rest tended to intermarry with one another, producing a web of relationship which might be called Byzantine if that would not exaggerate what went on in Byzantium.

It is a noticeable feature of Belgian life to this day that within a certain circle, everybody knows a great deal about everyone else. When I came to construct a web of related Walloon families living in Canterbury in the sixteenth and seventeenth centuries, I got the impression that it was a small world in more ways than one. In particular, I found as I extracted details from the registers of the Walloon congregation that there was a nexus of some thirty or forty families which seemed to take the lead. They provided most of the elders and deacons; they married off their sons and daughters within the circle, and witnessed each other's contracts and bap-tisms. The names of certain individuals from these families cropped up with great frequency over periods of time. What was even more helpful, some of these were families which could be traced moving from particular towns in Flanders to end up in Canterbury or in London, some of them stopping on the way for half or the whole of a generation in other Walloon communities which also sprang up in France and in the northern provinces of the Netherlands.

The network of related families is illustrated in the appendix. Among those families of special interest to me are the Caron, Caullet, de la Forterie, de Lillers, de Villers, de New, de Santhuns, de Winde, des Bouveries, des Marets, Dornion, du Bois, de Quesne, Fremaut, Galmar, Guesquier, Lombart, Maurois, Nicolas, Ogier, Ricard, Roussel, Six.

Anyone who is used to surnames from the north of France will notice at once that most of the names in this list are very common: how then is it possible to identify individuals? Often it is possible with the aid of an overall web or matrix of the sort I have described; and if people connected in the 1590s or early 1600s in Canterbury can be related to a previous generation in Flanders, then the odds in favour of establishing a genuine link, and against mere coincidence, are high.

In order to link families on either side of the Channel it is clearly important to be able to identify the place of birth. Where Christian names and surnames are common, the nearer the places of origin, the higher the natural probability of some relationship existing between them; and when people of the same name are found to come from the same place, the chances are increased. Final proof can only come from searching in the usual way, through records of baptism, marriage, death, wills and so on; but once this has been achieved for one person, then all that individual's known relations can be pinned down also. So, in each of the linked families, there are one or more individuals who fix the whole group in position.

For example, consider the fragments of evidence given above about people called de le Pierre who may or may not be my ancestors. There are traces in the records of convictions for heresy: at Tournai where Marie de le Pierre was executed in 1545 and four more de le Pierres were condemned in 1568; a possible link, perhaps, but not firm evidence. We are on slightly firmer ground with Mahieu de le Pierre, thanks to the intercepted letters from the Pays de l'Alleu; he came from near Armentières, possibly from Sailly, where his mother was still alive; his wife was with him in England in 1570, and they were likely to be in the company of Guillaume le Roy who was condemned in December 1568; all of which makes it reasonably likely that he was the same Mahieu de le

Pierre who, with his wife Elizabeth du Maret, was received into the Walloon church at Southampton on 2 January 1569. I had noticed additionally that a du Marets was condemned at Lestrem in 1568.

The Southampton registers are the earliest continuous series for any of the Walloon churches in England. They begin in December 1567:

> *Ensuyt les noms de ceux qui ont fait profession de leur Foy et admis à la Cène le 21 decembre 1567.*

So runs the heading on the first page, and Mahieu and Elizabeth are among the very first whose names have survived. The registers of baptisms and deaths at the Walloon church at Canterbury start on St John's day, 24 June 1581, while marriages begin to be recorded on 5 May 1583, and these are the lists which are probably of most interest to the descendants of the immigrant Walloons. The first entry seems to mention one of my ancestors: on 2 July 1581 Judith the daughter of Antoine de Lannoy and his wife Marie was baptised, and the witness was Laurent des Bouveries. Thereafter, except that the register of baptisms and marriages between June 1584 and July 1590 is missing, and that the schism caused by Minister Poujade in the next century resulted in a disruption, the records are continuous. Indeed the Canterbury registers contain thousands of names with relationships, places of origin and other material from which to construct a network linking families in Flanders and in England.[3]

Even in the case of very common surnames, it is sometimes possible to identify individuals from a surprisingly early date. For example, one of the family names which is found most frequently in the north of France is Six. However, the records in Flanders tell us a useful amount about a particular Six family from Wambrechies, a small town on the river Deule above Armentières. Jacques Six and his wife Jacquemine Lezaire were living there at the end of the fifteenth century; the next generation included Jacques, Jean and Guillaume Six, of whom Jacques married Valentine, daughter of Antoine de Thieffries, a well known family in the region some of

---

[3]The registers at Norwich begin on 22 June 1595, with baptisms. The registers at Threadneedle Street in London start in 1600, for marriages as well as baptisms: the first marriage recorded is that between Jean Duquesne and Sara de Franqueville, who later had a good deal to do with the community of Canterbury.

whose members, as we have seen, were notorious Protestants; Jean and Valentine died before the troubles began, but their son Jacques, who lived at Baisieux and inherited land at Rigalles, lost it all when he was hanged a heretic on 9 April 1568. Heresy, clearly, was well established in this branch of the widespread Six family, because on 14 March 1570 Jean Six of Wambrechies had his goods confiscated; soon after the family reappears on the other side of the Channel, on 1 June 1588 Pasquier Six, born at Wambrechies, married Peronne Ramery at Canterbury.

Hold on, you say, I thought there were no records of marriages in the Walloon registers at Canterbury between 1584 and 1590? Quite so: but some of the immigrants thought it prudent to get baptised or married in the Anglican parish church, and the registers of St Alphege's and the other churches in the parts where Walloons had settled contain a number of names of first-generation immigrants.[4] Later on we shall see that it became more common, indeed it was one of Archbishop Laud's injunctions that Walloons should attend the parish church rather than the services in the crypt. In 1582, however, so many strangers had by then entered Canterbury from Flanders, including the arrivals from Winchelsea and Sandwich, that the Walloon community may have numbered nearly one third of the entire population; and the city fathers thought it time to call a halt. They forbade any more Strangers to enter without special permission.

That makes a good point to leave for the time being the Walloon refugees who had crossed the Channel, and turn to those who had made the rather less traumatic journey into France. They did not have to travel very far, at least in the first migration, because there were three main centres for Protestants in the far north of France, at Marcq and Guînes near Calais and in the country near Boulogne.

The temple at Marcq seems to have been the first in the area; indeed it is said to have been built in 1563, soon after the recapture

---

[4] Baptisms in an Anglican parish church were not always reported to, or picked up by, the Walloon minister, which sometimes resulted in a rather sniffy note in the latter's register. For example, when Samuel de New had his baby daughter baptised at St Alphege's, the parish register records, "3 March 1635: Jane daughter of Samuel de New and Jane his wife". Over a year later, in July 1636 the Walloon register has, "*Jenne fille de Samuel de New et Jenne sa femme . . . Fut baptisé à l'Anglois à la paroisse de St Alphets. Obmis d'estre poses devant faute de billet*" (i.e. no card was made out).

of Calais from the English, and the French court allowed those expelled from Flanders and Artois by the Inquisition to come and worship there; French Calvinists had this right confirmed at the Treaty of Nérac in 1579. There was certainly a temple still in existence at Marcq in 1612; but in 1641, after the renewal of the war between France and Spain, a marauding Spanish force drove the inhabitants as far as Nouvelle Eglise and set fire to Marcq, destroying the temple and probably its records too. A visitor to Marcq in 1715, by name Bernard, said that the temple had been situated at the bottom end of the town and that the ruins were still visible. After the Spanish withdrawal the Protestants were allowed to rebuild the temple but it was no longer needed in Marcq because a very much bigger one was by then available at Guînes. This may have been built as early as the 1580s though it is not mentioned in a *terrier* of 1582, but there is a reference in 1602 to land "in front of the Temple"; the house in whose grounds it was built belonged to a Catherine Dornion, a prominent name in the community at Canterbury; and a Nicholas Dornion, (possibly Catherine's son or nephew) was a merchant in Guînes in 1619. Her house, according to a reference in 1606, had "a courtyard and garden in which is built the Temple which fronts the street going from the market place to the big windmill"; clearly the Protestants in the Calaisis had well-placed supporters, and the same was true further south in the Boulonnais.

I knew that there was at least one de le Pierre family in Boulogne at this time, but they were baptised in the Catholic church and I could find no connection between them and the de la Pierres of Canterbury except for the hint that the leading Protestants in the area were called Guiselin, like the mother of Pierre de le Pierre. The main centre for the Protestants was the Guiselin manor house of des Barreaux at Réty near Wissant; until recently there was to be seen there a memorial dated 1617 to Louis de Guiselin and his wife Judic de Licques, with a motto taken from Marot's version of the Psalms, *"En un seul Dieu m'atens, qui me rendra content"*. At least one incident during the 1580s involved a Guiselin, when a Protestant pastor called Jean Auber ministered at des Barreaux; because of the dangers of the time, de Guiselin and his people would escort the minister on the road to his next place of call. On 28 April 1585 a soldier called Fléchicourt tried to murder Auber, but de Guiselin and some other Calvinist gentleman managed to rescue him; Fléchicourt tried again later when Auber was unprotected, and this time killed the unfortunate minister.

This incident on the road from Réty was only one of a series; the rising storm of trouble for the Protestants of France was soon to drive many of them across the Channel to join their fellow-exiles in England, or to the north. The 1570s saw the beginnings of successful armed revolt in the northern provinces, and Holland and Zeeland began to look very attractive to Protestants in trouble further south. The Netherlands Reformed Church had been constituted by a synod at Emden in 1571, and it adopted a Dutch version of Guy de Brès's Walloon Confession of Faith. The first Walloon church in the north was established at Middelburg in 1574; and from that time onwards, while refugees from the south of Flanders headed for France and England, a steadily growing stream from the other parts of the province flowed to swell the Calvinist congregations in the north. A second mass migration was under way.

CHAPTER 8

The Second Exodus from Flanders
1580–1600

He stated that at the time of the death of his wife . . . in the year 1596 (which was a plague year) they had lost all their furniture, grain and animals in the war declared between our King and the King of Spain . . . and they took refuge in the lower town at Boulogne.

Disposition of Pierre Denguin
of Bazinghem (1623)

The years of the troubles had been bad: the 1580s and 1590s were even worse for the people of Flanders and Artois. In between, however, there came a brief respite. On 17 December 1573 Alva left the Netherlands after six years as governor and captain-general, to the relief of the government and the people alike. His successor, Don Luis de Requesens, a humane man, was careful to avoid further provocation of the local population. He ordered the bronze statue erected by Alva at Antwerp to be taken away and stored out of sight in the citadel. The scene of action moved to the north, where the rebels continued to hold out against the Army of Flanders. During this time many of the refugees who had left the south during the first exodus returned quietly home, leaving no further traces in England; indeed for the time being it was safer for Protestants to follow their cult on the Spanish side of the border, and some refugees came into the southern Netherlands from the north of France. That is perhaps how some of the Guiselin family from Réty came to be living in Aire-sur-la-Lys, just over the frontier, where the Guiselin mother of Pierre de le Pierre was born about 1575; there are no traces of the family in the town archives, or in surviving memorials there, which may be because their stay was short or because they avoided the Catholic parish churches.

In 1576 there was a sudden crisis in the affairs of the Netherlands. In March of that year Don Luis died unexpectedly, and the Spanish hold on the north of Flanders began to slip. By November a part of the Army of Flanders encamped outside Antwerp mutinied because their pay was in arrears, and decided to recoup themselves from the rich city which was known to be ready to accept help from the north. At dawn on Sunday 4 November, when the pious citizens had chosen to suspend work on a small gap left in the fortifications, Spanish troops stormed and sacked Antwerp with bloodshed and pillage such as had not been known in the province. Eight thousand people are said to have died: one of the survivors was a baby girl called Sarah Oeils, born the previous December, who was found by the troops and looked after by them until the trouble was over; later she went to England and was married in London in 1599 to a Dr Baldwin Hamey, who comes into the story later on. In the general revulsion against the ruin of one of the great cities of Flanders by troops supposed to be in the government's pay, the council at Brussels outlawed the mutineers and a general concordat known as the Pacification of Ghent already in draft was signed on 5 November. Holland and Zeeland united with the Catholic provinces to demand the expulsion of the Spanish troops. It was agreed that all religious prisoners would be released; the two Protestant provinces would not seek to convert the other fifteen; the placards were repealed, and the tribunals againt heresy were abolished. It was in this general mood of *détente* that the court records were destroyed, to the satisfaction of men of good will at the time, and the regret of family historians ever since. William of Orange (whose brothers Louis and Henri had been killed in battle at a place called Mook) was welcomed at Antwerp in September and at Brussels in October; then he stayed in charge until Don John of Austria arrived to take over as governor and captain-general.

In the interregnum there was a remarkable two-way flow of traffic into and out of Flanders. Besides French Protestants escaping persecution, numbers of Walloon refugees came home to Wallonia and the towns along the Lys valley; while the Army of Flanders – survivors of Alva's men and subsequent reinforcements – left the Netherlands for Italy. They went in style, riding not marching, and with such a huge accompanying swarm of women and camp followers that the scene was compared, rather inappropriately, to the march of the Israelites out of Egypt. For the surviving veterans everything had turned out well in the end: their arrears of pay came to so much money that most of it was transferred by letters of credit to Spain or Italy; they had the plunder of towns like Mechelen and Antwerp in their haversacks; to crown it all, their expulsion was so hasty that they had left their billets too quickly to settle their debts. The army whose first coming across the Alps had been so hard returned into Lombardy in comfort, with every soldier on horseback and 2,600 tons of luggage on their mules; and the ancient business of arms had taken another step into the modern world. The mercenaries, hired for a season, who had done the fighting since the Italian wars, were to be replaced by full-time professionals.

In Flanders the Protestants enjoyed a brief heyday. The last quarter of the sixteenth century marked the high tide of Protestantism everywhere in Europe; it would never reach so far again. The Calvinists and Lutherans took over churches and established temples in many places well south of the "Protestant" provinces. A synod in 1576 listed Protestant congregations in twenty-seven places in the Netherlands including ten in Wallonia.[1] In Antwerp the Calvinists had seven churches and the Lutherans three; and the cathedral was shared between Calvinists in the nave and Catholics in the transept. Alas, as was usual between different Christians, such tolerance was short-lived. The Protestants given the opportunity were as high-handed as the Catholics; at Bruges on 19 March 1578 there was a Protestant take-over and the Jesuits and Franciscans were expelled. In the same year a Calvinist university was established at Ghent and the Professor of Protestant Theology gave an inaugural lecture there on 6 October. For a little while it must have looked as if the Netherlands, south as well as north, were bound to go the same way as Germany, or as France where the court was distracted by quarrels among the royal favourites; the provinces were unruly, and the duke of Anjou was ready to intervene in the Netherlands on the Protestant side.

All this was too much for King Philip to stomach, or for his new governor in the Netherlands. Don John of Austria who had beaten the Turks at Lepanto was not a man daunted by difficulties. Less

---

[1] Armentières, Commines, Lille, Tournai, Valenciennes, Mouscron, Tourcoing, Bondues, Linselles and Roubaix.

than a year after the Spanish veterans left the Netherlands (for good, as everyone had hoped) fresh troops arrived from Italy to reinforce him; Figueroa covered the distance with 4,000 Spanish infantry and 1,300 cavalry in the record time of thirty-two days, arriving in Namur on 27 March 1578. It was the writing on the wall for the Protestant cause. Don John like his predecessor died unexpectedly before he could take matters in hand; but his successor was a man of rare ability who found how to succeed where Alva had failed.

Alexander Farnese, later duke of Parma, son of Margaret of Parma, the former governor, was in his early thirties in 1578. He combined the qualities of a good governor with those of an excellent captain-general. He realised that the people of Flanders, with their preference for good order and their great dislike of throwing good money away, would always grumble at a governor but were not natural revolutionaries. The liberal religious settlement made possible, at least in theory, by the Pacification of Ghent two years before had not been generally accepted either by the Protestant provinces of Holland and Zeeland or by the Catholic provinces of Hainaut and Artois. Quite quickly the two sides fell apart. French Flanders and Luxembourg joined Artois and Hainaut, and the Confederation of Arras was sealed on 2 January 1579; three weeks later the northern provinces responded with the Union of Utrecht. All the Calvinist towns of Flanders adhered to the Union, all the Walloon towns were Confederate. The final separation of the Netherlands into the northern Union and the southern Confederation was confirmed in July 1581, when Philip II was formally deposed at the Hague, an act and a date now taken to mark the formal foundation of the Dutch Republic; while the southern Confederation formed the basis of the kingdom of Belgium today.[2]

---

[2] Another distinction between Catholic and Protestant resulted from the reform of the calendar. In 1582 Pope Gregory XIII replaced the ancient Julian calendar, which had lost ten days as a result of reckoning each year too short by eleven minutes; he left out ten days in February and initiated the new Gregorian reckoning which became general in the Catholic states. Protestants were not prepared to accept a papal innovation, and not only in England the old style remained in use; a Protestant writing in a Catholic country would date his letters in the Julian style. King Philip like a good bureaucrat marked the new calendar by stopping ten days pay to the Army of Flanders; oddly enough, no one seems to have mutinied as a result.

If it had not been for Parma, Belgium would be much smaller than it is and the kingdom of the Netherlands much larger, because throughout the 1580s he managed to push the frontiers of the Confederation steadily northwards. This was made possible by two developments: Philip made a truce with Sultan in 1579; and the first really large shipments of Spanish bullion began to arrive from the New World. The Army of Flanders was regularly paid, indeed in 1584 and 1585 the money arrived in advance instead of in arrears; and the quality of its Spanish veterans soon told, from the capture of Maastricht in June 1579 to the recovery of Antwerp in August 1584. It began to look as if the Seven Provinces, like the Ten, would soon be restored to obedience to Spain.

In the south Parma set to work to consolidate the Confederation by a policy of allowing Protestants a fixed time in which to settle their affairs and to emigrate, whether to the north to Union territory or west to France and England; and he maintained the pressure by keeping up his drive to the north, recovering one city after another for the king. By 1585 Tournai, Brussels, Ghent, Antwerp, Bruges in succession were secured, and their Protestant citizens (at least the more substantial ones) sold up and left. By the time that Parma died in December 1592, worn out at the age of forty-seven, he had created a secure base in the southern Netherlands, and turned them into the *Pays-bas Catholiques* which have remained predominantly Catholic to this day.

Parma's period of office as governor and captain-general there-fore marks the start of the second great exodus of Protestants from the southern provinces of the Netherlands. Whereas Alva had frightened them away, so that when he left the country many of them came back again, Parma removed them more humanely but ensured that men of substance would leave for good. During his time, therefore, the fate of Protestants in Flanders depended on which part of the province they lived in, and also whether they were prosperous enough to be able to leave with their possessions. Many humbler people who could not afford to leave had to return to the clandestine practice of earlier days, travelling from Catholic to Protestant areas to marry and to baptise their children by forms not officially accepted in the home towns to which they returned. Like the spread of dissent in England in the eighteenth and nineteenth centuries, the survival of Protestantism underground in

Flanders makes life difficult for the family historian, because the short-lived congregations were soon suppressed and any records the pastors kept were lost. Once again, therefore, we depend mainly on court registers for details, and some strange tales emerge from these documents; the bored clerks of the court enlivened them with little drawings in the margin which lend a touch of immediacy to the bare details. The penalties on conviction for heresy were no longer the final ones, but they were still severe.

One convict was Jehane de Lobel from Lille, the daughter of Jehan and wife of Nicholas Duquesne, a saye-maker who had moved to Antwerp from Lille "for religion". From Antwerp she returned home disguised as a man to bring messages to the Protestants still in hiding. She was arrested by a band of soldiers and searched; she had no passport and was carrying a heretical book: had up before the court and found guilty on 23 June 1582, she was banished for two years, and probably went north again.

On the river Deule, between Lille and the Lys, are the small towns of Wambrechies and Quesnoy-sur-Deule; they provided several Protestants for the court at Lille to try. For example, on Thursday, 3 October 1585 Denis Romery of Wambrechies, son of the late Guillebert, who had earlier taken refuge like many others over the border in the Boulonnais and then returned to Wambrechies during the Pacification, was charged and found guilty of having married in 1578 a woman called Catherine Six, the widow of Loys Hedbault. His offence was that they were married by the Protestant minister at Courtrai; Catherine Six, if she too came from Wambrechies, was probably a cradle Protestant, because the Six family of that town, as we have seen, were deeply dyed in the new opinions. Ten years after Catherine Six married Denis Romery, Pasquier Six married Peronne Ramery. This can hardly be a mere coincidence: it is therefore quite probable that the two couples were related, and that another small piece of Protestant family network may be conjectured.

The similarity between "Romery" and "Ramery", both in the written form and presumably in the pronunciation, is a feature very common in all the records. For every common surname there are several written variants, and quite frequently the same individual appears in different guises. De le Pierre or de la Pierre, for instance, is not a particularly common name; nevertheless it is tantalising to see the obvious similarity between these variants and other names found just as frequently in the same parts of the country, like Delespierre and Despierre. On the same day in October 1585 that Denis Romery was had up before the court in Lille, the next case in the list was that of Jean Delespierre, otherwise known as "Jean Mahieu" because his late father's name was Mahieu.[3] Jean was born at Wambrechies and like Denis was charged with having been married in 1577 or 1578 by the Protestant minister at Courtrai: his wife was Anne le Cocq of Quesnoy-sur-Deule. Jean compounded this offence by having his son baptised by another Protestant minister, this time at Menin; he was banished for six years and was also sentenced to be beaten three times round the fountain in front of the Exchange at Lille; the clerk of the court relieved the tedium of his job at this point by making a little sketch of a bundle of birch-rods in the margin of the records.

A man like Jean Delespierre who was banished on pain of death would probably have emigrated out of Spanish controlled territory, and many such must have gone to Canterbury. The constant pressure on Protestants to leave the southern provinces during Parma's successes coincided with a marked growth in the size of the Strangers' church; in 1582 when the city fathers tried to halt new immigration the Walloons numbered some 1,750 souls, but in 1592 the congregation had grown to over 3,000, something like half the population of the city. However not all the new arrivals stayed for long; and again the court records at Lille give some interesting glimpses. One of the Protestants convicted at Lille on 18 June 1586, Jean Laigniel, was accused on two counts; not only had he married Marie Pare in the Protestant church at Alembon, but she had then taken their child across the Channel when he was four months old to get him baptised at Canterbury. On 3 December 1594 Michel le Mesurier was banished from Lille because he had been in England several times; he must therefore be a Protestant because "they do not have Catholics there". He broke this ban, and was found in Lille again in February the next year. Ten years later, on 21 May 1604 Jacques des Bouveries, son of the late Antoine, from St-Gain-en-Mélantois, was also banished from Lille for three years; it seems

---

[3] Tempting as it is to connect Mahieu Delespierre, father of Jean, with Mahieu de le Pierre who fled to England with Guillaume le Roy, the dates tend to be against it.

likely that he spent his exile with the members of his family already in England. Such cases suggest that many of the entries in the Canterbury register refer to temporary visitors.

So the Protestants were squeezed out of Flanders by Parma. In France, they were now being expelled more violently as a result of the growing crisis in the struggle between Protestant and Catholic and the involvement of outsiders. In particular, Philip subsidised the Catholic League (formed in 1584 to oppose the Protestant succession in the person of Henri of Navarre); the eighth outbreak of the religious wars in France in 1586 was followed by the murder of the last of the Valois kings without an heir, and the eventual succession of Henri was contested to the last. Until the final exhaustion of all the participants at the end of the century, the last years saw continual warfare of a sort which devastated the frontier regions, and which turned some of the richest parts of the Netherlands into a desert bleaker than the troubles had created a generation before.

What sort of warfare this was can be gauged from the observations of two generals who knew their business, Montluc and Alva. Montluc was a sort of walking demonstration of sixteenth-century warfare: he had been a soldier for fifty-five of the seventy years of his life, and had sustained twenty-four wounds in the course of five battles, eleven sieges, seventeen assaults and two hundred fights and skirmishes. From his own experience he said that war had become a matter of fights, encounters, ambushes, an occasional battle, minor sieges, assaults, escalades, surprises – guerilla warfare rather than the regular campaigns of old and of the military textbooks. Alva remarked in praise of his Spanish veterans that any sort of soldiers could fight a battle, but it took a trained man to win a skirmish. Throughout this period small parties of troops in the pay of the States or the kings of France and Spain skirmished, ambushed, tricked and killed each other for possession of villages and hamlets. In the north, between the king of Spain's territory and the Dutch rebels, was a sort of floating frontier, running from one fortified town or village to another, from Liège to the sea coast of Flanders; while in the south French Flanders, Artois, the Calaisis and the Boulonnais were ravaged by the continual passage of small marauding armies. In 1580 Parma besieged Cambrai; in 1582 d'Alençon burnt Lens and St Pol; so it went on. In 1587, 1588 and 1589 the harvests in Flanders and Artois failed for three years in succession, and a Dutch blockade prevented supplies from arriving by sea; famine followed by plague was inevitable, along with epidemics of other diseases just as deadly as the *peste*. In vain the Estates of Artois complained about the ravages of government troops, just as bad as French incursions; in Flanders the army was instructed not to pillage (forlorn hope) and to make do with a pound and a half of bread and a pound of meat a day. Taxes could not be raised because of the insolvency of most of the farmers; the peasants in some places had to take refuge in underground shelters to escape the troops. In the spring of 1597 they could not even sow their fields, the final disaster for an agricultural community; and in that year Artois, once the richest producer of food in the Netherlands, had to import corn. It was the worst moment of the century.

At such a time of disasters, any people who were able to move, whether Catholic or Protestant, went and took refuge with their families either in the nearest *ville forte*, or in the neighbouring French provinces of Ponthieu and the county of Eu in Normandy. As soon as the rival armies had moved on, they returned to their homes and tried to make a living once more. The flavour of the time is given in this affidavit sworn years later before Maître Gillon, a notary of Boulogne, on 27 June 1623.

> There appeared in person Pierre Daguin (Denguin) master *mesurier* living at Bazinghem who stated that at the time of the death of his wife Catherine Le Boide in the year 1596 (which was a plague year) they had lost all their furniture, grain and animals in the war declared between our King and the King of Spain, whose army took the towns of Calais, Ardres and Mont Hulin: for which reason the said Pierre Daguin was forced to abandon the house where they lived, belonging to his said wife in the village of Leullinghem, and they took refuge in the lower town at Boulogne; and when peace came in the year 1598, he returned sometime afterwards to live in the said house at Leullinghem with his six children. . . .

This dry lawyer's account has two points of special interest. First, and more obviously, the year of 1596 must have been memorable enough for poor Pierre Daguin: war, plague, the loss of his wife, the loss of all his possessions and means of livelihood, and survival (just) looking after six children destitute in the crowded slums inside the walls of Boulogne: there must have been many such families by the end of the wars. The second point, which may not register at first reading, is the reference to the capture of Calais by the Spanish army. Among the many disasters of those grim years, one of the worst for Protestants sheltering there was the unexpected over-running of the Calaisis, including the temples at Marcq and at Guînes and full of refugees from Flanders, by the Army of Flanders in 1596.

Most people know about the recapture of Calais by the French from the English in 1558; it is sometimes overlooked that the Spanish army, no longer in alliance with England, retook Calais for a short time at the end of the century. It was as much a surprise as the French feat of arms nearly forty years earlier. The usual marching and countermarching was going on, interspersed with various skirmishes and engagements. A French army under Maréchal d'Humières had seized a château called de la Montoire, then Tournehem (8 May 1595); the Spanish garrison was massacred, and its commander hanged at the castle gate, the sort of thing that happened in this guerilla campaigning. In 1596 the Spanish had their revenge. The Cardinal Albert, archduke of Austria and now the captain-general of the Army of Flanders, advanced suddenly at the head of a strong Spanish force and arrived outside Calais, weakly garrisoned with 600 men, on 9 April. Some French reinforcements managed to get into the town through the Spanish lines; but the forts were carried, the town was taken on 17 April, and the citadel on the 24 April, reversing the order of the capture in 1558. Henri IV, now king of France, brought an army to the relief but too late to save Calais, and too late to save Ardres where the French garrison surrendered on 23 May. Henri therefore avenged himself by ravaging Artois; the Spanish army took Amiens; the French retook it; and so it went on until, in total exhaustion, peace between France and Spain was signed at Vervins on 2 May 1598.

During the calamitous years of the 1580s and 1590s Protestant refugees from the Calaisis and the Boulonnais, most of them already refugees from Flanders, took ship to join the communities in England and the north. The fall of Calais triggered off a final wave of emigration. A typical entry in the Canterbury register of this period records the marriage on 27 December 1596 of Pierre Fremaut from St Pierre near Calais and Jeanne le Grand from St Etienne near Boulogne. The clerk noted that Jeanne's husband had been "*entre les refugiés en Canterbury l'an 1596*"; she too was probably displaced at about the same time. Several times in the last decade of the century the number of baptisms registered in the Walloon church at Canterbury exceeded 100 a year, indicating a community of about 2,500.

Because the second exodus of Protestants from the frontier took place in the time of the surviving Walloon registers at Canterbury and other centres, it is possible to plot the movement of families much more fully than in the first migration. Indeed there is some danger of being swamped by the flood of information. From it I tried to extract the details of the families related, then or later, to the de la Pierres, among them many who seem to have moved from Flanders to France during the first exodus, and then from France to England in the second.

The name of Elaine de la Pierre occurs in the Canterbury register in the 1590s. She had married Guillaume Caron of Estaires in the early 1560s, before the troubles, and two of their children, Françoise and Marie, were born at Estaires on the Lys. Then three more children, Moyse, Israel and Judith, were born at Clainleau in the Boulonnais in the 1570s; the biblical names of the latter three (compared to the orthodox Françoise and Marie) and their birthplace are evidence that the family had become openly Protestant and had taken refuge from Alva in France. Moyse, Israel and Judith were married in the Boulonnais; but their children were born in Canterbury in the 1590s, which indicates a second expulsion by the Army of Flanders. The family stayed in England thereafter.

Two related families who moved in the same way were the Ogiers and the des Marets. Charles Ogier was regarded by the historian Agnew as related to Robert Ougier, who with his wife and two sons was burnt a heretic at Lille in March 1557, so the family may have moved to France even before the troubles began. Charles was the cousin of Salome des Marets of Cormont who married Moyse Caron already mentioned; Cormont is also in the Boulonnais, so the Protestant families in exile there were clearly keeping in contact with each other. Charles and his second wife Jeanne Trupin had children born at Cormont in the 1570s; these children were married at Canterbury in the 1590s, and they and their children remained there subsequently. So did Jean des

Marets,[4] brother of Salome, who married Moyse Caron; and his brother Esaie, and his other sisters Judith, Susanne and Anne, all born in Cormont and later married in Canterbury; Anne married Charles Ogier's son Jacques.[5]

Then there was the Roussel family. Adam Roussel married Jeanne Chiroutre, the aunt of Susanne who married Pierre de le Pierre. They came from Estaires on the Lys; but they had children born in Maninghem-en-Boulonnais about 1590; later the family moved to Canterbury, where it remained. A Jeanne Chiroutre died in Pierre de la Pierre's house at the Blackfriars in 1654.

Therefore it looks as though the Protestants who were pushed to the south out of Flanders tended to arrive in England via France; while many of those pushed out to the north tended to arrive in England after a stay, sometimes brief, in the northern provinces. One centre which attracted many of those expelled by Parma towards the north was Middelburg in Zeeland: we have seen how the first Walloon church in the north was established at Middelburg in 1574, after the troubles. As the reconquest of the southern provinces pressed on, more Walloon churches were founded: Leyden (1584), Delft (1586), Rotterdam(1590), the Hague (1591); in all, fifteen such churches were founded in the north down to the year 1600, and some of them were very large. As Parma pushed on, whole congregations left their homes and moved ahead of him. In 1584 so many refugees arrived in Middelburg from Ypres and Douai that three ministers were needed to look after them; in the same year 450 refugees arrived in Leyden from Bruges complete with their own minister and consistory, and the church, where services in French had been started three years earlier by the Protestant professor Lambert Daniau, was officially established there.

The congregations at Middelburg and at Leyden have the distinction that they have survived to this day. At Leyden, the

[4] Pierre des Marets, father of Salome and the others, came from Sailly; so it is not unlikely that Elizabeth du Maret wife of Mahieu de le Pierre from Sailly was one of the clan.

[5] Jacques Ogier, son of Charles, married three times, and each time married a widow. First, Jenne de Rome, born at Vimy-en-Boulonnais, widow of Jean Slinghe; second, Michelle Caron, born at Lille, widow of Jean Cappron; and third Anne des Marets, widow of Philippe de Mortagne: a nice nexus of in-laws.

present Walloon church is the old chapel of St Catherine's Hospital, Breestraat 64, and services are held on Sundays at 10.30 a.m.; close by are two very important addresses, Boerhaavelaan 37, where the pastor lives and which houses the Secrétariat de la Commission de l'Histoire des Églises Wallonnes, and Pieterskerkhof 40, which houses the Bibliothèque Wallonne. The Walloon synods decided that they should keep their *actes* and documents centrally, and chose the church at Leyden as the repository; the Bibliothèque was established there in 1852. It houses a card index, the *fichier des refugiés*, which includes nearly two million separate records of births, professions of faith and other *actes*, and so it is an indispensable reference point for family historians whose Walloon ancestors may have taken refuge in the northern provinces. It is thanks to the *fichier des refugiés* that I can trace the movements of my own ancestor Michel de le Pierre (after his brief visit to England) from Calais to Middelburg, where his son Pierre was born; and of Pierre who later moved from Middelburg to Canterbury. There were very many links between the Walloon communities in England, France and the northern provinces, and constant movement between them, sometimes of merchants and professional men in pursuit of business, sometimes of families moving to escape trouble or to seek a living.

Thus a number of families who later formed part of the Canterbury network arrived there from the Walloon centres in the Netherlands as Parma's army came too close for comfort. By 1585 the recapture of Antwerp must have given a nasty shock to the Protestants in Holland and Zeeland; the Canterbury registers mark their arrival in England.

We pass suddenly from a dearth to a surfeit of facts. Jacques Ricart and his wife Peronne le Rouge had at least one child, Susanne, born in Middelburg in the 1580s but married in Canterbury in 1611. Jacques's sister Philipette was married at Canterbury in 1587; his granddaughter Judith married Pierre Roussel, and their daughter Judith was a cousin of Pierre de le Pierre. There was François Lombart, who married Anne Chiroutre, a sister of Susanne, wife of Pierre de le Pierre; he had at least one child, Marie, born at Middelburg in the 1600s, and married in Canterbury in 1639, assisted by her uncles Pierre de le Pierre and Philippe Chiroutre and her great-uncle Adam Roussel. . . .

But by now, any reader who has only so much interest in family relationships will begin to feel he has had quite enough to be getting on with. Quite so: to avoid more of the same, the connections are summarised in the appendix where anyone who is interested can trace the cross connections. However the tables come mostly from the English side of the Channel. There is still the problem I started with, to find out where in Flanders the de la Pierre family came from. By now I had a fairly good idea, and so will the reader who has picked up a number of hints in the preceding pages; but there is still a little way to go before definite proof can be found. First, the events of the sixteenth century had to be played out; one after another the main parties reached the point of exhaustion, where it was simply a question of who would be the first to settle and on what terms.

In the Netherlands the archduke Albert was barely able to hold his own against Maurice of Nassau in the north; it was becoming clear to all that the Seven Provinces were now effectively a new independent state in the north Netherlands. A similar consolidation took place in the Ten Provinces of the south. In 1599 the archduke Albert married Philip's daughter the Infanta Isabella: Philip had renounced to his son-in-law all his rights in the Netherlands, which would revert to the Spanish crown only if Albert and Isabella died childless. The grand inauguration of the "archdukes" at Brussels in September 1599 marked the beginnings of an ultra-Catholic state in which more than three hundred new churches would be built, the number of convents tripled, the Jesuits would assume the ascendancy, and all traces of Protestantism (including the holding of secret assemblies, and the possession of heretical books) would be formally abolished. Nearly all the Protestants had left Flanders, and Protestantism in Europe had passed its zenith.

In France, where Henri IV had at last secured his throne, he became a Catholic; and even though the Edict of Nantes, given on Monday, 13 April 1598, appeared to mark a gain for Protestantism, its effect was to forbid the Huguenots to look for new converts; they would be on the defensive from the beginning of the new century. France and Spain made peace at Vervins the following month. On the French side the peace marked the end of forty years of upheaval and of civil and religious war which no one could contemplate starting again. On the Spanish side the settlement in Brussels and the treaty of Vervins both had the same cause: Philip II was close to death, and he needed to put his affairs in order. His end, physically at least, was a wretched one. Dropsical, fevered and covered with boils and sores, he lay for weeks unable to move, his coffin at his bedside; to comfort him he had his father the emperor's penitential scourge, a crucifix, and many holy relics. At last the monk sitting at his bedside on 13 September noted, "He died slowly, so that with only a faint motion, giving two or three small gasps his saintly spirit left him." It was an appropriate end: and the condition of the Netherlands by now was not much better than that of its ruler. Exhausted by the continual campaigns, famines and epidemics of the final years, Flanders and Artois were practically at the end of their resources. To the lasting credit of Albert and Isabella, they provided the breathing space which allowed recovery to begin, and incidentally the puzzle of Pierre de le Pierre's birthplace to be solved.

CHAPTER 9

Armistice and Recovery:
Gorne Found

Bailleul, Estaires and Merville are old market towns . . . the other
villages are small and surrounded by orchards, hedges and elm-trees;
those on the rivers Lawe and Lys contained very old houses, well built
of grey stone.

Official History of the First World War, IX

Saturday, 2 May 1598, the date of the treaty of Vervins between
France and Spain, was the first day of formal peace that the people
of the southern Netherlands and northern France had known for a
generation. The Army of Flanders, no longer obliged to campaign
on two fronts, turned its attention to the north and quickly recovered more lost ground. In 1604, after a three-year siege, it
forced the surrender of Ostend; in 1604 and 1606 it crossed the
Rhine and the Maas and captured several Dutch-held towns. At
last, in April 1607, the archdukes and the northern provinces agreed
to negotiate an armistice on the basis that the independence of the
north would be respected; Spain agreed, reluctantly, and in April
1609 a twelve-year peace was signed between Spain and the Seven
Provinces. Now the whole of the Netherlands, north and south, was
at peace after forty years and more of civil, religious and foreign
war.

The armistice of 1609 proved to be only a truce between wars;
but it was a watershed that marked a broad new political pattern. In
the Netherlands this was not to be upset from that day forward. The
people on both sides of the armistice lines began to pick up the
threads of normal life in some sort of security. The refugees returned
home, or else settled down for good in their new countries; the

battered towns and villages of the war zones began to recover. There was an immense amount of work to be done.

Although conducted on a small scale by modern standards, the warfare in Flanders during the last quarter of the sixteenth century bears many resemblances to that of following times including the first world war itself. Michael Howard, in his *War in European History*, makes the point that the sort of trench warfare involved in the investment of towns in Flanders, "tedious, dangerous, murderously unhealthy", would not have seemed unfamiliar to Tristram Shandy's Uncle Toby in the eighteenth century, nor to the British troops on the Western Front in the twentieth; after men had been forced to spend months in waterlogged trenches, desertion and disease took a greater toll of the Army of Flanders than wounds, and casualty lists reached the proportions of 1914–18. There are other resemblances across the centuries.

In Alistair Horne's splendid trilogy about the Franco-German crises of 1870, 1916 and 1940, there is a passage in which he describes the aftermath of another war which ravaged the plains and hills of Flanders and northern France to an extent which we in England have never experienced since the eleventh century.

> Superficially, the regenerative powers of Nature are immense. Soon even the blasted trees began to put out new shoots. . . . Slowly the city of Verdun, perhaps half of its houses destroyed or damaged to some extent, came back to life. The *Verdunois* returned whence they had been evacuated to set their town in order and retill the ravaged fields. To nine villages around Verdun . . . the inhabitants never returned. The villages had literally vanished. The deeper scars of Nature took longer, far longer to heal. At the tragic cost of still more peasant lives lost when ploughs detonated unexploded shells, Champagne, Artois, Picardy, Flanders and even the Somme eventually came back into cultivation, with little trace of the horrors that had been enacted there. But Verdun defied man's peaceful amends longer than all of them. . . .

In the same way, when peace returned at last to Flanders and Artois at the start of the seventeenth century, the pace of recovery varied according to the depth of the preceding disasters. There was then no aftermath of unexploded shells and bombs to interrupt the farmers' work; but neither was there any machinery nor massive reparation funds to help them. Sir Thomas Overbury, entering the southern provinces at the start of the truce of 1609, wrote:

> As soon as I entered into the Archduke's territory . . . presently I beheld . . . a Province destroyed with war. The people heartless and rather repining against their Governors than revengeful against their enemies. The bravery of that gentry which was left, and the industry of the merchants, quite decayed. The husbandman labouring only to live, without desire to be rich to another's use. The towns (whatsoever concerned not the strength of them) ruinous. And to conclude, the people here growing poor with less taxes, than they flourish with on the States' [i.e. the northern] side.

It has been reckoned that perhaps 100,000 people (the same magic number as Guy de Brès had claimed for his Protestants) had emigrated from the southern province, most of them to the north or to England, between the troubles in 1567 and the truce in 1609. Many communities had lost between one third and one half of their people, as at the time of the Black Death. In southern Flanders, only a tiny proportion even of the tenacious peasant farmers had stayed on their land throughout the terrible 1580s and 1590s. Marauding soldiers and bandits destroyed the farms, burnt the crops, murdered the peasants; packs of wolves roamed around the ruined countryside. The people of the Brugse Vrij, once some of the richest farmland in the whole of the Netherlands but now exposed on the new frontier between the northern and southern provinces, offered to pay protection money to the north; this was, they said, to allow the people "to return to their accustomed occupations after having been confined to walled towns, exhausted, and subjected to so many miseries, including the deaths of over two-thirds of them".

In spite of all this, somehow or other, with the prodigious industry which had created prosperity out of the flat lands over the centuries, the damage was repaired, and life returned to normal. The centre of the southern provinces had escaped the worst effects of the campaigning on either frontier and recovered first; from there, life returned to the outlying regions too.

For the family historian the coming of peace and the recovery in nothern France and the southern provinces of the Netherlands in the first quarter of the seventeenth century marks at last the beginning of reasonably continuous records. On both sides of the frontier surviving parish registers begin to record the *état civil* of members of the Catholic faith, while the records kept by the ministers of the Protestant churches are also a source of growing usefulness. The Walloons in particular are well documented, with the registers of the communities in England and the *fichier des refugiés* in Leyden which I described in the last chapter.

This, then, is a crucial period for family historians who are hunting Walloon ancestors. It is the time when stray clues from previous generations can at last be pinned down with some hope of a continuous record thereafter. For instance, I knew that Pierre de le Pierre and his wife Susanne Chiroutre were born about 1600, and married about 1625, and research into the troubles and travels of the Protestants had indicated a place of origin somewhere in the frontier region between the Spanish Netherlands and France. The records of the troubles and of the warfare and migrations which ensued suggested there were two particularly promising areas to search: at Tournai, where Marie de le Pierre was executed in 1545 and Pierre "Cra Cul", Gervoys, Simon and Catherine had been condemned at the assizes in 1568; and the Pays de l'Alleu from which Mahieu de le Pierre and his friends and relations had fled at the time of the troubles. Armed with these clues, it was time to try for answers to the two key questions: where exactly was "Gorne in Flanders", from which place (according to Pierre's naturalisation) he and his son Jean had come; and was Gorne a place for which records in the first quarter of the seventeenth century were preserved? Without a clear and positive answer to both questions the prospects of making a positive identification were not bright.

In fact by this stage in the search I was reasonably sure of the answer to the first question, which had baffled my father. He had had the very sensible idea of asking the Belgian Railway Office in London for advice, and a helpful Mr Mertz had replied that while he was unable to find the name Gorne among Belgian towns, villages or localities, he suggested as possibilities Goore (part of the commune of Linckhout in the province of Limbourg), Gooren (part of the commune of Deurne-lez-Diest in the province of Brabant), and Heurne near Audenarde in east Flanders because "Gorne" was quite possibly a contraction of the name used for that village in the seventeenth century. I wonder if a Belgian writing to an office of British Rail for help in locating a seventeenth-century village in England would receive as helpful a reply? Mr Mertz sent his letter

on 14 June 1938; there was no opportunity for my father to follow
it up across the Channel. It was nearly forty years later, when I was
living in Brussels and able to explore the Belgian countryside, that
these and other possible sites could be visited and explored at ease.
Each was ruled out fairly quickly: Limbourg was too far to the east,
and none of the background history nor the places themselves
provided any positive links with Gooren or Heurne. I could therefore be fairly sure that "Gorne" was a corruption of some other
place-name, and it was time to start hunting for a place with a
similar name in the likely areas, preferably in which there was some
positive indication that people called de le Pierre had once lived
there, indeed, by a fluke of chance might be living there still.

For this stage of the hunt three sources of information were
essential, the first naturally being a good map. As remarked earlier,
Belgian maps are not very good, but luckily the excellent maps
produced on the 1:100,000 scale by the Institut Géographique
National in France (especially No. 2) cover the area and extend far
enough over the Belgian frontier to be of invaluable help. The other
two indispensable aids for sweeping an area, especially in France,
are the telephone directory, which is obvious, and the war memorial
which may be less so. The great thing about telephone directories,
besides the fact that they are readily available in reference libraries
in England as well as everywhere in France, is that skimming
through them helps to grasp the types of surname predominant in
a region. If you were an Australian called, say, Boothroyd or Ent-
whistle, you would probably be wasting your time if you hunted for
your ancestors in Dorset;[1] in France too there are names that go with
regions and names that do not. The directories of the two northern Départements, the Nord and the Pas de Calais, showed that
de la Pierre was not a common name; indeed it hardly occurred at all,
whereas "Delpierre" turned up a little more often, and usually along
the line of the Lys valley, at Calais and in Tournai. So far, so good.

War memorials are even more useful than telephone directories.
Not everyone is on the telephone, whereas the massacres of the First
World War left few families unscathed in France, and the names are
all there, carefully listed, in the parish church and on the base of the
statue in the village square. We are familiar in England with the

[1] Whereas the Wigan telephone directory lists 40 Entwhistles.

difference in length between the lists of names on the memorials of the First World War and the Second: in France the contrast is much more stark. In England there are, I believe, thirty-two "Thankful Villages",[2] so called because every single one of their servicemen returned safely after November 1918; in the whole of France there can hardly be so many. The slaughter of the war years – especially the battles of the frontiers in 1914, Verdun in 1916, and the final convulsions of 1918 – are still commemorated in many French villages by bands and processions on Armistice day; and the names on the war memorials record a complete cross-section of the community. So in my travels I made a point of reading the war memorials in a succession of villages along the line, and this gave useful guidance, especially as the communities at the beginning of this century had more continuity with the past than is likely to be reflected in the present-day telephone directory. By these means I arrived at one very likely possibility for the location of Gorne. It was at last confirmed by two quite unexpected strokes of luck.

The first happened when I noticed that an exhibition of the works of the great sixteenth- and seventeenth-century mapmakers was arranged in Brussels. Brussels is a first-rate centre for exhibitions of all kinds, and there had been several cartographic shows during my stay. This one looked especially promising. I was very busy at the time with ministerial meetings, and day after day went by without an opportunity to visit the down-town gallery where the maps were being shown. On the last day of the exhibition I was able to snatch some time, find a place to park the car and get to the gallery while it was still open – only to find the whole exhibition-room completely packed with noisy school-children being given a cultural outing. I went in and was carried along in the crocodile, barely able to stop at any of the exhibits. I was just being swept past a splendid Mercator map of Flanders dated 1540 when suddenly, just where I wanted it, appeared the word "Gorghe"; and that was the answer. The name of La Gorgue on the Lys had cropped up frequently in the accounts of the troubles, but I could not see how any parliamentary draughtsman, however insular, could have managed to translate "La Gorgue" into "Gorne" in the naturalisation Bill. I had overlooked the fact that the Lys was pretty close to the

[2] Seven of them are in Somerset: I have seen only one such memorial.

language frontier, and that there would be a Flemish form of the local place names; and there is no difficulty at all in misreading Gorghe (or more likely Gorhe) in seventeenth-century handwriting as "Gorne". The war memorial at La Gorgue had shown a couple of Delpierres; the telephone directory for La Gorgue listed a Delpierre and a Chiroutre both living at La Gorgue, what is more, they both lived in the same rue de la Gendarmerie. It seemed very likely that Gorne was La Gorgue; but the harder question still remained, could I prove to the satisfaction of a respectable family historian that there was a definite connection between La Gorgue and Pierre de la Pierre of Canterbury?

That is where my second stroke of luck comes in. I had naturally written to the municipal and provincial archivists of the Département du Nord, which includes La Gorgue since Louis XIV swallowed Artois at the treaty of the Pyrenées in 1659, and I soon discovered that the records of the early seventeenth century were frequently patchy, sometimes non-existent. I had been advised by a friendly local antiquarian how best to phrase enquiries to the archivist: the rules are very much the same as in the game of Happy Families. If you can come close enough in your question to secure an identification, then by law the archivist must supply you with copies of the entry in the *État Civil*; but if you are at all adrift, there is no one who takes more relish than a French civil servant in replying, "Sorry, not at home." So when I posted off my crucial question about the baptism of Jean, son of Pierre de le Pierre and Susanne Chiroutre, at La Gorgue in about 1625, I knew there was a very good chance that no records would exist, however likely it was that the event had actually taken place in the Catholic parish church which was the only authorised place of worship in 1625.

When the reply came back from Monsieur Guy of the Direction des Services d'Archives of the Département du Nord at Lille, the first sentence was so familiar that I hardly bothered to read on.

> Sir, I have the honour to inform you that the parish registers of La Gorgue do not start before 1694.
>
> However, there is an alphabetical list of the *actes* of Baptism covering the years 1605–1792.
>
> And one finds in the year 1626 mention of the baptism of J. B. Delepierre, son of Pierre (Petri) and of Suzanne Giront (Chiroutre).

He enclosed a photocopy of the alphabetical table for the year 1626, and a bill for six francs for the copying. And that was that; the right name for the father, and the mother, and for the son, in the right place at the right time, is as near as anyone can get to perfection in the hunt for ancestors. I could have kissed M. Guy on both cheeks; instead I wrote off post haste to thank him and to ask him for the other cards in the Happy Family de le Pierre; such as Pierre's marriage to Suzanne about 1624, and the baptism of Pierre's brother Michel about 1605; or, since there was an alphabetical table, perhaps the best thing would be for him to send me a copy of the pages covering the Ds (if not the complete alphabet) for every year between 1605 and 1640. Though I did not know it such an unsporting demand was soon to be ruled offside by the French authorities; nevertheless with considerable patience Monsieur Guy sent me a photocopy of the first eight pages of the volume containing the D registrations of baptisms at La Gorgue. It arrived on the evening of a dinner party at our house in Brussels and I had time only to glance at the pages while waiting for the guests to arrive. I could hardly believe my eyes. "Delepierre", though hard to find in the local telephone directory or the war memorial, seemed to have thronged the parish church at La Gorgue in droves between 1605 and 1642 to baptise their children. All at once, from having just one obscure couple to hunt, I was submerged in the de le Pierre family.

I suppose it was only to be expected. Once you strike oil, you may be inconvenienced by the results, and prompt measures have to be taken to cap the gusher and control the flow. La Gorgue and the other little towns nearby looked like being the place of origin of a fairly large number of families now scattered far and wide in Europe and the New World. Before going any further it was necessary to read the local history, so as to identify the main features of the place and its inhabitants at the beginning of the seventeenth century. Straight away a new difficulty presented itself: from the material point of view nothing in La Gorgue suggested that it had any history to speak of. The reason is, paradoxically, that it has had rather too much history for its own good.

La Gorgue today is a drab little town on the south bank of the river Lys, just upstream from Estaires. That means that it is really in Artois, though Flanders is only a short bridge's length away. It has the look of all the towns in northern France which were rebuilt after the Great War, and for the same reason: it had been totally destroyed. In April 1918 the British Second Army was holding a line only a few kilometres to the east of La Gorgue. The position of the front line had hardly altered since the winter of 1914, because, in the words of the Official History, "the surface soil everywhere is clay: the water table is always fairly high, and any depression or excavation quickly fills with water." Not a good place for trench warfare, therefore, in the twentieth century any more than in the sixteenth; but even worse for attack than defence, and the sector had been quiet for a long time. It was so quiet that the inhabitants, who had joined the refugees in 1914, had returned to their farms and were cultivating the land within two or three kilometres of the front line, very much like their predecessors in the sixteenth century who had come back to till the fields and harvest the crops under the nose of troops of the Army of Flanders. Suddenly, on 7 and 8 April 1918, the front line erupted. The German artillery fired 40,000 gas shells into Armentières; the battle of the Lys, part of the German spring offensive, had begun. On 9 April, after a heavy bombardment, eight fresh German divisions with six in reserve attacked up river, and by the evening of that day the German 42nd division, opposed by the British 151st brigade, had pushed the front to Estaires and the river Lawe. "Towards 7 p.m.," says the Official History, "it had become evident that the enemy had brought up field guns and was systematically destroying the bridgeheads south of the Lys," such as La Gorgue. On 10 and 11 April the front line pushed slowly through La Gorgue and finally came to rest beyond Merville. By now La Gorgue, like the other towns of the Pays de l'Alleu, was smashed to pieces; the river Lys, which in peacetime could carry barges drawing 5 ft of water, was simply an extra wet area in the wasteland of mud and wreckage. So it remained for the rest of the war.

After the war La Gorgue, along with many other small towns and villages in northern France, was rebuilt on reparations money. Today it has a population of about 2,000, a new church, a fine war memorial (with the names of three Delpierre inscribed on it) and a British Commonwealth war cemetery. If the truth must be told I found it on the whole, apart from the war memorial, rather depressing and certainly my wife was not impressed with my discovery of the birthplace of my ancestors. However even a wife's lack of enthusiasm should not put off any family or local historian worth his salt. After all, that classic work by Rowland Parker, *The Common Stream*, unfolds layer after layer of detailed history from a patch of Cambridgeshire countryside which looks no more exciting to a casual passer-by than the Pays de l'Alleu; possibly even less so.

As I dug further into the archives it became clear that part of La Gorgue's problem, and also part of its attraction, was the fact that it was a frontier town: frontiers are dangerous places in time of war, but can be convenient in peacetime. The systems of law in Artois and in Flanders were different, and just as anyone in trouble in the United States could find it convenient to cross the line between one state and another, so in the Burgundian and Spanish Netherlands it could be helpful (for Protestants, for example) to move from one jurisdiction to another, by passing from the county of Flanders to the county of Artois. Indeed, soon after the de le Pierre family arrived in Canterbury the bridge over the Lys at La Gorgue became the frontier between France and the Netherlands: *de facto* in 1640 when the French army occupied Artois, *de jure* after the peace of the Pyrenées of November 1659 which finally ceded Artois to France. When Pierre de la Pierre in England had to give his place of birth to the parliamentary draughtsman for the naturalisation Bill at about that time, he made prudent use of the in-between status of his birthplace, by claiming to come from "Gorne in Flanders". It was no lie, because to anyone in the *pays* La Gorgue was well within the ancient territory of Flanders; moreover it allowed Pierre to claim (depending on how the wind veered about) that he was a subject of the king of France, or of the king of Spain; or even, since Flanders extended to the region finally incorporated into the Seven Provinces, of the Dutch Republic. England had been allied to Spain in the 1630s, and to France in the 1660s; who knew that a Dutch connection might not come in handy? It was not only the Vicar of Bray who had to be ready to steer about.

However, the frontier region was an uneasy place to live in for many centuries before the convulsions of the sixteenth and seventeenth, and the references in the few surviving documents about La Gorgue and the other little towns along the Lys tend to be uniformly depressing. A *draperie* or textile industry had been established at Estaires before 1250, but the English Edward III's Flemish allies had pillaged the towns along the Lys on their way to help him at Calais in 1347, and the following year the Black Death had done an even more thorough job of destruction. In 1359 an *acte de pouvoir publique* created a *draperie* at La Gorgue on the same basis as the one at Estaires.

> We Louis de Male, Count of Flanders, desiring the common profit and expansion of our town Le Gorghe and of those living and dwelling in it and the surrounding country; and considering that if the *draperie* there were lawful and approved, our said town could recover from the many setbacks which have been and are besetting it; and that it could then better serve us and our heirs, Counts of Flanders, so we grant to our said good people, the provost, *eschevins* and community of our said town of Le Gorghe . . . that they and their successors can make, and have made, and work, all sorts of lawful draperies, by the same *"loy esward et preuve"* as the people of the town of Estaires make, work and are accustomed to do.

They were to pay the count's steward for every whole piece of cloth, 12*d* of Flanders money, and 6*d* for a half-piece; half of any fines levied would go to the count and his successors for ever, one quarter would go to the town and the other quarter to the *"eswardeurs"*. This imposing, and for the count and his heirs profitable, document was "given at Bruges the XVIII day of May, the year 1359, by you, Monseigneur, and master Jehan de le Delft, Receiver of Flanders, here present", and signed in their names by a clerk called Lambin.

During the next three centuries, down to the eve of the troubles, the town continued to subsist on the textile trade. In 1428 Estaires, La Gorgue and Merville belonged to the *"privilège yprois"* in which new rules were set for the wages of the textile workers: for fulling cloth of English wool the master was to have 13*s* 6*d* in Flanders money, while two *varles* working for four days were to get 32*s*, and so on; for working Spanish and Scottish wool there was less pay. We next hear of the towns on the Lys in 1469 when the duke of Burgundy called for a report on the number of households there, for the usual purpose: he wanted to tax them. The *baillis, eschevins* and *avis* being sensible men laid much stress in their replies on recent outbreaks of fire, and the large number of poor people to be supported. In terms of size, Merville headed the list with 450 households (compared with 106 in Armentières); the *curé* of Estaires reckoned the number of households at around 300 (about one third of them "poor"), and the *bailli* of La Gorgue reported "about 60 hearths". During the Burgundian prosperity between 1469 and 1485, the towns expanded rapidly; the population of Walloon Flanders as a whole is reckoned to have increased from some 8,000 to about 10,000 households during the period. However, Estaires suffered a disastrous fire in 1474, and then the whole region was devastated again in the war between Louis XI of France and Maximilian of Austria; down went the number of households to about 7,000. In Armentières, which had grown from 106 to 350 between 1469 and 1485, there were only 150 households after that war; once again, one third of them were reckoned too poor to tax.

For thirty years after 1485, the *pays* and the textile trade were in a depressed state; then in May 1516 the emperor Charles V decided to try to revive their prosperity, and the tax revenue with it. This *octroi* restoring a free annual market at Estaires contains the usual references to past disasters:

> During the wars and divisions that have reigned in our lands of Flanders and Artois since the death of our very dear lord and ancestor Duke Charles of Burgundy (whom God absolve) the said town of Estaires and the châteaux there have been several times burnt and destroyed, and the letters and charters lost and burnt, and the cloth-making which used to take place there has been discontinued.

Charles's measures were successful, and the sales of Frisian butter used for treating the wool (*l'ensuinage des laines*) revived with the textile trade: at Estaires, ten to twenty *tonneaux* of butter were used yearly, and since each piece of finished cloth had needed about a pound of butter, annual production must have amounted broadly to between 2,500 and 5,000 pieces of cloth a year. That was about the year 1540, when the persecution of heretics began in earnest; soon the Pays de l'Alleu was plunged into a new round of troubles, and the first mass emigration was under way.

The alphabetical table of baptisms at La Gorgue starts in 1605, after the second exodus but before the truce and the revival of the frontier provinces. What sort of picture can be deduced from this bare list of names about the region which Sir Thomas Overbury had described in such depressing terms?

What I had to work on were copies of four large sheets of paper on which a clerk had transcribed details of the baptism of children whose family names began with the letter D, as recorded at La Gorgue between 1605 and 1642. I had hoped to get a full table from A to Z, but the archivist quite properly declined; they could not all be my ancestors, and the table was fragile and should not be photocopied too often. This material, though seemingly limited, had two considerable advantages. In the first place the writing was legible, with very few doubtful readings in some 800 entries. The second advantage is that the letter D is the most common initial of family names in northern France. If you study the telephone directories for Lille, Armentières and Estaires, you will find that the overall proportion is about 100 D entries to 666 of all others combined. Therefore the list of D baptisms provides a reasonably good sample: good enough for some rather obvious and elementary statistical analysis of the kind which local historians call "aggregation" and "reconstitution". Aggregation means counting monthly totals for births, for example, and annual totals for the calendar year and for the "harvest year", so as to be able to assess such things as population size and changes linked to outside historical events, for instance the truce of 1609. Reconstitution is much closer to family history because it means sorting out information by families and analysing it in social terms: for instance, is there evidence of deliberate birth-control?

The scope for aggregation was fairly limited because the table showed years but not months, but at least it allowed an estimate of the size of the population of La Gorgue in the first half of the seventeenth century, and of the extent to which it was affected by changing circumstances. The overall annual average of births to the D families was about 21, which suggests a total average for all families (at the ratio 1:6.6) of something like 160; and Braudel assumes that *ancien régime* families had a birthrate of about 40 per 1,000 (lower in the towns, higher in the country) which further suggests a total population for La Gorgue of some 4,000, or twice as large as today. Considering that the number of hearths reported in 1469 was only about 60, that many families from La Gorgue had been included in the Lists of the Condemned between 1567 and 1573, and that the town had been in the military zone for the disastrous last quarter of the sixteenth century, this is somewhat surprising. What is more, the number of baptisms in any one year did not vary very markedly from the overall annual average: neither the truce in 1609 nor the resumption of war between France and Spain in 1635 seems to have made much difference. It looks therefore as if the south of Flanders, and Artois which conformed quickly at the start of Parma's period of office, may have come off more lightly than the parts further north. As for the apparent stability of population, that could be accounted for by newcomers taking the place of families squeezed out by the pressures of conformity or the fear of trouble in store; such an assumption could only be tested by moving from aggregation to reconstitution, sorting out the family groups (each pair of parents with children baptised during the period) to make a better analysis of the sample. Here I should explain that in the Pays de l'Alleu the baptismal register usually includes the mother's Christian name and maiden name, so that it is possible to identify families even though many of the surnames are very common and the same Christian names tended to be used by the same family groups. (Even Christian names, used with care, may be useful as indicators of cousinship.) As soon as the sifting and sorting was done some interesting points began to emerge.

There are half a dozen surnames, or groups, each represented by around a dozen separate family groups, as follows:

    13 families d'Assonville
    13 families de le Pierre or Despierres, Despierre, Despier
    12 families de le Place or de le Plache
    12 families du Bois or du Bus, Buce, Buz, Buche, Busche, Busle
    11 families du Croquet
    11 families de le Rue or de le Ruelle or des Ruel or des Ruelle

Now, on the same principle that local historians use to date hedgerows, it is a reasonable assumption that if in a fairly small place one finds a number of families of the same name (even more, with surnames which seem to have developed varieties of their own) then those families have probably been settled in that place for some time. Indeed, in spite of all the upheavals in Flanders and northern France in the sixteenth and seventeenth centuries, it seems that a large majority of people showed remarkable resistance to being removed from their ancestral villages. In his *Early Modern France 1560–1715* Robin Briggs remarks on this as a reason why regional diversity survived so long.

There was one particular factor which maintained this diversity, while itself being common to the whole country (France). The village community had demonstrated remarkable coherence and strength during its long past, putting up continued resistance to excessive demands from outside, whether they originated from the seigneur, the church or the king. . . . While most people lived in nuclear family units, their primary loyalties were to their lineage – the extended family – and to the community. Country dwellers might extend their horizons to include the *pays*, a group of perhaps 10 or 20 villages associated by similar geographical features and local traditions. . . . The enormous majority of marriages were between members of the same village or two immediately adjoining villages . . . in practice population mobility was only possible within very strict limits. . . . Movement to towns was another (possibility) and here the immigrant would expect to find help from other members of his original community who had preceded him.

All of this is very apposite, not only to the community of a small town like La Gorgue, but also to the Walloon migrations. We have seen already how those forced to flee from the Pays de l'Alleu had gone to places where they "would expect to find help from other members of their original community who had preceded them", to Canterbury, Frankfurt, Middelburg, the Boulonnais, the Calaisis or the other centres for refugees of the great migrations. At La Gorgue we see the home territory and the network of related families from which the refugees came, to which they returned if circumstances allowed, and to which they looked for support to help them establish themselves in their new homes if it became clear that there was no going back to Flanders. It looks as if the stability of population suggested by the table of baptisms was a real feature of a society which not even the upheavals of the sixteenth and seventeenth centuries could seriously undermine. Nevertheless, the migrations too were fact, and many of the families at La Gorgue had members living in exile overseas. In one case in particular, the family of Louis de le Pierre and Jeanne Guiselin, we can be precise about their movements; and it is time to look more closely at them and their closest relatives, many of whom were about to leave Flanders for good.

CHAPTER 10

The de le Pierre Family Joins the Third Exodus

1625–35

Besides, an acquaintance with the names, connection, and characters of individuals that compose the body whose actions are recorded in history, and with the places where those actions happened, gives a distinction and precision to the knowledge of general events to be obtained by no other means.

Topographer, I (1789)

Now that I had at last located Pierre de le Pierre and Susanne Chiroutre as a young married couple at La Gorgue in 1625, it was possible to introduce them at the top left hand corner of the family chart which my father had registered in 1938. There were two main aspects to this task: to trace the way in which this couple, and any others of the family at La Gorgue, had made their way to England; and secondly to see if there was any prospect of tracing how they had got to La Gorgue in the first place. After all, having found unexpected evidence which carried the family back to the sixteenth century it seemed a pity to stop there. As a result I found there was more to the name de le Pierre than met the eye. This arose from my analysis of D surnames. Out of well over a hundred entries all but a handful are recognisably derived from place-names or geographical features of some sort. About half have the prefix "de" (and all its variants), and half "du" (and plural variants). Such styles are of course very common in France, and names like "de le Rue" and "du Bois" cause no identity-problems. But what did de le Pierre mean, and if it was a place-name, what was a "lepierre"? The obvious answer seemed to be that the first bearer of the name worked in a quarry, but this was unlikely: how many quarries are there in the Lys valley? Another puzzle was the existence in the same small town of families called de le Pierre, Despierres, Despierre and Despier.

As in the case of Gorne, it was brooding over a map which produced a convincing answer; there were several place-names which seemed entirely to fit the bill. There is a little town on the river Escaut just before it changes its name to Scheldt, which is called Spiere in Flemish and used to be called Espierres in French. Running into the river at that point is a tributary (now a canal) called L'Espierre, by which it is possible to reach the river Deule and thence the Lys. Several smaller streams flow into the Espierre: today they are called Grande Espierre and Petite Espierre and Espirillon. Now, this group of names seemed to me very useful. A man from Spiere might be called de Spiere (later Despier); from Espierres he would be d'Espierres (later Despierres). And from l'Espierre? Surely (alas) he would be not de le Pierre but de l'Espierre.[1]

I happened to come across a list of tenants paying *rentes* in about 1200 to the Seigneur of Mouscron, a town between the river Escaut at Spiere and the river Lys at Menin. Six of the names were represented in the baptismal list of La Gorgue four hundred years later: de Lattre, des Hayes, des Camps, du Mont, du Pont; and de Lespierre. Therefore I thought it worth going to the excellent map department in the Bibliothèque Albert Premier in Brussels to investigate the area. I explained to the assistant that I wanted an early map of the area around Mouscron (pronouncing the "s"). "You mean Mou'cron," he said in the nice Belgian way of correcting a mistake, so unlike the schoolmarmish French style. People, it seemed, do not pronounce the "s" in Mouscron; or in l'Espierre. So a man moving from the Escaut to the Lys in the thirteenth century, asked where he came from, would probably have said, "de Le'pierre".

The moral of the story is that family names are more complicated and eventually more revealing than they look. So de L'Espierre turned into de la Pierre over the centuries; de la Pierre turned into Peters all at once. Back at La Gorgue in the first quarter of the seventeenth century, the various families de le Pierre (or something like it) could be plotted in detail, thanks to the

[1] In 1515 or thereabouts Marie de l'Espierre married Nicholas Mullier at Roubaix, and two de l'Espierres were *baillis* at Tourcoing at the end of the century; these places are near Mouscron and half way between Spiere and La Gorgue.

alphabetical table of baptisms; since it covered nearly forty years from 1605 it could fairly be assumed to embrace the whole of one generation without leaving serious gaps, as well as providing clues to the previous generation and the subsequent one.

As luck would have it, the family which I had been hunting for so long was not only numerous but also among the very first to be listed. Louis de le Pierre and his wife Jeanne Guiselin had three children baptised and recorded in the list, Michel (1606), Nicholas (1608) and Marguerite (1614): here at last was my direct ancestor Michel, his Guiselin mother Jeanne, and his father Louis; a new generation to be added to the family tree. Pierre's birth was not recorded nor had I expected to find it, since the table began in 1605 and he was almost certainly born earlier, having married before 1626. Another couple in the table was Maximilian de le Pierre and his wife Florence le Candle, whose children were born about the same time as Louis's and Jeanne's: Anne (1607), Louise (1608), Jeanne (1610), Pierre (1612), Antoine (1614), Florentine (1616), Jacques (1620) and Laurent (1623). Another Pierre de le Pierre and his wife Jeanne Saumon had a son baptised François in 1613; and Antoine de le Pierre (whose wife was not named) had a son baptised Jean in 1608. Then Louis de le Pierre and Peronne Defief had a son Jacques baptised in 1617, and a daughter Louise in 1618; Louis de le Pierre and Marguerite Lebrun had Pierre (1620), Marguerite (1622), Louis (1624), Jacques (1626). . . .

But that was running into a new generation; Louis the elder had a son Pierre alive in 1620 and there is enough information to make the point that in La Gorgue children would appear regularly every two years (sometimes faster) for twenty years or so, and as soon as the first wife succumbed to the strain her husband would marry a second wife (Louis and Peronne Defief), and perhaps a third. Children were the most basic form of social security.

Another feature the list of baptisms illustrates is the surprisingly small incidence of illegitimate births. Whatever had happened during the passage of armies, births out of wedlock were comparatively rare in the small towns and villages of Artois once the truce was in operation and the parish clergy were firmly back in control. In most cases the premature arrival of a baby resulted in the hasty marriage of the parents; the system of trial marriage was not suppressed until later in the century. Thus in La Gorgue, out of some 800 entries over nearly forty years, representing perhaps one in seven of the population of child-bearing age, only fourteen illegitimate births are recorded. One for 1624 is "Marie de le Pierre daughter of Pierre and of Marie Mars, illegitimate", adding an unexpected note to Pierre's biography. Marie Mars was clearly a thorn in the curé's side because she accounts for two such entries.

There were other biographical links to be deduced, none with complete certainty, but it was possible to construct a reasonable table of de le Pierre contemporaries in La Gorgue at the beginning of the seventeenth century and to draw some conclusions. Thus it seemed likely that the elder Louis and Maximilian were closely related, possibly brothers: Maximilian gave the rare name Louise to his second daughter; Louis and Maximilian themselves are rare Christian names, significant when given to children born in the 1570s. Louis of Nassau was the Protestant hero killed at Mook in 1574; and the emperor Maximilian II died the following year, having earned the gratitude of Protestants of the Netherlands by his appeal to Philip to ease the repression of Alva, suggesting (through the archduke Charles) that it would be politic to stop the executions and aim for a reconciliation. Less probably Pierre and Antoine, of the same generation, may have beeen brothers of Louis and Maximilian, as Maximilian gave those names to his first and second sons: I place no weight on it but when men of the same surname, living in the same small town and producing families at about the same time, go on giving their children the same set of Christian names, it would after all be somewhat surprising if they were not cousins, if not brothers.

Armed with all this new information, the next step was to see how many of the de le Pierre families could be identified in England later on; having secured one line across the Channel, it would be a pity not to consolidate it if that could be done. It was noteworthy that Pierre de le Pierre and Susanne Chiroutre were not the only couple to disappear from the register after the baptism of their son Jean-Baptiste in 1626: there is only one more baptism recorded for any de le Pierre, that of Jeanne, daughter of Jean de le Pierre and Peronne Pilize, in 1633. What became of them all and the children already born to them?

There were various possible traces to be considered. Besides the arrival of Michel at Dover in 1635 and of Pierre with Susanne

Chiroutre at Canterbury in the same year, a Nicholas de le Pierre witnessed a baptism in the Walloon church at Threadneedle Street in August 1635. Canterbury has several references to François Delepierre "son of the late Pierre"; my father had conjectured that he might be a cousin or even a brother of Pierre and Michel; I now knew that he could not be a brother, but he might well be a cousin; the François born at La Gorgue in 1613 might be this François of Canterbury. Other connections came to light: in particular, it was clear at La Gorgue that Pierre's wife Susanne Chiroutre came from a fairly prolific local family. Joddine Chiroutre was married to Nicholas Descamps, and their son Philippe was baptised in 1617; Catherine Chiroutre married Mahieu Descamps (a cousin) and their son François was baptised in 1639. At Canterbury Susanne's sister Anne Chiroutre was the wife of François Lombart, born at Estaires next to La Gorgue; and Susanne's brother Philippe, an elder of the Walloon church at Canterbury, was married to Jeanne Becqu, another very frequent name in the Pays de l'Alleu.

That was all I needed to extract from the material available at La Gorgue. Two questions now remained: why did those families and individuals move from La Gorgue to England in the 1620s and 1630s; and what were they doing in the decade between the last record of their existence in the Spanish Netherlands and the first in their new home? By now there were plenty of leads, and a good chance of evidence with which to follow them up.

It is worthwhile taking another look at the Walloon community in Canterbury, where by good fortune we have a more or less complete list of the heads of families taken in 1622 as part of a census ordered by James I. The list was collated by W. Durrant Cooper for the Camden Society. It is headed in the original, "The Catalogue of the Names of the Artisans, Strangers, Denisens and English-born, of the Walloon Congregation of Canterbury"; and there is a footnote explaining that "These are the names of the Masters and Journeymen of silk weavers, silk rash and stuff weavers, wool combers, spinners, quillmakers and of the Dyers, Tailors, Bakers, Loom and Wheelmakers for the Congregation." This suggests perhaps that the list excludes the small number of professional men in the community, such as the minister and any doctors or notaries. It is invaluable because it provides information on a number of key points: the size of the community after the effects of the second exodus had begun to die away; its relation to the births and deaths in the Walloon registers; and the distinction between Strangers (born abroad) and English-born points to the different waves of migration. The names of those born in England show how rapidly the form of name in use changed in the process of naturalisation. There are 284 names recorded in the list, including 189 Strangers, 93 English-born and two "denisens" – that is, foreigners who had lived in England long enough to acquire the right to reside there permanently. The clerk who compiled the list had done so with care, so that the spelling of family names is reliable, and he took the trouble to distinguish "the elder" and "the younger" in cases where fathers and sons (or other close relatives) shared the same Christian and surname. The date of this record is particularly useful. It is shortly before the third great migration out of Wallonia. To appreciate the important respects in which this was different from the previous migrations we must return to the continent.

The community at La Gorgue, and hundreds of others like it, now formed part of a new state, which remained formally independent under the rule of the "Archdukes" until Albert died in 1621. The Confederation of the southern provinces was intended to be a successor to the Burgundian Netherlands of happy memory, and the only link with Spain was to be the family connection of the rulers; a link which was to prove surprisingly strong, and long after Lille had been absorbed into France loyalists would drink toasts to the king of Spain as warmly as Jacobites to the Stuart pretenders "over the water". The archduke Albert was a pious Catholic, and under his rule the Jesuits quickly became more numerous and influential in relation to the size of the population in the Netherlands than anywhere else in Europe. In 1630 when there were 3,000 members of the Society of Jesus in Spain, 2,200 in France, there were 1,700 in the *Pays-bas Catholiques*. They conducted a lively propaganda war with the Calvinists in the northern provinces, but both sides were obliged to temper their zeal to the urgent claims of reconstruction, and there was *de facto* tolerance on both sides of the border. Once the truce of Antwerp of 1609 came into effect, the large number of Catholics still living in the north was revealed by the numbers coming for confirmation to Antwerp or to s'Hertogenbosch (then still south of the border); and considerable number of Protestants from the northern parts of the Archduke's territory, especially around Antwerp, made their way to worship at the nearest Calvinist temple at the States' fort of Lillo on the Scheldt.

For those of Protestant sympathies still living in the south, like those of the Pays de l'Alleu, the main centres for the exercise of the reformed religion were still the temples of Marcq and of Guînes near Calais, just over the border in the territory of the king of France. The two-year Spanish occupation of the Calaisis between May 1596 and July 1598 had scattered the Protestants, and all their records were lost; but the new French governor of Calais, Dominic de Vicq, was a friend of Henri IV and favoured the Protestant religion. He granted free entry and exercise of their religion to many refugee families from Flanders; and in the general atmosphere of tolerance and reviving prosperity, people must have hoped that their problems were on the way to solution, and that there would be no more enforced migration of people out of the *pays*.

What ruined their hopes, and those of so many other people in Europe, was the endless succession of campaigns in Germany which formed the Thirty Years War, and the determination of the new rulers of France – Louis XIII and his minister Richelieu – to seize every opportunity to turn affairs to their own advantage. Many innocent people died to earn Richelieu his place in the history books: for example, in Franche Comté a whole prosperous and semi-independent province was ravaged by the French and their Swedish allies, while in the Netherlands there seemed to be an equally tempting opportunity to partition the southern provinces between the French and the Dutch. The first plan was simply to divide up the southern Netherlands along the language frontier; but there seemed to be no hurry as long as the Habsburgs were preoccupied with the war in Germany, which they seemed sure to lose as Gustavus Adolphus led the Protestant armies from one victory to another. Then there was a startling change of fortune; on 6 September 1634 at Nordlingen the combined Catholic armies won a crushing victory in return. The French and the Dutch, alarmed at the prospect that they might lose their opportunity, quickly made a treaty to seize the southern provinces.

Naturally it was not presented quite like that in public. The "oppressed" people of the south were invited to liberate themselves from Spain, failing which the Allies would do it for them. This time the partition line would not lie along the language frontier, but would favour Richelieu; almost the whole of Flanders was to go to France, along with the Walloon provinces. The frontier would run from Blankenberge to Brugge and Rupelmonde; the great Flemish cities, Bruges itself, Ghent and Ypres would all become French.

The two partners drove a hard bargain with each other. France insisted that once fighting started the Dutch would not make a separate peace, so locking them into many more years of war. In return, the French made no attempt to gain freedom of religion for Catholics north of the partition line: Richelieu the pragmatist was not the man to let a small matter of religion stand in the way of national advantage. The time allowed to the southern provinces to obey the ultimatum was brutally short, just over three months in fact, before the French herald formally declared the resumption of the war between France and Spain in the Grand' Place at Brussels on 19 May. Flanders and Artois found themselves once more in the front line. Once more the people of the two provinces faced the prospect of skirmishing armies and the loss of their painfully recovered prosperity. For many of them, especially those close to the frontier, those with Protestant sympathies and those with property in France as well as in the province, it was time to pack up and seek shelter beyond the Channel or the Maas, as so many of their friends and relatives had done before them.

That was the way the third exodus began. It was different in some respects from the previous ones. The first great migration in the 1560s was "for religion", or "because of the oppression . . . or because they despair of pardon, or through dread of miseries to come", as Margaret of Parma described it to Philip; probably the refugees themselves would have recognised all of these motives. The second exodus during the 1580s and 1590s was also driven by a combination of religious pressure (Parma's policy of conformity or expulsion) and the more basic instincts of self-preservation. But by the time the third migration took place, the world had moved recognisably closer to the one we live in ourselves, where rulers (like Richelieu) saw the interests of the state as predominant, and the ruled had learnt enough to take precautions accordingly. Indeed there are some distinct similarities between the 1630s and the 1930s. The people of the southern provinces were well informed, much better than their grandparents, about what was going on in the world, and the plans of Richelieu and the Dutch were as obvious in advance to its potential victims as the German and Russian plans which ushered in the Second World War. Those who were most likely to be affected, and had the means of doing something about it, reacted in the same way; in fact the third exodus was spread over a number of years before the formal declaration of war in 1635, as the flow of refugees from Central Europe had begun years before 1939. In the 1930s some of the refugees tended to move in stages, keeping ahead of the growth of German power: so too the families who decided to leave the Pays de l'Alleu in the 1630s did not all proceed directly to England. As noted earlier, there is a gap of nearly ten years between the last reference to Pierre de le Pierre and Susanne Chiroutre in the Catholic register at La Gorgue and the first reference to them in the Walloon register at Canterbury. For at least some of the time they were in France, probably in Calais. There are several pieces of circumstantial evidence for this.

When the refugees arrived at Dover in 1635 they came from Calais; as Mayor Luke Pepper told the Lord Warden of the Cinque Ports, they were people "whose dwellings were in or near Calais, but have lands and tenements in Flanders and fly hither for security of the same". They were Protestants, and though the records of the temples at Marcq and at Guînes do not survive from this period, we know that Michel de le Pierre, for one, had become a Protestant at Calais, because it was the church at Calais that recommended him to the congregation at Middelburg when he arrived there in January 1637. When Jean de le Pierre was registered at Leyden University on 2 November 1639 his nationality was "Gallus", a Frenchman, whereas the proper designation of someone from the southern Netherlands was "Belga", and the clerks at Leyden were always meticulous about these matters; the French had not yet occupied Artois in 1639, but if the de le Pierres had lived in France since the time of Jean's birth it would have been prudent (and very nearly true) to claim that he was French, like the brother and sisters he had acquired before the family came to England in 1635. After all, the Dutch Republic and the French king were bound to remain allies for many years to come.

So the de le Pierre and many other families like them lived for some years on the mainland until the dangers of renewed warfare at last impelled them to cross the Channel. Anyone like me who has a healthy respect for the Channel even in these days of large and comfortable ferries must blench at the thought of the crossing in earlier times: certainly no one ever took it lightly, even though some made a virtue of necessity.[2] In the days of sail the short Channel crossing might take an unconscionably long time and no description of a visit to England was complete without an account of it. Thus, when Frederick, duke of Württemberg travelled to Dover from the Ems river in August 1592 his secretary Jacob Rathgob kept an account which was printed in 1602:

> Not being accustomed to the sea, we were seized with horrible vomitings, and most of the party [with the exception of His Highness, the courtier hastened to add] became so dreadfully ill they thought they were dying. . . . Nevertheless, the merciful God graciously looked down with fatherly eyes on us, so that on the morning of the 9 August, towards mid-day [they had left the mouth of the Ems on the afternoon of 7 August] we arrived happily and well near Dover. . . . We were about some 1,000 paces from the port when the Master ordered the anchors to be cast, and gave those on shore a signal to fetch us off in small boats, because he did not want to go into the harbour but to set sail immediately for France and La Rochelle. Thereupon several Englishmen soon came with boats . . . and some of our party were in terror at seeing themselves in such little boats among such awful mountains of salt water, but the Almighty assisted us.

So too Pierre de le Pierre must have prayed for assistance from the Almighty as he took Susanne Chiroutre and the children on the boat to join their relatives and friends in England. The crossing took place, most likely, some time in the nine months before his baby daughter Marie was baptised in the crypt of Canterbury in November 1635; perhaps the family was part of the large batch of arrivals early in May which Luke Pepper the mayor of Dover reported to the Lord Warden of the Cinque Ports. Pierre and Susanne had at least two children before Marie, including Jean-Baptiste, the eldest. It was a daunting undertaking to arrive in this very vulnerable state to establish themselves in a new country: just as well that they could not foresee quite how daunting it was going to be.

[2] Henry VIII's minister Thomas Cromwell seriously contemplated a voyage to Calais and back for the sole purpose of purging his stomach; this confirms my generally unfavourable impression of Cromwell himself and the suspicion that though seasickness may be nasty enough, the medical remedies of Cromwell's day were even nastier.

PART III

———⟨⊗⊗⊗⟩———

Home from Home
1635–1700

CHAPTER 11

⊗

Toil and Trouble
1635–50

The people are not so hard-working and industrious as the Netherlanders or French. The most laborious, difficult and skilled work is chiefly done by foreigners.

Emmanual van Meteren,
visiting England from the Netherlands in 1575

He knew their doctrines, and that they were all hardy fellows well met . . . that they sat at the communion as in taverns . . . and that their churches were nests which he would reduce to canonical obedience. . . . Their ministry and discipline was not *secundum Evangelium* as the English was.

Archbishop Laud addressing Pastor Bulteel
of the Walloon church in 1634

The de la Pierre family arrived in Canterbury in the year that Bell Harry was hung in the great tower of the Cathedral, thereafter known as Bell Harry steeple: "That stately tower . . . which, for the elegant proportions of the building itself, and of its ornaments, is perhaps the completest beauty of that kind anywhere to be seen", as Canon Gostling described it in his "A Walk in and about the City of Canterbury" and as many generations of men of Kent have thought before and since. Canterbury was the largest of the score of little towns in Kent, but it was still pretty small with a population of not much over 5,000 of which the Walloons now made up perhaps one-third. Among the English, families tended to be fairly small: Gregory King the demographer made the average size four or five; only a few of his sample had more than five in the family, and none had more than eight. This comparatively low rate of fertility was the result of fairly late marriage, high infant mortality and a high death rate. In the first half of the seventeenth century, the average age at marriage in Canterbury was twenty-six for the bridegroom and twenty-three for the bride, slightly younger among the tradesmen of the city; up to one-half of the children died before the age of sixteen. In the 1620s and 1630s burials slightly exceeded baptisms in the five central parishes (St Alphege, St Dunstan, St George, St Mary Major, St Paul and St Peter); and indeed throughout Kent as a whole, numbers remained fairly steady throughout the century, with a population of about 130,000 in 1600 rising to perhaps 150,000 by 1700. There is no mystery about this rather poor record: malnutrition, cramped and stuffy houses, no sanitation, no pure water, all gave an easy run to epidemic diseases, and consumption, typhus, typhoid, smallpox and influenza were as deadly as the plague in Kent, as everywhere in the kingdom.

Within the city of Canterbury the Walloons were noticeable not only for their numbers, their language and their Calvinism, but also for their un-English industry; and their large families aroused the fear that they would swamp the native population. There was also a constant suspicion that new arrivals from foreign parts, crowding into already crowded tenements, would bring infection with them, especially the plague. Such outbreaks were severe. The Walloon register at Southampton for 1583 records on 17 April, "*Peste a commencé*"; there follow seventy numbered entries of deaths, each followed by the word "*Peste*". In Canterbury the years 1576 and 1596 were marked by severe outbreaks, and it would have seemed no coincidence that the city was then crammed with refugees of the first and second migrations. However, 1635 was mercifully spared the plague. That was very likely due to the previous bitterly cold winter which William Whiteway of Dorchester noted in his diary in February of that year:

> This year we had an extreme hard winter with much frost, severe hails, cold rains, so that the Thames was frozen and men went and rode over it. 22 January the ink did freeze in my pen while I did write. Countrymen could not labour and therefore 1 February there was an extraordinary collection in the Town to relieve the extraordinary necessities of the poor. Many drowned in the snow.

The respite did not last very long, and the de la Pierre family together with the rest of the Walloon congregation were soon facing a succession of threats to their survival. The first that happened to them was a return of the plague; next, ecclesiastical persecution; and then the civil war. At times they must have wondered if they had really done the right thing in crossing the Channel.

When Pierre de la Pierre and Susanne Chiroutre first lived in Canterbury they had three living children, including little Marie, baptised in November 1635. The eldest son Jean-Baptiste was baptised at La Gorgue in 1626; and there was a son Pierre two years younger than Jean-Baptiste. The existence of the other children is marked simply by their deaths. On 4 January 1637 the death of Susanne de le Pierre was registered in the Anglican church of All Saints; on 20 July in the same year the death of *"un enfant à Mr Pierre Delapierre"* was listed in the Walloon register. The summers of 1636, 1637 and 1638 were blazing hot, and 1637 was a bad plague year at Canterbury: the entries in the Walloon register follow the characteristic pattern. There were 6 deaths in May, 9 in June, 12 in July, 32 in August, 21 in September, 20 in October, 6 in November; the plague always flourished during the warm weather.

Pierre and Susanne appeased their sorrow by naming another daughter Susanne, who was baptised in the crypt on 24 February 1639; and a second Marie (the death of the first is not recorded unless she was the child who died in 1637) was baptised on 26 November 1640. The plague returned in 1638, and again in 1639. However no more deaths were recorded in the de la Pierre family in this period. Whether or not it was plague which carried off their children in 1637, it was a grim enough introduction to Canterbury for Pierre and Susanne. The physicians and surgeons, with the "searchers" and bearers of the dead, going around carrying the white sticks which identified them and permitted them to move about; the streets washed down morning and evening; the fires of pitch and sweet herbs; the boarded-up windows and the red crosses on the barred doors of the houses where the plague had struck. Pierre is called "Mr" (for *maître*) in the entry of the death of his child, and the witnesses at the baptisms of his children come from the *gratin* of the community, which may suggest that he was already practising as a surgeon. If so, the plague epidemics put him doubly at risk. Many of those who ministered to the victims died of the plague themselves, like Raphael Thorius, doctor to the Walloons in

London during the plague of 1625, whose end is recorded by Wood in his *Athenae Oxonienses*:

> He acted more for the public (by exposing his person too often) than for his own dear concern. Wherefore, being deeply infected with that disease, he died of it in his house in the parish of St Benet Fincke, in July or August 1625, but where he was buried I know not, unless in the church or churchyard of that parish.

In such harrowing circumstances the job of the mother of the family was even more demanding. As a housewife from Flanders, Susanne Chiroutre's place was central.

Another immigrant family in London at the time of Thorius's death was that of the doctor Baldwin Hamey, who had married the girl Sarah Oeils who had survived the sack of Antwerp when a baby in 1574.[1] Many years later her son remembered in his old age the way she had looked after her young immigrant family.

> As each of us became of age to learn, it was she who first taught us our letters, not only to read but also to write. . . . She also instructed us in the rudiments of arithmetic. . . . When we had been prepared in this way, she handed over to my father the further education of his sons, reserving for herself the care of diet and clothes. . . . The care of her daughters was nearer to her and occupied her daily: in addition to the teaching already described, she wished them to excel with the needle . . . nor did she neglect to teach them how to sing and play stringed instruments; and she permitted them to dance with their friends of similar age.

It was also the mother who undertook the children's religious instruction, and taught them manners and how to keep accounts. No wonder that Susanne Chiroutre, as is clear from the registers at Canterbury, came to be just as important a member of the Strangers' church as her energetic husband; it was the result of hard work and only after much distress. The first generation of immigrants, then as now, had an uphill task establishing themselves in the new country.

[1] Later on, a portrait of Charles Oeils hung over the staircase of Pierre de la Pierre's house at the Blackfriars beside "great grandfather Gisling"; but I have not been able to trace any connection between the families except the study of medicine at Leyden.

From now on the details of the Walloon community are well established in the surviving documents. The 1622 census records every head of family who practised the trades formally permitted to the immigrants, but not the handful of professional people, the ministers Delmé and Bulteel, the doctors and surgeons de la Rivière and Dubois or the notaries, the Springhe family. A total of less than two hundred does not sound enough to account for a community several thousand strong, until one remembers the web of relationships; every one of those men was supporting not only his wife and children but also parents, uncles and aunts, cousins, nephews and nieces as well, to say nothing of apprentices, servants and destitute travellers.

The size of the Walloon community is documented in 1635, after the main influx of the third migration. That year Secretary Sir John Cook called for returns of the communicants in all the Strangers' churches in England, and received the following:

French and Walloons of London	1,400
Dutch of London ['Dutch' includes Flemings]	840
Walloons of Canterbury	900
Dutch of Colchester	700
Walloons of Norwich	396
Dutch of Norwich	363
Dutch of Maidstone	50
Dutch of Sandwich	500
Dutch of Yarmouth	28
Walloons of Southampton	36
Total	5,213

To turn the number of communicants into a total for the community one has to choose a multiplier, which some set as low as two and others as high as four; it mainly depends on how many families had children too young to be communicants, which is a tricky thing to try to estimate. Sir John Cook was interested in the number of communicants; the ecclesiastical authorities were more worried about the way in which the Strangers took communion, sitting down (and with their hats on too) exactly "as in taverns", as it seemed to the more formal of the Anglican divines. Quite soon it was not only hardship and disease that was pinching the Strangers at Canterbury; the ecclesiastical climate too had turned very sharp. Good Archbishop Parker had been succeeded by a very different man. Dr Laud, the terror of nonconformists, was resolved to restore good Anglican discipline in his archdiocese just as he had done before as bishop of London. Laud was a man of whom little good was spoken in his life, and less afterwards; so before recording very briefly how he made himself unpleasant to the Strangers, let us note one point which is undoubtedly in his favour, as recorded by Aubrey:

> W. Laud AB Cant. was a great lover of Cats. He was presented with some Cyprus Cats, i.e. our . Tabby-cats, which were sold at first for 5 pounds a piece: this was about 1637 or 1638.

Aubrey could not resist adding another fascinating irrelevance: "I do well remember that the common English cat was white with some blueish piedness, so a gallipot blue." No man who is a great lover of cats, whatever their colour, can be all bad; but Laud certainly gave a most unfavourable impression to any fellow Christian who incurred his wrath by actual or suspected nonconformity. So vivid was the impression that the accounts of meetings with him carry clear signs of recording the actual words and phrases used. Here is a description witten in 1630 in the aftermath of a very unpleasant interview: Thomas Shepard had preached an unwise sermon at Earl's Colne in Essex and was at once summoned to London to see the bishop.

> December 16, 1630. I was inhibited from preaching in the Diocese of London by Dr Laud Bp of that Diocese. As soon as I came in the Morning, about 8 of the clock, falling into a fit of rage, he asked me *what degree I had taken in the University*? I answered him, I was a Master of Arts. He asked, *of what college*? I answered, of Emanuel. He asked, *how long I had lived in his Diocese*? I answered three years and upwards. He asked, *who maintained me all this while*? charging me to deal plainly with him; adding with all, that he had been more cheated and equivocated with by some of my malignant faction than ever was man by Jesuit. At the speaking of which words he looked as tho' blood would have gushed out of his face, and did shake as if he had been haunted with an ague fit, to my apprehension by reason of his extreme malice and secret venom; I desired him to excuse me; he fell then to threaten me, and withal to bitter railing, called me all to naught, saying *You prattling Coxcomb! Do you think all the learning is in your brains?* He pronounced his sentence thus: *I charge you that you*

neither preach, read, marry, bury nor exercise any ministerial
function in any part of my Diocese; for if you do, and I hear of
it, I'll be upon your back, and follow you wherever you go, in
any part of the Kingdom, and everlastingly disenable you. I
besought him not to deal so in regard of a poor Town [i.e. Earl's
Colne] and here he stop't me in what I was going to say; *A poor*
Town! You have such a company of seditious factious
Bedlams; and what do you prate to me of a poor town? I
pray'd him to suffer me to catechise in the Sabbath Days
in the afternoon; he replied, *Spare your breath, I'll have*
no such fellows prate in my Diocese; get you gone, and
now make your complaints to whom you will. So away I
went.

All of this has the authentic ring about it: after an interview like that
all of us can remember the words that were used uncomfortably
clearly; it is not often that we have from the seventeenth century the
exact sayings of a man in authority and out of control, a sort of
Nixon tape. Unfortunately for Laud he was reported more or less
verbatim by more than one witness, hardly to his credit as a
shepherd of souls. Among those who fell foul of him were the
pastors of the Strangers' church at Canterbury, John Bulteel and
Philippe Delmé, and the quotation recorded by Bulteel at the head
of this chapter shows that the former bishop of London had lost
none of his vigour of expression on his translation to the
archbishop's throne. However, in trying to browbeat Bulteel and
Delmé he had picked two pretty hard nuts to crack.

Bulteel's family came from Tournai, and settled in London in
the 1560s during the first exodus, making a living as merchants. He
had been a theology student at Leyden from 1603–10, and worked
there for a couple of years after his ordination. He was pastor at
Canterbury from 1617 to 1640, and one of his first tasks was to lead
the delegation which politely but firmly resisted an injunction from
the bishop of Norwich, Dr Overell, that communion should be
received kneeling not sitting ("as in taverns"). That was in 1619,
when Bulteel was joined as associate minister by Philippe Delmé,
whose father had come from Lorraine to Norwich and who left
Philippe in his will "my great Bible, the Decads of Mr Henry
Bullinger and the Institutions of Mr Calvin". Delmé, like Bulteel,
was ordained at Leyden; he married Elizabeth Maurois on 29
December 1616, thereby joining an ecclesiastical tribe rather like
the Fishers of Lambeth.

Generally the Leyden-trained Protestant pastors were a considerable cut above the home-grown Anglican clergy, just as their predecessors had out-gunned the Catholic parish clergy in France; and when the archbishop tried to cow them, as he had the English nonconformists, he soon found that they were made of sterner stuff. This did nothing to sweeten his temper. Indeed Laud had good arguments on his side. He objected to the idea of churches within the Church, and to the Strangers not marrying English people so that their children, though born in England, remained alien in outlook; and so he decided to lay down the law to the Walloons and Dutch within his jurisdiction. On 14 April 1634 he summoned to the dean's house at Canterbury delegates from the Dutch churches at Maidstone and Sandwich, and Bulteel and Delmé from the crypt of Canterbury Cathedral. He proceeded to ask them three questions (in which he was being rather moderate, since in 1638 Bishop Wren sent 146 questions to the barely-literate churchwardens of Foxton in Cambridgeshire, as Rowland Parker records in his classic "Cottage on the Green"); Laud's questions were: "What liturgy do you use; for how many descents are you 'born subjects', that is, born in England; and will those who are English-born conform to the Church of England?"

The Strangers replied that they used the same liturgy as the reformed churches in France, Germany and Holland, and that King Edward's patent exempted them from conformity; at which Laud resolved that the French and Dutch churches should be forbidden any English-born among their members. On 19 December 1634 an injunction was given to the Strangers,

> that all natives (i.e. born in England) of their Walloon congregations must resort to their several parish churches to hear divine service and sermons. . . . That the Ministers and others who are alien born shall have and use the liturgy used in the English churches . . . translated into French.

However the Walloons remained their usual stubborn selves. On 31 January 1635 Bulteel and Delmé were summoned to Archbishop Laud's presence to receive another scolding.

> You regard yourselves as the wise and the religious, and as Israel in Egypt and the bishops of the Church of England

as superstitious and idolators. (Your churches are nests and occasions of schism, and my intention is to hinder the schism in Kent.) It would be better if there were no foreign churches nor Strangers in England than to have them thereby give occasion or prejudice to the church government of England.

All this was duly reported by the pastors to the elders. The elders at Canterbury in January 1635 were Samuel du Bois, Jean Despagne, Vincent Ferrot, Quintin Galmar, Nicholas de Santhuns and Eleazer de Jonghe, of whom the first two and the last were English-born and all except Ferrot were related to each other, and to the de le Pierre family not yet arrived at Canterbury. It must have been rather depressing for them to emigrate from La Gorgue, only to find in England that the authorities were shaping up for trouble on the religious front, as well as in politics. The Walloons were careful to keep their heads down as regards the political troubles; it was not so easy to keep clear of Archbishop Laud, and he continued to harass them, along with his ally Bishop Wren of Norwich, who in 1638 turned the Walloons out of his episcopal chapel which they had been allowed to use for many years, and presented them with a large bill for the damage which, he said, their congregations had done to it.

The Walloons stuck to their guns, and on 12 February 1635 presented a petition to Charles I. Their spokesmen were the Huguenots Sir William St Ravi and the duc de Soubize, and Sir Theodore Mayerne, a famous Protestant and physician to the king. The king and his archbishop in due course agreed to amend the injunctions, which were read out to the assembled congregation in the crypt on 11 October. On that occasion Pierre and Susanne de la Pierre were probably among the congregation. In 1636 Laud wrote in his annual report to Charles I:

I have received information from my officers that the Walloons and other Strangers in my Diocese, especially at Canterbury, do come orderly to their parish churches, and there receive the sacraments and marry etc. according to my injunctions with the limitations your Majesty allowed.

In this case Laud's officers were deceived or else diplomats, because there is little sign that the Strangers did as they were told. In 1635 and the following years the small number of Walloon entries in the registers of St Alphege and the other parishes tell their tale, compared with the proliferating and entangled hatches, matches and despatches which are listed in the Walloons' own records. Certainly the churchwardens of St Alphege's noted in 1635 that there were more Walloons attending their services than before; but they did not take communion, or get married or baptised there, and parents feared that their children would have no religious instruction, especially as there were no sermons in most English parish churches. In 1638 Laud's annual report said only that "The Strangers at Canterbury do reasonable well obey my injunctions for coming to our churches". There was no mention of the Strangers in the report for 1639.

Archbishop Laud had other and more pressing worries. In 1641 when he was impeached one of the articles charged him with the hostility he had shown to the French and Dutch churches. On 10 January 1645 the archbishop was beheaded on Tower Hill. His old foe Pastor Bulteel was already dead but had long since arranged to have the last word: in 1645 Samuel Enderbie, at the Star in Pope's Head Alley, published, *A relation of the Troubles of the three Forraign Churches in Kent caused by the Injunctions of William Laud Archbishop of Canterbury Anno Dom 1634 Etc.* "Written by JB Minister of the Word of God."

At Earl's Colne in Essex, where Thomas Shepard had been debarred in 1630, Ralph Josselin, his Puritan successor, wrote in his diary for January 1645:

> The Archbishop that grand enemy of the power of godliness, that great stickler for all the outward pomp in the service of God, lost his head at Tower Hill London by ordinance of Parliament. This week the great snow melted gently, never were houses in many years so filled with snow and puddled when it melted away.

Even religious animosities melt away in time. Three hundred and fifty years after Laud persecuted the Strangers, his successor the archbishop of Canterbury preached to the French church in the crypt; and in the same year of 1982 the pope visited the cathedral for an ecumenical service. Laud, Bulteel, Josselin must all have turned in their graves; or perhaps it is just possible that when they met in the next world, they behaved to each other with more civility than they had managed in this one.

At a level below the exchanges of bishops and pastors, the elders and deacons were busy during the 1630s helping the poor of the community through a series of disasters. In 1630 the crops failed and, in the famine, prices for wheat and barley caused riots in Canterbury: naturally the immigrants, who as cloth workers could only suffer and not profit from dear food, became the target for attacks. They were charged with being spies, and "merchants and tradesmen who came over to take the profits of ours, to eat up and make dear our victuals, to spoil our manufactures by making them in such slight and base fashion as is used in their countries"; and they were unfair competition "by reason they do live 5 or 6 in one tenement, the rent whereof is daily paid and causes them to take money when Englishmen cannot".

These are the familiar tones of natives talking about immigrants. Luckily the townspeople of Canterbury knew better and continued to support their fellow citizens against attacks from the outside. In particular the Walloons earned credit for the way in which they helped their own poor. Lancelot Andrews noted in London that the Strangers' churches managed "to do so much good as not one of their poor is seen to ask [i.e. beg] in the streets"; and the Kentish justices of the peace urged that the Walloon system should be used as a model for poor relief in England as a whole.

In Canterbury, as in the other Calvinist churches, it was the deacons under the supervision of the elders who were responsible for looking after the poor and the sick. Statements of the money that passed through their hands take account of income from special and regular collections, legacies and fines.

	Total income			Total expenditure		
	£	s	d	£	s	d
1631	426	5	8¾	437	10	10¾
1633	505	3	6¾	311	8	0½
1635	580	6	8	326	16	6
1637	641	9	3½	437	17	11¾
1639	528	17	3	364	13	6

The difference between income and expenditure in some years was made up by the deacons; there must have been many times when the elders too had to dip into their pockets. Sometimes there was a special collection for an individual: for instance, in February 1631 thirty shillings was raised to pay the doctor, M. de la Rivière, to cut for the stone; but the unfortunate patient remained ill until at last he was carried off by the plague, a more lethal hazard than even M. de la Rivière's knives. Expenditure mainly took the form of regular payments ("ordinary") to the aged, widows and orphans, and special payments ("extraordinary") for doctor's bills, or helping travellers on their way. The deacons' detailed accounts at the start of 1641 are preserved: the summary for January is a good example.

Income	£	s	d
Collection on New Year's Day	4	2	9½
Collection on Communion Sunday	3	16	0½
In the plate during the month	3	15	1¾
Collection in Dover Quarter	1	3	3
Collection in London quarter	1	19	0
Collection in Rye Quarter	1	8	9
Collection in North Quarter	1	19	0
Fines by the Politic Men	1	1	3
Gifts of fuel for the poor		11	6
From the sale of goods		3	0
Found in the box			11
Total	£20	0s	7¾d

Expenditure	£	s	d
(Ordinary)			
Payments to 27 people (including 11 widows)			
Payments for orphans under care			
Bread and wine for communion			
Sundry payments			
(Extraordinary)	8	2	7
Payments to 41 people "in want", "ill", "out of work", "grievously afflicted", "his wife ill", "for rent", "for mending shoes", "for schooling", "for a burial", "for 62 faggots"			
Payments to "*passants*" (i.e. refugees passing through)	2	7	4
"*Estrennes*" (New Year's gifts to the poor)	3	13	0
and other payments, all to a total of	£29	18s	2d

The details of some of the extraordinary expenditure recorded by the deacons give us information which is sometimes useful for genealogy as well as for family history in general. Thus:

	£	s	d
To Jean Bonardel being in need		3	9
To Jacob Pout being out of work		9	0
To Bartholemy Pout grievously afflicted with the stone		8	0
To David Laffroy for rent of his house		4	0
For mending Pierre Six's shoes			6
For food to Rebecca Delamare		2	0
For burial of Luc du Bacq's wife		5	9
For a chemise for Louis le Roy's daughter		1	6
For watching and nursing David Martin & his wife		3	6
For 3 ells of cate to make a petticoat for David Martin's widow		4	6
To Jean Gourdin for making the said petticoat		1	0
For 2 ells and a quarter of linen to make a shirt for Jacques Honer		1	4
For a pair of shoes for Michie du Pire		2	10
To the said du Pire to go to Holland		7	0
To Jean du Bois the doctor for Eloy Bouhart's foot and his wife's arm		16	0
To Robin Garçon which the Church of Calais promises to repay us:			
For his necessity		12	0
For tools for his work	1	4	0

The entry about Michie du Pire's going to Holland is interesting as an example of the large numbers of refugees who went back across the Channel to one of the congregations in France or the United Provinces in the early 1600s helped on their way by the Strangers in England. There are many such entries about "travellers":

	£	s	d
Given to Balthasar de Robecq to return to France with his family		6	0
To Marguerite Petit returning from here to Holland with 3 children		8	0
To the wife of Pierre Miny going to Calais		3	0
For a pair of old shoes for the wife of Pierre Miny			7

The crushing poverty of so many of the congregation, and the absolute need for them to support one another in a foreign land, must have been one of the main reasons for the strong cohesion of the Walloon community during the hard times of the seventeenth century. To the hardships caused by poverty and disease were now to be added the miseries of civil war; something from which the refugees must have been particularly anxious to escape.

The Strangers who came to Canterbury in the third exodus of the 1630s were unlucky to find themselves once more in a nation close to civil war; but at least they had the good fortune to live in a county which kept out of trouble most of the time. Majority opinion in Kent during the Civil War was Royalist, but the county because of its position remained firmly under Parliamentary control; the city of Canterbury was both independent and Parliamentarian, but local loyalty was stronger than any other, and when the troopers tried to desecrate the cathedral one day they were soon seen off.

If the events of the 1630s had foreshadowed, on the continent, some of the happenings of the 1930s, the 1640s in England gave a foretaste of some of the arrangements of the 1940s. For example, there was a Kent County Committee in the 1640s: this was about as popular as the Kent War Agricultural Executive Committee that set up its East Kent Office in my uncle's house at the Home Farm, Betteshanger in 1941; and there was a Canterbury Committee which was supposed to raise taxes and recruit soldiers. The mayor of Canterbury was *ex officio* on both committees; no Walloons served on either, though some of them signed the protestation just before the war began, some joined the local militia under Captain Thomas Belke, and some may even have served in the two companies of foot which were raised for the Parliament army in June 1643 and paid by the city. At least one of the strangers was a firm Parliament man, the minister Philippe Delmé; he was a friend of the Puritan preacher Herbert Palmer, an excellent French speaker whom he sometimes invited to address the congregation in the crypt; Palmer was evidently a baby-faced man, and his eloquence came as a surprise to his listeners. There is a story that "An ancient French gentlewoman, when she saw him for the first time coming into the pulpit . . . cried out '*Hola, que nous dira, cet enfant ici*' but having heard him pray . . . lifted her hands to heaven with admiration and joy". In return, Palmer got Delmé appointed as a member of the Westminster Assembly of Divines, as a result of which he got the opportunity for such exciting war-work as preparing a new Catechism, and drawing up rules for excommunication.

As the war went on, people in Canterbury seem to have been put off the Parliamentary cause by the self-righteousness of its proponents – a fairly constant feature of British political life through the centuries. When a Puritan mayor in 1647 announced that "Christmas Day and all other superstitious festivals should be put down, and that a market should be kept on Christmas Day" there was naturally a riot. Only twelve shops opened, and the mob soon forced them to close again, effectively seizing control of the city. Royalists flocked in from the countryside around and closed the gates; and there was great excitement when news of Charles I's attempted escape from Carisbrooke Castle arrived in the city on 29 December. In the end the revolt had to be suppressed by force. Sir Antony Weldon arrived in January with the county trained bands, the city gates were removed, breaches were made in the walls and cannon were mounted on them pointing inwards. However the authorities soon found that it was not as simple as that. When the ringleaders of the Christmas riot were brought to trial the juries refused to convict them; and in May 1648 there was a general Kentish revolt in support of a petition calling for a treaty with the king, disbandment of the army, government according to the rule of law and an end to extraordinary taxation. Knights and gentry assembled at Canterbury on 23 May, arms and ammunition were issued, and Colonel Hannon (who had raised a company by beat of drum) gave a rendezvous at Barham Down where ten thousand are said to have assembled under arms.

For a little while it looked as if the "Insurrection of Kent" would succeed: the fleet which was lying off Deal declared for the king, and the castles at Deal, Walmer and Sandown were taken over by the Royalists. However, the Parliamentary troops defeated some of the rebels at Maidstone, and those who pressed on into Essex were eventually brought to bay at Colchester. In the meantime they had given a fright to the good Puritans of Essex, as we know from the diary of Ralph Josselin, vicar of Earl's Colne. The arrival of the Kentish rebels near Earl's Colne was one of the most exiting things which ever happened to Ralph Josselin and for once in a way he forgot about his aches, pains and spiritual unworthiness and gave a blow-by-blow account of events.

> June 4. We began to send out parties of horse this way and that, brought of the magazine from Braintree, the way was stopped that we could have no intelligence, Goring and the Kentish men were come into Essex, we were all young and raw men, yet God in mercy disposed our spirits to resolvedness and a willing laying out ourselves, we had many alarms but all false, the enemy never attempted us at Coggeshall.
>
> June 11. The enemy marched on to Braintree *die* 10 and this day being up and down plundering and taking away . . . our people assembled in arms, we were not able to draw into Church for the keeping of the Sabbath but were deprived of that opportunity: we set good guards in the town, at 8 of the clock that night the enemy advanced from Braintree to Halstead: we heard they intended Colchester, but we knew not for certain this.
>
> June 12. On Monday morning the enemy came to (Earl's) Colne, were resisted by our townsmen, no part of Essex gave them so much opposition as we did. They plundered us, and me in particular, of all that was portable except brass, pewter and bedding. [Afterwards Josselin received £12 compensation from the Essex County Committee.] I made away to Coggeshall, and avoided their scouts through providence . . . this day I borrowed money for to buy hose, and borrowed a band to wear having none in my power. . . .
>
> June 13. I returned home met with danger by our own men: who by some sudden accident mistaking me sought for me, but I escaped their hands through God's mercy, who in their fury might have done me wrong . . . that night the General marched to Colchester, where there was a sad skirmish, we retreated to Lexden, and resolved to draw a line about the town, I went divers times to the Leaguard, but through God's providence, I met with no danger, yet the muskets divers times and the Drake bullet flew with divers noises near me. . . .
>
> June 18. I preached at Markeshall and Mr Clopton for me, I preached in my little coat as I go every day; I could not with that confidence venture to Colne at first as afterwards, but being wonted to the troubles and rationally considering the same . . . I was daily more and more emboldened.
>
> June 25. This Lord's Day I preached at Earl's Colne to my own people who were glad to see me preach to them.

The Insurrection of Kent comes into the story of the Strangers because a minority of the Walloon community was involved in the affair. When the drums were beaten at Canterbury on Christmas day 1647, a Walloon called Jacob Halluin was the first to begin, and the mob raised a cry of "The King and Poujade". This was the most notorious sign of a schism which divided the Strangers into two factions for many years, so that the name of Poujade became synonymous with trouble.[2]

Poujade was first elected as an assistant minister for one year only from November 1638 to November 1639, in order to help Bulteel and Delmé cope with the rapid growth in the congregation resulting from the third exodus from Flanders. He soon turned out to be a vexatious colleague and began to quarrel with the ministers; but they were reconciled for a time, and when Bulteel at last retired in 1640, Poujade was confirmed in his place. It was a bad mistake, and soon he had split the Strangers into two parties. The better sort of people sided with Pastor Delmé and, by implication, tended to support the Parliamentary side of the national quarrel; Poujade and his supporters therefore inclined to the Royalists. In fact both sides were more concerned with personalities than with national politics, and charges and counter-charges flew back and forth, until at last it looked as if the Delmé party had scotched their foe with a charge of evil living: Poujade was living with someone else's deserted wife. In 1646 a Colloquy at Norwich found Poujade guilty, but he prevented their findings from becoming public knowledge; the elders (by now Pierre de la Pierre was one of them) therefore took it upon themselves to read the letter from Colloquy in front of the congregation, at which there was uproar in the crypt. During the following year Poujade tried various manoeuvres against his enemies but was stymied by them, and by the mayor of Canterbury who supported Delmé. On 9 March 1647, in a reply to an appeal by the Consistory, the House of Commons Committee for Plundered Ministers ordered Poujade to obey the authority of his church; he ignored them, and when the serjeant-at-arms was ordered to arrest him for contempt of the House, Poujade managed to dodge him. In

[2]The register of the Walloon church was disrupted, as a note in it records, *par les grans et incroyables troubles advenu par Poujade et la faction en la Rupture et Descirement de l'église.*

September the synod in London tried again: they ordered Poujade to repent and the congregation at Canterbury to be reconciled; the answer was the cry of "The King and Poujade!" at the Christmas riots. In February 1648 Poujade rejected the orders from the Consistory and led his supporters in secession to the church of St Dunstan's outside the city walls; he was reported again to the Committee of the House of Commons. At last, after the suppression of the Kentish revolt, Poujade admitted defeat, and in March 1649 he left England for Calais. Delmé carried on but fell ill in the spring of 1653, and died; Poujade's supporters continued in schism until 1654, when the community was at last restored to peace.

By the time of the Commonwealth, the Strangers like the rest of the people of England must have been exhausted. Wenceslaus Hollar, the man from Bohemia who made the great perspective drawing of London, a traveller and a skilled observer, told John Aubrey that

> When he first came to England (before the Civil War) which was a serene time of peace, the people both rich and poor did look cheerfully. But at his return (after the war) he found the countenance of the people all changed – melancholy, pitiful as if bewitched.

The immigrants might well have been tempted to return home, except that home was now formally part of France and the French authorities had long since unmasked their batteries against the Protestants. The frying pan or the fire? The de la Pierre family decided to stay; as things turned out, they had taken the right decision.

CHAPTER 12

❧

Commonwealth, Restoration and Prosperity
1650–70

Upon this purchase (of the Blackfriars) Mr De La Pierre took into his possession that side of the Quadrangle which had formerly been inhabited by the Hovedens, but had lately been neglected and let into small tenements, which, as well as the Friars, were then principally inhabited by Walloons. This he repaired, and according to the depositions in a famous Tithe Cause ... "built himself a stately home" which now remains much in its original state.

Topographer, II (1790)

Item, I give unto the poorest people of the Walloons congregation here in Canterbury the sum of twenty pounds. . . .
Item, I give unto Peter De La Pierre my brother Michael's son the sum of five and twenty pounds.

Will of Pierre de la Pierre
dated 7 October 1666

Almost at the end of the hard decade of the 1640s an event took place which marked the beginning of better times for the de la Pierre family. On 18 October 1649 Jean de la Pierre, the eldest son of Pierre and Susanne, qualified as M.D. at Leyden University in the Dutch Republic under the name "Johannes Peters (La Pierre)". His dissertation was "*De Empyaemate*" and it was dedicated to his father, to Dr Otto van Huerne of Leyden and to Dr Richard Gibbon of London. Every part of this statement is full of clues to a family historian, and when my father received his parcel of books from Sotherans after breakfast on a January morning and started to leaf through the *Topographer*, it gave him particular pleasure to find

173

that not only John Peters but also Peter Peters his eldest son had taken his degree in medicine at Leyden.

Besides the discovery that the practice of medicine was well rooted in the Peters family, a pair of medical degrees from Leyden indicated to my father that this was likely to be a source of information almost as fruitful as membership of one of the Walloon churches. The medical fraternity are assiduous in keeping records, in the normal professional interest of restricting profits to the qualified, and Dutch doctors are more meticulous than most; and my father, by consulting the lists of *alumni* of Leyden and Cambridge, was indeed able to find out a fair amount about the Peters's who became doctors during the seventeenth century. When I was following the same traces I came across some unexpected extra information about the Leyden connection, particularly about Pierre de la Pierre and his son Jean; this means going back for a moment to the period after Pierre had left La Gorgue and before he turned up in Canterbury.

I had been trying to find out where and when he had become a member of the Reformed Church. The *fichier des refugiés* at Leyden told me that a "Pierre del Pierre" had been received a member of the Walloon church at Leyden *"par confession"* in February 1633; it therefore seemed possible that he had learnt his medicine at Leyden, like his son and his grandson after him. I thought it would be worth asking Leyden University what they could tell me, and so I wrote to the Bibliothecaris der Rijksuniversitat. I was not disappointed. Mr J. van Groningen sent me back a splendid letter, with information gathered by himself and colleagues from the *Album Studiosorum Academiae Lugduno Batavae 1575–1875* and the University archives.

> I am unable to find any trace of Pierre de la Pierre [he wrote], there is only a Petrus de le (!) Pierre, *Coloniensis*, 19 years old and a student of Law, living with the widow van den Dyck; he was enrolled on 12 July 1603 . . . Jean de la Pierre was enrolled on 2 November 1639 at the age of 14 years; no study is given. He lived with Jan la Fort.
>
> There seems to be a curious thing in the matriculation book. The inscription just before Jean's runs: *Petrus Petri 't Kind, out 12 jaer, woont bij sijn ouders* (P.P. the child, 12 years old, lives with his parents). Maybe this is a brother. . . . On 14 August 1645 Joh. de la Pierre is (again) matriculated now at

the age of 20 and for the study of philosophy; he lives *apud D. Joh. Bachysium op de lange brugge*. Peter/Pierre Peters was enrolled as an "Anglus" on 28 June 1677 at the age of 20 for the study of Philosophy; from the manuscript I gather that he lived with Andrews Belon op de Clocstraet. He was "recensed" (*recensio* is the word for the yearly inscriptions in February of the members of the University) twice, i.e. in 1678 (living with Joh. de Laurière) and in 1679 (living with Lambert Gromm). He took his degree on 27 October 1679 with a treatise *De Diarrhoea*.

I blessed Mr van Groningen and his colleagues for providing me, out of pure kindness of heart and academic industry, with a glimpse of the de le Pierre family at Leyden, including even addresses of their student digs and the names of their landlords: Clock Street and Long Bridge are still there at Leyden, with fine houses of the seventeenth century. I lost no time in paying them a visit, and in sorting out the implications of the new evidence. First of all, I had to admit that Pierre de le Pierre (clearly the admissions clerk in 1603 had spelt the name right, in spite of Mr van Groningen's exclamation mark) was not Pierre from La Gorgue: he was too old, he was a lawyer not a doctor, and "Coloniensis" meant that he came from Cologne (not from "the colonies" because 1603 was too early for that: the first colony of the United Provinces was at Amboyna, established some years later). However, Jean de la Pierre and his son Pierre were clearly identified; and best of all was the news about "Petrus Petri the child". Assuming that Pierre de le Pierre and Susanne Chiroutre would have produced children every two years or so, there had been space for several (not necessarily live births) between Jean in 1626 and Marie in 1635; a son called Pierre born in 1627 fitted one of these slots very neatly. (As subsequent events showed, Pierre and Susanne went on naming baby sons Pierre as untimely death carried off their predecessors.) Very interesting too was the description of Pierre de la Pierre as "Petrus Petri", which confirmed my suspicion that our surname Peters was awarded by the clerks at Leyden long before any Act of Parliament in London; what seems to have happened is that when the surname had to be Latinised (for academic purposes) from the French, de la Pierre became "Petri", the nearest translation; and when Petri had to be turned back into a current form for normal purposes, the most obvious was "Peters", a very common type of surname in Holland and Zeeland then and now.

The thing that interested me most of all was the reference to young Pierre "living with his parents". I had all along been puzzled by two things: when had Pierre the elder learnt medicine, or rather by what process had he become first a surgeon and then a physician; and was it really likely that a refugee family living in England would ship off a young son, on his own, to a university in what was still a war zone? Now there were two pieces of evidence – the Walloon register and the Leyden archives – to suggest that Pierre, Susanne and their children were in Leyden possibly before and certainly after the first references to them in the Canterbury register, and that made much more sense. In particular, it suggested that Pierre's medical education had been acquired at Leyden, even though he had gained no formal qualification from the university there. To explain how this was possible would require too long a diversion into the remarkable story of the medical revolution and the large part played in it by the University of Leyden; to cut the story short, it was possible for visitors to Leyden to attend the lectures in the Anatomy Theatre, as well as lessons in the Botanical Garden; while at Canterbury the regular arrival of the plague stifled any questions about medical degrees: you did not ask to see the qualifications of the man going round with a white stick attending to the victims. As long as he stayed within the Walloon community Pierre de la Pierre was safe from any inquisition by the Royal College of Physicians in London, who kept a very sharp watch for anyone practising medicine without a licence – even someone who had qualified M.D. at Leyden, like Baldwin Hamey the elder.

The arrival of young Jean de la Pierre back at Canterbury in 1649 armed with his brand-new qualification from the best medical school in Europe meant that there were now two members of the family practising medicine in the Walloon community; prosperity was in sight. Pierre started to be described as *chirurgien* in the Canterbury registers in 1641; in 1642 he was shown as *medechin*. By that time the family was living in the Blackfriars, and young Jean was coming home from Leyden for the holidays. How do I know? Because of some useful minor vandalism committed by the de la Pierre family.

One sunny afternoon in September 1941 my father took my

sister and me to visit the Blackfriars. We took the boat down the Stour and moored alongside the archway between the river and the refectory building, where we were shown some initials carved on the stonework. I can clearly remember the scene, and at least one set of initials which was very easily to be discerned "IDLP" with the date 1649. I remember that my father was very put out to hear the guide explain that these letters meant, "I Defy the Lords of Parliament", and had been carved by one of the Kentish rebels; he took him aside afterwards to put him right, and was duly gratified on a subsequent visit to hear the guide telling his visitors about the Walloon doctor Jean de la Pierre. Going back with my own family nearly forty years later, I was delighted to find that the initials were still easily legible; what was more, IDLP seems to have carved his initials three times, in 1642, 1646 and 1649, and there were what looked like the letters "MD" on the last available stone of the archway to complete the series in 1649. I also made out beside "IDLP 1642" another stone carved "PDLP 1642": since the first Pierre (the one who was at Leyden in 1639) was dead before 1642, and his successor little Pierre was only a year old, it was presumably Pierre the father who carved that set of initials alongside his son Jean, home on vacation from Leyden – just as my father and I strained our eyes side by side three hundred years later, to see what was written there.

All through the 1640s and into the next decade, Pierre de la Pierre and Susanne Chiroutre had gone on producing children and (perhaps because the practice of medicine began to bring in fees and raise the family's living standards) more of the babies survived. From the Canterbury records of baptisms and burials we can compile a pretty complete list of the children born, and lost, to Pierre and Susanne; time after time they used the same Christian names in memory of the dead. The second Susanne survived, but the second Marie died in infancy in November 1640; the second Pierre, born 1641, died in October 1642 but a third Pierre was baptised in October 1643 and survived. Another son was baptised Benjamin (though he was by no means the last of the brood) in 1647, and died the same year; a third Marie was baptised in 1648, and she survived. When another daughter was born in 1651 it was time at last (after twenty-five years of marriage) for Pierre and Susanne to think of another name as Susanne and Marie were alive; they chose

Elizabeth. And when the last son was born in 1652, and since Jean and Pierre were booked, he was called Michel, and he too survived.

Therefore, by the time of Michel's birth early in the 1650s and the Commonwealth, his parents were well past their silver wedding, and both were probably close to fifty years old. Nowadays that would be considered a remarkable (if not ridiculous) age to have children, but among the Walloon community in the seventeenth century it was by no means unusual for parents to go on producing offspring until their eldest child was married and the grandchildren had begun to appear. I suspect that it was not simply a matter of obeying God's will, or of providing for old age (in any case Pierre de la Pierre was prosperous enough by now to provide very adequately for his family) but there was also a more basic instinct of survival at work: after nearly a century of disasters, men perhaps needed to feel sure that they would leave a new generation to succeed them. Now that Jean was back from Leyden, it was high time for the new generation to establish itself.

In February 1652 Jean was married in the crypt of Canterbury Cathedral. He was now "Mr Jean de la Pierre, *Docteur en Médecine*", a good catch; the girl who caught him was Jeanne du Bois, the daughter of Samuel (by now the late Samuel) du Bois by his first wife Judith de New, and related by blood or by marriage to much of the *gratin* of the Walloon community. The match was therefore a good one; it must have given equal pleasure to Pierre and Susanne to welcome the birth of their first grandson in the autumn of 1654. Jean, son of Jean de la Pierre and Jeanne du Bois, was baptised on 16 November; the witnesses are recorded as "*son Grampere Mestre Pierre de la Pierre, Susanne de la Pierre sa Gramere*", and Judith du Bois, sister of Samuel and wife of Pierre le Noble. However, and this is a sign of the times, Jean was baptised not in the crypt but in St George's parish church, and appears in the register there; he was baptised by minister le Keux "*à l'anglais*". The following year, on 29 November 1655, the baptism of Pierre, son of Jean and Jeanne, appears in the Walloon register; the same baby seems to have been baptised twice, the second time "*à l'anglais*", because the register of St George's has "Peter son of Jean (Doctor of Physick)" baptised 8 May 1656. By this period of the Commonwealth the affairs of the Church of England had been put into considerable disarray; but the registers indicate too that the process of anglicisation of the second generation of the de la Pierre family at Canterbury was now well under way.

It was not long before the de la Pierres proceeded to full-scale Naturalisation with a capital letter. Most of the Walloons turned almost imperceptibly into Englishmen by the process of "denisation", but those who wanted to do the job properly had to apply for full naturalisation by means of an Act of Parliament. Pierre de la Pierre had decided by 1656 that his future lay in England, and so had Jean; the problem was that Parliament was currently under a cloud. In November 1656 an abortive Naturalisation Bill failed to pass: among the names in it were "John de la Pier alias Peters" and his father Pierre. This is the first time that Peters is given as the official alias in England and it can be seen from this entry and those in the Walloon register that Pierre and his family had taken to spelling their surname "de la Pierre". In the event, the family had to wait seven more years before turning into regular Englishmen. A second try was made in 1660, when the Naturalisation Act passed the Lords on 23 August (12 Car II No. 14); the details had been altered to "John de la Pierre alias Peters, born at Gorne in Flanders, son of the abovesaid Peter de la Pierre alias Peters"; but this was the Convention Parliament, and a third Act was needed to confirm the second: it passed the Commons on 3 July 1663, the Lords on 24 July and at last received the Royal Assent on 27 July (15 Car II No. 26m).

On the eve of the Restoration, on 29 November 1658, Pierre de la Pierre had satisfied the first desire of any Walloon, once he had established himself and had acquired more than was needed for bare subsistence, namely to buy property. Even today a Belgian is said to be born "with a brick in his belly" and the object of any good bourgeois of Brussels is to build himself a comfortable mansion in the suburbs, which he leases out at once to foreigners so as to provide the means to build again. The better-off Walloons in the community at Canterbury had just the same impulses, and the decayed fortunes of the city at that time offered some good opportunities for investment. Pierre de la Pierre, once his medical skills had provided the means and the Poujadist faction had lost its leader, bought up the old buildings of the Blackfriars monastery, which for some time past had been used as a centre for lodgings, workshop and trading hall by the Walloons. There, as the *Topographer* recorded, he took for himself one side of the quadrangle, removed the tenants (presumably), and "built himself a stately home". The family of de la Pierre, or Peters, had arrived, and arrived for good.

After the hardships of the 1630s and 1640s and the hard slog of the 1650s, the 1660s were a time of prosperity for the new Englishmen at the Blackfriars; they began to move out of the confines of the Walloon community and put down deeper roots in England. True, Pierre remained enough of a Walloon to fight a long rearguard action against paying rates and taxes like an Englishman. The Walloon community as a whole had maintained a successful resistance over many years, claiming (with justice) that they supported their own poor, and paid their share of special taxes, and employed six or seven hundred poor Englishmen who would otherwise be destitute; so they should not also be called on to pay English rates to support other English poor. Proposal and counter-proposal were made; the matter was still in dispute in 1663, when it was charged that Walloons (like Pierre de la Pierre or Peters) occupied many great houses which would otherwise be taxed for the support of the poor; they engaged counsel to argue that their houses had never been taxed "until the late disorderly, usurping and confounding times". In spite of his efforts, the Walloons were at last obliged to yield, at least as regards rates; but Pierre still maintained a stout resistance to paying tithes to the rector of St Alphege's, on the grounds that the Blackfriars had never been part of the parish. Indeed he was able to maintain that particular struggle until he bequeathed it to his son.

By now the younger generation had started to become naturalised in fact as well as name, and to leave the Strangers' community for the great world outside. Jean, as the eldest son, had married a girl from a Walloon family though she had been born in England; when Jean's sister Susanne, Pierre's eldest surviving daughter, reached the age of twenty in 1659 it was time to look further afield. Next in importance for a good Walloon, after acquiring property, was the use of that property to acquire good matches for his daughters. Then as always, money tended to marry money, so that elders' daughters would marry the sons of elders, and heiresses whose husbands died would not be left widows for long. The more enterprising families (or the ones with the prettiest daughters) had no objection at all to marrying outside the Walloon community provided the young man was well off, and preferably a gentleman.

On 6 September 1662 the Walloon notary at Canterbury drew up a marriage contract between

> *Edward Crayford fils de deffunte Mr George, natif de Mangham, et Susanne De La Pierre fille de Mr Pierre natif de Canterbury. Avec consentement de leurs père et mères. Contract mariage ce jour.*

The consent of Pierre and Susanne to their daughter's marriage was probably given readily because the defunct George Crayford of Mongeham and his son were members of a very respectable Kentish family, whose monuments can still be seen in Mongeham church. Their lucky break came when William Crayford fought on the winning (Yorkist) side at the battle of Northampton in 1460 and Edward IV made him a knight banneret. From him the estate descended to a William Crayford who was the uncle of Susanne's fiancé Edward. The marriage between Edward and Susanne took place at St Alphege's church on 25 September 1662. The register records the wedding of "Mr Edward Crawford" (at least the Walloon clerk had got the bridegroom's name right) "and Mrs Susan Peters". So John Peters now had a married sister with an equally English name. The match seems to have been a happy one: the Peters's liked Edward to judge from their wills, and the Crayfords must have liked Susanne because her name continued in the family for several generations. When Susanne and Edward had their first son they named him William after his uncle; his eldest son was also named William, and became Recorder of Canterbury.

From this point onward the members of the de la Pierre (alias Peters) family tend to appear more often in the register of St Alphege's, the Anglican parish church as well as, or instead of, the Walloon records. This was hardly surprising, because after the Restoration the former supporters of Poujade, now led by Minister Jannon, stole a march on their rivals by offering to adopt the liturgy of the Church of England, and the supporters of Pastor le Keux were excluded from the crypt. For a while after 1661 baptisms took place at his house, or at the churches of Holy Cross or St Martin's, until they were at last restored to the crypt and their privileges confirmed by order of the King in Council dated 14 November 1664 – the basis on which the French church holds services in the crypt to this day.

At this stage both le Keux and Jannon withdrew, and Elie Paul d'Arande became pastor in 1664, being joined in 1666 by Vital de Lon.

By this time persecution of the Reformed Church in France was general and systematic. Temples were closed down, privileges taken away, and the *dragonnades* – "conversion" by the dragoons or *missionnaires bottés* of the royal army – took their toll of the congregation. When at last in October 1685 the Edict of Nantes was revoked, the final suppression of Protestantism in France began. Huguenots were liable to imprisonment, their property was confiscated, their children converted and their pastors banished or sent to the royal galleys. In April 1687 Vital de Lon was replaced as pastor by Pierre Trouillart, who had been the last minister of the great temple at Guînes and who took refuge with many of his flock in England; and the next month a new heading appeared in the deacon's account book: *Les Français*. From that time onwards, the number of French Protestant refugees grew while the number of Walloons in the Strangers' churches of England dwindled away. They had left the ghetto and turned into Englishmen.

Young Susanne had been the first of Pierre and Susanne's children to marry outside the Walloon community but she was not alone for long. On 18 August 1668 a marriage licence was issued at Canterbury for the marriage of her brother Pierre to Margaret, the daughter of Richard Jacob of Dover; four years later their sister Marie was married at St Alphege's to Robert Jacob of Dover, possibly her brother-in-law. These too were good and appropriate matches; the Jacobs were a medical family, and one which had several connections with the Walloons at Canterbury. The Peters's and the Jacobs were doctors, and the Crayfords were lawyers, and doctors and lawyers can usually make a living. Soon a new generation was sprouting up. Jean and Jeanne produced four more children, Pierre in 1655, Susanne in 1660, Jeanne in 1663 and Charles soon after. Edward and Susan Crayford had William, Edward and Peter. Pierre and Margaret Peters, and Robert and Marie Jacob, also had families – but by then old Pierre the patriarch and old Susanne his wife were no longer there to enjoy them.

Susanne was the first to go. She died in 1664, when she was probably in her sixties; she had seen her older children married and her grandchildren start to appear, and she must have been kept busy to the end by her work among the Walloons and in transforming the Blackfriars into a "stately home" fit for a gentleman to live in. Pierre, in traditional style, was soon married again: his second wife's name was Mary, and she may have been English, her maiden name is not known. However, he soon had a reminder of mortality, because of the Great Plague in 1665; perhaps it was because of this that he made his last will and testament on 7 October of the following year. In fact the danger passed, and it was nearly two years before the will was proved, and its maker buried at St Alphege's.

This was the will which had given my father so much pleasure when he found it among the diocesan records. It is a remarkable testament to the success of a first-generation immigrant in planting his family in English soil. Pierre left twenty pounds to the poorest members of the Walloon congregation (a tidy sum, and twice as much as Archbishop Laud had left to the poor of his own flock in the city) and his second wife and all his children were well provided for. She was to have an annuity of forty pounds a year, free use of the mansion for six months and then a house and garden in the Blackfriars, and

> all the furniture and goods that are now in the lower
> bulkhead chamber over the great kitchen in the house that I
> now dwell in, that is to say the featherbed and bedstead,
> curtains and valence with counterpane and blankets thereto
> belonging and also the couch, chairs and stools with two
> tables, and the brass andirons and chest of drawers.

The children divided up between them the rest of the Blackfriars property and also the "rents, issues and profits" of the Manor of Grove at Woodnesborough, near Sandwich, which with the Blackfriars had been Pierre's main purchase of property. One half of the manor went to Jean and his heirs and assigns, along with "the house I now dwell in" (that is, the Blackfriars mansion after Mary moved out of it) "with the orchard garden and enclosed slips of land on each side of my house porch". The other half of the Manor of Grove was left equally to Peter and Michael the younger brothers, and their heirs, together with property at the Blackfriars; Michael's legacy was not to be handed over until he reached the "full age" of twenty-three. Susan Crayford was to have "the upper and lower part of the house or great hall where Samuel De New and Mary à la Vigne live", and also a house and garden let to a Mr Sutton; Mary

Jacob inherited the house with gardens let to tenants (one of them "formerly called the Churchyard of the Blackfriars") and a timber-yard hired by one Rigsby. Clearly "the Blackfriars" made up a whole estate, and thickly populated: Pierre's will shows that at least half a dozen Walloons and three Englishmen were his tenants there.

To this last will and testament Pierre signed himself "Peter de Lapierre", and he sealed the document with the self-awarded coat of arms which my father made respectable at the College of Arms nearly three hundred years later. The will was Pierre's memorial, because surprisingly enough there was no monument to him at St Alphege's church; and it marks an appropriate place to leave the family of Pierre and Susanne, and the Walloon congregation at Canterbury. The last entry for a de la Pierre in the register of the Walloon church was made on Christmas day 1714.

Besides his own wife and children, Pierre left legacies to a nephew and a niece. The niece was Ester Chiroutre, daughter of Susanne's brother. The nephew was Pierre, son of Michel de la Pierre of Middelburg, who is first mentioned at Canterbury in 1665. On 30 January 1671 he was married at St Alphege's to Elizabeth Coot; the ceremony was performed by Mr Stockar, the rector who later sued Pierre and then Jean for back-payment of tithes. Their son Edward Peters was born at Canterbury on 26 July 1679; and his son Peter baptised in 1714 at Ripple,[1] married Elizabeth Barling of Dadmans in Lynsted. Their son Peter was baptised at Lynsted in 1745; his son John was baptised at Throwley in 1795; his son John was baptised at Barton le Clay in 1831; his son Frank was baptised at Sittingbourne in 1864; and his son Gordon, baptised at Sittingbourne in 1894, was my own dear father who set to work one day in the 1930s to find out where the Peters family came from.

---

[1] The manor house of Grove was about two miles across fields from Ripple.

CHAPTER 13

Brief Lives

In short, instead of describing your characters, you exhibit them to the reader. He finds himself in their company.

> from an admirer to James Boswell, on publication of
> his *Life of Johnson* (1791)

The job my father set himself, namely to trace where his direct ancestors came from as far as the records would take him, is finished. However, he knew that an account which dealt only with genealogy would be incomplete; general history and local history are needed to make sense of the dates and places, and the other essential ingredient of family history is biography.

It is not enough that so-and-so was born at X on such-and-such a date, that he married and died; to bring him to life we want to know something more personal about him. Jean Michel Pardon, a genealogist who has written an entertaining and useful guide to ancestor-hunting in Belgium and the North of France, gives a list of questions about them with an appropriately French slant.

> What were their occupations, their convictions, whether philosophical, religious or political. Were they rich or poor, happy or unhappy? Did they play an important part in the history of their village, the prosperity and greatness of their country?
>
> Were they robust, healthy in mind and body? Did they live to old age, were they often ill? Did they have many children, and lose many in infancy?
>
> Were they fond of life, food, pretty girls? Or were they sober, austere, severe?
>
> What careers did they choose: did they marry above them, or beneath them? Were there more girls than boys? What were their physical and mental peculiarities? Did they like music and poetry? What was their favourite hobby? Did they coin good

185

phrases? Did they play practical jokes? Did they paint or
sculpt, or did they prefer hunting, fishing, gardening? Were any
of them inventors?

Were they hostile to the clergy, or were they altar-boys?

These are indeed the things we would like to know about our
ancestors, and it is surprising how much can be gleaned from scraps
of information picked up on the way, so that an individual may
come back to life even after the lapse of centuries. Best of all perhaps
is to be able to quote the words they used; not a careful composition
(an educated man writing a letter in the seventeenth century tended
to write in Ciceronian Latin and in polite forms which strain out any
individuality) but words spoken or written in anger, like those of
Philip II when he heard of the image-breaking; or the letters written
in haste from their families to the refugees in England. I have tried as
much as possible to quote people's actual words: a sentence or two
of quotation is worth pages of one's own prose. Among the obvious
primary sources are diaries, letters and wills; and then there are
portraits, locks of hair, the other stray personal mementos that
people leave behind them.

As to diaries, it is certainly unlikely that you will be so lucky as to
find anything of this sort left by your ancestors from so long ago; a
good deal of help can still be got from diaries written by someone
living at the same time and sharing some of the same opinions and
events. I have made some use of the diary of Ralph Josselin, a
non-conforming Anglican clergyman who was also a farmer and a
hypochondriac, who lived at Earl's Colne in Essex and kept a diary
starting before the Civil War and continuing until his death in the
1680s; he tells us about the weather, the state and price of the crops,
the intrusion of national affairs (political and ecclesiastical) into the
countryside and even into the pulpit – in fact, the same sort of things
which loomed large in the lives of the nonconformist Walloons on
the other side of the Thames, whose world came into direct and
unfriendly contact with Josselin's during the Insurrection. Josselin
also tells us about his wife and family: his rows with his son, his grief
when children die young or in infancy, the likelihood of nasty
accidents in houses where open fires and sharp knives could never
be kept out of the reach of young children, quite apart from the
perennial fear of typhus, smallpox and the plague; all these give the
flavour of life and help us to recognise real people.

Another help provided by Josselin's diary is that he gives days of the week to go with dates – the Lord's day in particular never goes unmarked – which saves making calculations from the universal calendar. It may seem a trivial matter, but it is frequently revealing to know the day of the week on which family occasions took place, or to know how much (or how little) a feast like Christmas meant if it fell on a weekday.

Sometimes a family biographer is lucky enough to have a portrait of the person he is studying. (The earliest photograph I have is of my great-great-grandfather: when in the course of fashion I grew long sideboards, I suddenly recognised his face in the shaving mirror). There was a Peters family portrait gallery at the Blackfriars at the end of the seventeenth century, as the will of Pierre's grandson Peter, who died in 1697, shows:

> To my said brother John ... the pictures of my great-grandfather[1] Gislin and of Carolus Olusius and the copy of my grandfather's picture all which are now hanging in the gallery of my house ...
>
> To my said daughter Ann the original pictures of my grandfather and grandmother and also the pictures of my father and mother now in the said gallery. . . . All the pictures on the staircase of my house except those that belonged to my wife before I married her, to remain and continue there as the proper ornament of the staircase.

My father did his best to trace these portraits – of Jeanne Guiselin's father, and Charles Oeils, and of Pierre de la Pierre and Susanne Chiroutre, and of John Peters and Jeanne Dubois – which were probably still hanging in the mansion at the Blackfriars in 1790 when Elizabeth lived there, but the trail was cold. They must have disappeared long since into some jumble sale or antique shop; however there is always the chance of a lucky accident, and if any reader happens to have in his attic some dirty old painting with the words Gislin or Olusius or de la Pierre on it, I would be delighted to hear of it. There are many such contemporary portraits about; in the sixteenth and seventeenth centuries it was popular in the Netherlands for the well-to-do to decorate their living-rooms with

---

[1] Actually his great-great-grandfather, but he may have made a slip, or the solicitor's clerk may have been impatient.

portraits, as well as the land and sea-scapes turned out in hundreds by travelling artists, which were of a very high quality indeed: a Van de Velde which goes for thousands of guineas in the auction-room today was well within the reach of a prosperous farmer, or doctor, when it was first painted.

There are other opportunities, more sinister, of coming by chance on the likeness of an ancestor. I have mentioned how the clerk of the court at Lille had the habit of sketching in the margin of his records the faces of the miscreants hauled up before the magistrates during the dark days of Alva's rule; some of these macabre little sketches are clearly portraits. For instance, Loys de le Tombe of Watrelos, banished as an image-breaker and caught breaking the ban, was sentenced on 12 May 1569; clearly this caught the clerk's imagination, and so he made a little drawing of the head of the unfortunate Loys, eyes closed as if after the event, and added a sketch of the long sword which was used to behead him. There are no de la Pierres in this rogues' gallery; perhaps the clerk of the court at Tournai lacked the talent of his colleague at Lille to sketch Pierre Cra Cul and other members of the family who were hauled before the tribunal, unless, more likely, they had the sense to clear off before there was a chance to arrest them.

But perhaps the most useful source for family details are wills, and these are the personal memorials most likely of all to survive. They provide a good deal of information indirectly as well as directly. The will of Peter Peters, Pierre's grandson, already quoted, contains the following legacies.

> To my brother Charles such of my books of physic or chirurgery as are in the English and French tongues as are of use to him . . . I give to my beloved wife all such books of practical Divinity or history in the English tongue wherein I have wrote her name, Elizabeth Peters, and other books of Divinity or history as she shall choose or desire . . . I give to my brother Lewis all my mathematical instruments and books as are in the English and Dutch tongues . . . To my brother-in-law Gilbert Innes all my books of controversial divinity which he hath not at the time of my decease . . . To my brother John all my other books usually in the room which is now my study . . . To my said brother all my Quinical (chemical) glasses. . . .

These extracts provide personal information about Peter himself – M. D. Leyden, with plenty of books and wide interests – his happy relations with his wife, his brother-in-law who was clearly the sort of person who borrows books and does not return them; and it is interesting to see how these third-generation immigrants still read easily in three languages, unlike their English relations. And of course where there is a will there is a signature: I know how Peter de la Pierre signed his name, and that is the only piece of his authentic manuscript I know to have survived. Wills are not the only places where people leave their mark: the initials IDLP and PDLP in the archway at the Blackfriars give me for some reason a closer feeling about the people who carved them than signatures inscribed with care on a will in the lawyer's presence.

A more respectable sort of inscription, though somehow less personal, is the gravestone or the epitaph on the wall or the floor of the parish church. Occasionally such an inscription gives us a glimpse of a real person. When Peter Peters died he was still a young man, barely forty years old, and his wife was as fond of him as he of her. Their surviving daughter had the following memorial, in Latin, carved on a stone in the north aisle of St Alphege's church.

> Here lies Peter Peters of the Blackfriars next to this Parish, Doctor of Medicine, eldest son of Dr John Peters of the same place. . . . He was an excellent doctor who took great care of other people's health and seriously neglected his own. When he was suffering severely from illness, he paid too much attention to the needs of his patients, and worked harder than his own weakened strength could stand. So in the year of Salvation 1697, aged 40 and loved by all, he peacefully died.

Not a bad epitaph for a doctor.

Besides all these fairly obvious sources of information about individual people, there is always the chance that you will come across treasure trove in the form of the "Brief Lives" which other people besides Aubrey were fond of writing. Baldwin Hamey the younger, who may have been a contemporary of the first de le Pierre at Leyden, left a collection of some eighty short lives of people he had known; these are still in manuscript, in Latin, in the splendid library of the Royal College of Physicians in London and one day I read through them; there were several Walloon doctors but, alas, no de le Pierre. The chances of coming across a Brief Life actually dealing with an ancestor are small indeed, but Aubrey mentions in passing a lot of otherwise forgotten people and details (like the "gallipot blue" cats which used to live in England) and it is these oblique references which are most likely to be helpful.

I suspect that in fact something like a Brief Life of Pierre de la Pierre was written, or at least that the material for it was collected. Right at the start I mentioned the *Topographer* with its references to Pierre, the essential clue which put my father on the right track. There is quite a lot about the de la Pierre family in the various articles dealing with the Blackfriars; from the internal evidence, I suspect these pieces were written by someone who knew the family as well as the place. Indeed it seems fairly likely that the articles were written by someone living at the Blackfriars, possibly related to the de la Pierres; which narrows the choice to two splendidly-named people who were living there in the late eighteenth century: the Reverend William Dejovas Byrche, M.A. and Mr Ciprian Rondeau Bunce.

Byrche was married to Elizabeth Barrett whose mother Elizabeth was the daughter of the Peter Peters who left all the books and paintings, and the great-granddaughter of Pierre de la Pierre and Susanne Chiroutre. By then (1790) Elizabeth was the senior survivor of Pierre's descendants, and so she lived with her clergyman husband in the "stately house" which Pierre and Susanne had made for themselves and which was still in much the same state as they had left it. Nearby on the little island in the Stour, reached by a wooden bridge, stood the former monastery infirmary; this had passed to another of Pierre's children, thence to the de la Noy family; and then in about 1786 the house was bought by Mr Bunce. It is a reasonable assumption that the neighbours were well-acquainted; also that a comfortably-off clergyman, and a well-off gentleman of leisure, were the sort of people likely to contribute to a newly-established periodical "containing a variety of original articles illustrative of the Local History and Antiquities of this Kingdom."

Whoever it was who wrote the pieces for the *Topographer*, he or she (because it could just as well have been Elizabeth Byrche) was able to describe the various parts of the Blackfriars estate in detail, and had seen "several testimonies" of Pierre's "eminent skill" in the practice of medicine which "now remain in his family"; and also to repeat the details of the "famous tithe-case" of Rector Stockar versus Dr John de la Pierre in about 1680 (but "I do not exactly recollect the year"), and to give the details of Pierre's descendants, down to

> Elizabeth, heir to her mother, who carried this estate in marriage to the Rev. William Dejovas Byrche AM (son of the Rev. William Byrche, formerly Minister of St Mary's, Dover, and Rector of Mongeham, Kent who died at Bath, June 24, 1756) formerly Fellow of Sidney College, Canterbury, who now continues to possess and inhabit it, having had issue a son Thomas Peters Byrche, who died 1784 *sine prole* and a daughter Elizabeth, born in 1767, who is married and has issue.

All of which suggests to me that there are a number of authentic biographical details about the family, back to Pierre de la Pierre, in the articles in the *Topographer*; and from these it is possible to construct Brief Lives of members of the family in England; just as it is possible to do something similar for the time they spent in Leyden, in Middelburg and at Calais. But that is another story. When Thomas Peters Byrche died without children in 1784, he was the last of Pierre's descendants to bear the family name.

Epilogue

There are two things which I am confident I can do very well: one is an introduction to any literary work, stating what it is to contain, and how it should be executed in the most perfect manner; the other is a conclusion, shewing from various causes why the execution has not been equal to what the author promised to himself and to the public.

Samuel Johnson

Ancestor-hunting is a very sporting pastime. In each generation the odds against a particular pair meeting, marrying and having children are pretty high. (As for the odds against each one of us being who we are, they are so astronomical that they could not possibly be worked out by the largest computer in existence.) There is the growing element of difficulty caused by the accidents which befall the records the further back one goes. On the other hand, the further back one goes, the more ancestors there are. Everybody has two parents, four grandparents, eight great-grandparents, and so on; so that by the time you reach the seventeenth century the chances that your family researches will bump into those of another family historian get progressively higher. The odds, in fact, are not all one way.

The fact that communities in the country (which means the vast majority of the population until the nineteenth century) tend to be very stable helps the searcher: in some cases generation after generation of the family are found in the same village, often in the same farm and working the same land. But in each family there are the exceptions: the enterprising ones who get bored with the same old life, the bad hats who get given a one-way ticket to the colonies, who move to another county or another country. And there are the occasional mass migrations of the sort described in this book, which result in whole families moving from the place where they have been settled for generations, and establishing themselves in a new place for generations more.

So when you sit down to start hunting your ancestors, as my father did one day in the 1930s, you have no idea at all what you may discover. The first moves on the board are well prescribed: back to the 1840s it is reasonably plain sailing, thanks to the central registers and the census returns, though even these recent generations will give you some surprises. From the early 1800s backwards, one move may still lead safely to the next; or else you may suddenly find yourself left in mid-air, with a real brain-teaser to solve. One of my wife's ancestors had the idea of running away from home and changing his name to John Smith, and if anyone can think of a better way of throwing the hounds off the scent, I would be interested to hear it. Or else you may discover, as I did, that your earliest traceable ancestor arrived off the boat from France one day long ago, and had his name misspelt on his very first contact with the immigration officer: in which case you will need the help of someone who has had to tackle the same problem. That is one reason why I wrote this book.

If you have had the patience to read through to this point you will not need much more advice that I can give you; there will I hope be hints enough to set you off on various possible trails. However, it may help if I summarise the sort of question it is worth asking, and the way to look for answers.

The first question is, do you know or suspect that some of your ancestors came from northern France or the Spanish Netherlands? A surprising number of families have the tradition of a "Huguenot ancestor", and family tradition is seldom ill-founded, but you will have gathered by now that there are different sorts of "Huguenot". Not all Protestants with French names come from France; and if your family comes from East Kent or East Anglia, or arrived in England before 1650, then it is more than likely that your ancestors were Walloons. There are two useful ways to check quickly if you are not sure about this. If your name still has a French sound, is it one of the names (or like one of them) that has cropped up in my story; and does it appear in the Appendix? Do not be put off if you cannot find a quick or exact correspondence; strange things happen to French names as they cross the Channel. Remember what happened to my own unremarkable surname: starting off as something like Delespierre, then smoothed to Delepierre, then "corrected" to de la Pierre, then Latinised by the clerk at Leyden to "Petri", then Hollandised from Petri to Peters; and solemnly confirmed as Peters by the House of Lords, though the clerk unfortunately misspelt the place my family came from as "Gorne" which does not exist.

If you have good reason to think that you may have Walloon or Northern French Protestants among your ancestors, you are lucky as a family historian, because there are more records to search in, and because the hunt on the other side of the Channel adds a new dimension to the search. You may be baffled but you will never be bored.

You begin, as for any holiday abroad, with maps and directories; the maps are the usual ones, Michelin and the Institut Géographique National; the directories are the sort you are less likely to consult on normal business: the telephone directories of the French Départements, the lists of names in the Walloon registers; the Index to this book. Do not disdain to use "sky hooks"; the odds in favour of your descent from one of the families settled in Canterbury in the seventeenth century are quite favourable, and it is much easier nowadays than it was in my father's time to trawl the parish registers to make the connection. Do not be put off by paucity of information (such as no information at all) about certain key figures in your plot: find a way round the gaps by constructing a network, of the sort illustrated in the Appendix, so that information about related families will help to make good the deficiency.

The members of the Société de l'Histoire du Protestantisme Français play an elegant game called "We are all cousins", in which Member X proves by climbing up one family tree, then jumping across like a squirrel and coming down another, that he or she is an umpteenth cousin, so many times removed, of Member Y. The same sort of game is harder to play with Walloon ancestors, because they merged into the landscape of their new homes sooner and more thoroughly than many of the French Protestants who succeeded them. But you will find it invaluable, as I did, to become a member of one of the vigorous genealogical societies which flourish in France and Belgium, whose members spend a good deal of time corresponding and helping to answer one another's questions, and are often interested to hear from the descendants of some ne'er-do-well ancestor who fled from his native *pays* to England and never came back. The most useful of these societies for those who hail from French Flanders is the Groupement Généalogique de la Région du Nord.[1] It was the former President of the GGRN, Paul de Behault, who helped put me on the path to La Gorgue with his good advice, and whose death in 1982 was sad news for very many family historians in his own country and abroad.

With that final piece of advice, probably the most useful of the lot, I leave you in peace to carry on with your own researches. When you get stuck, as you will, remember that travelling hopefully is better than arriving; though arriving can be pretty exciting too. If you have studied a period of history previously unknown to you and visited strange places; if you have been able to collect scraps of information about the lives of ancestors when before you did not even know they existed, and helped to recover their memory from the past; then, like the farmer's sons in the old story, who dug the fields over in the search for hidden treasure and found not gold but a bumper harvest, you will have profited more from your labours than you expected. Good hunting; and as the French say on many of those war memorials which you should scan in the course of your travels,

HONNEUR À NOS MORTS

John Peters,
60 Scotts Lane,
Bromley, Kent.

[1] Correspondence should be addressed to Boîte Postale 547, 59060 ROUBAIX CEDEX 1, France.

Family Network in
the Walloon Refugee Communities

The registers of the Strangers' churches in the main places of settlement, especially Canterbury and London, contain a mass of raw material – baptisms, marriage contracts and marriages, burials, wills and property transactions – from which it is fairly simple to construct a large number of family trees. Two main features soon emerge: the large families, and the complex web of connections between families. Nearly every couple had several children at short intervals, many of whom died young; those who survived to adulthood married and had families in their turn; and marriages were made within a restricted range, especially in the enclosed refugee communities; therefore many families were soon linked together by widespread cousinage.

To illustrate the network examples are taken of some typical families involved in the three main migrations from Flanders. The sample is restricted to two or three generations after the arrival of the patriarch, and to one or two main lines of descent per family, or it would be too unwieldy. To help distinguish individuals, each member of the stock family is numbered.

The First Exodus

The families which settled in England about the time of the troubles in 1567 include the DE LA FORTERIE, the DES BOUVERIES and the DU QUESNE. (Most immigrant family names took different forms in England: in what follows, only the main original form is used.) These names are very widespread but the main families in England were founded by three men, Jean DE LA FORTERIE, Laurent DES BOUVERIES and Jean DU QUESNE, who are typical of this wave of migrants: born about the middle of the sixteenth century; comparatively young when they removed in haste from Flanders; once in England moving between Canterbury and London.

DE LA FORTERIE of Lille

Jean DE LA FORTERIE (1) left Lille in 1567: his wife's family name was probably BOUTRY. He went first to Canterbury where he signed the petition to the Court of Berghmote the same year; then moved to London; he may be the "John FORTREE" listed in the subsidy rolls for the Tower Ward in 1568 along with the "widow FORTREE", perhaps his mother.

Among Jean's children are Jean (2), Nicholas (3) and Rebecca (4). Jean (2) married Elizabeth PASSET at Canterbury: their marriage contract (11 Dec 1589) mentions his father, his uncle Melchior BOUTRY, and his godfather Michel COUSIN; Elizabeth's step-father Pierre GUESQUIER and her mother Antoinette ROSE are also mentioned. Nicholas (3) was "born on shipboard as they came" in 1567 and married Margaret, daughter of Guillaume THIEFFRIES and Hélène BOUSIN. (This was probably the Guillaume THIEFFRIES who was a spice merchant and a prominent Lutheran at Tournai in the early years of the Reformation; his brother Pierre THIEFFRIES married Marie, daughter of Francqis Cousin, perhaps related to Jean's godfather. Guillaume was arrested for heresy and imprisoned in the church of Notre Dame at Tournai, but escaped to England by the connivance of a sympathetic official called Martin FOURMANOIR.) Rebecca (4), the third child of Jean the elder, also married and had children.

The children of Nicholas (3) and Margaret THIEFFRIES were Pierre (5), Jean (6), Samuel (7), Marie (8) and Elizabeth (9).

Pierre (5) was born in London; he married Leah DES BOUVERIES (of Canterbury) at Threadneedle Street on Tuesday, 17 August 1613. Twenty years later the family was living in Aldgate Ward. Pierre died in 1639 and was buried at St Dionys Backchurch; Leah survived him by twenty years. Their eldest son and heir James (10) was a captain of Trained Bands in the 1660s; he founded the FORTRYE family of Wombwell Hall. Other children baptised at Threadneedle Street were Leah (11) (1615), Marie (12) (1618), Pierre (13) (1620) and Susanne (14) (1621). Young Leah (11) married Jean HUGESSEN at St Dionys Backchurch on 25 June 1634, and they had a son John; his father died soon afterwards and Leah then married Edward ADYE of Barham: their daughter Dorothy was the great-grandmother of Elizabeth BARLING who married Peter PETERS. Young Susanne (14) married Pierre BULTEEL.

Jean (6) married twice, first Mary BISCOP and second Anne DE FRANQUEVILLE. Jean and Mary had a son Abraham (15), a merchant living in Aldgate Ward in the 1630s, who married Jane VAN DER PUT. Jean and Anne (like Peter and Leah and Abraham) lived in Aldgate Ward; their children were baptised at Threadneedle Street: Sara (16) (1603), Catherine (17) (1613), Anne (18) (1616) and Ester (19) (1617). Another daughter, Jeanne (20) married a Jean LETHEILLIER; and another, Marie, married Salmon GORIS.

Samuel (7) married at Utrecht on 7 June 1612 Catherine, daughter of Jacques DE LATFEUR (? DE LA TOUR) of Hainaut; they were living in Walbrook Ward in the 1630s: their children were Catherine (21) (1613), Samuel (22) (1622) and Marie (23).

Marie (8) married at London on 16 April 1618 Jacques DE LA TOUR (possibly her brother-in-law).

Elizabeth (9) married Samuel DES BOUVERIES (definitely her brother-in-law).

There are plenty of signs, besides the marriage of Samuel at Utrecht, that some members of the DE LA FORTERIE from Lille had settled in the northern provinces. For example, Vas DE LA FORTERIE was received a member of the Walloon Church at Leyden on 2 Dec 1590, on the recommendation of the chuch at Lille (the "Olive" church); Jean "DELFORTERIE" and his wife Marie LE GROSE had a son Jean baptised at Leyden on 17 September 1651; it is possible that Jean the elder was the "Jan LA FORT" who took in the young Jean DE LE PIERRE as a lodger when the latter was first entered at Leyden University in 1639.

DES BOUVERIES of St Gain-en-Melantois

Two of the DE LA FORTERIE (see above) married DES BOUVERIES; and the Protestant members of this family settled in England and the northern provinces, and also in Germany. They first appear in England in 1567; Laurent (1) (see pp. 86, 87) came to England from Frankfurt-on-Main while his brothers Jean (2) and Antoine (3) probably arrived direct from St Gain. Their father Le Sieur DES BOUVERIES, Lord of the château of Bouvines (probably related to

Jean DE LA BOUVERIE the eighth Chancellor of Brabant in 1478) seems to have been a severe Catholic, because others besides his own sons turned up as refugees from St Gain during and after the troubles.

Laurent (1), his wife Barbara VAN DEN HOVE (or possibly VAN NINOVE) and his brothers Jean (2) and Antoine (3) arrived in Sandwich in 1567. They moved to Canterbury in 1576 with the other Walloons from Sandwich. Laurent was an elder of the Canterbury church in 1577 and again in 1598; Barbara died at Canterbury in October 1591; Laurent married the second time in 1594, to Catherine PIPELART (born at Peronne-en-Mélantois) the widow of Michel CASTEL; Laurent died in 1610. Laurent and Barbara had five sons, Samuel (4), Jacob (5), Edouard (6), Valentin (7) and Jean (8); and three daughters, Elizabeth (9), Jeanne (10) and Leah (11).

Samuel (4) married Elizabeth, daughter of Nicholas DE LA FORTERIE (see above) and had sons baptised at Threadneedle Street: Jean (12) (1600) and Samuel (13) (1613). The witnesses at Samuel's baptism were Elizabeth's brother-in-law Jean DE FRANQUEVILLE, her sister-in-law Catherine DE LA TOUR and her sister-in-law Leah DES BOUVERIES.

Jacob (5), born at Canterbury in 1586, studied theology at Leyden, where he joined the Walloon church in 1604. His widowed step-mother Catherine PIPELART joined him there in 1611. After becoming a minister, he married at Threadneedle Street in 1630 Catherine daughter of Jean LE THEILLIER of the Walloon community at Cologne (possibly a relative of the Jean LE THEILLIER who married Jeanne DE LA FORTERIE about the same time (see above).

Edouard (6) married Marie DE FOURMESTRAUX, also of the Walloon refugee community at Cologne. Their children were baptised at Threadneedle Street: Elizabeth (14) (1619) and Jeanne (15). Edouard died in 1625.

Elizabeth (9) married at Canterbury on 11 February 1594 Elias MAUROIS, whose father Elias came from Houplines-sur-la-Lys. Their marriage contract, dated 17 February, says she was born at Sandwich, daughter of the "honorable personne" Laurent DES BOUVERIES and the late "Barbe VAN NYNOVE"; her brother Samuel was a witness. Elias was an elder of the church at Canterbury in

1601. Their children were baptised at Canterbury: Elizabeth (16) (1595) who married Philippe DELMÉ the minister; Marie (17) (1599) who married Jacques DE NEW; Elias (18) (1600) who married Jeanne DE LA TOMBE; Jacques (19) (1604) who married Anne BULTEEL; Jeanne (20) (1605) who married Pierre DU QUESNE and Anne (21) (?1610) who married Jean DE LILLERS (his second wife).

Jeanne (10), born at Canterbury, married there in 1604 Thomas DE LA TOMBE (her brother-in-law).

Leah (11), born at Canterbury, in 1613 married in London her brother-in-law Pierre, son of Nicholas DE LA FORTERIE (see above).

Jean (2) and Antoine (3), the brothers of Laurent who also came to England in 1567, seem to have returned home after the troubles; but some of their children crossed the Channel again. Thus Antoine had a son Jacques (22) who was born at St Gain, but was banished for three years on a charge of heresy in May 1604; he stayed longer in England, and is listed among the Strangers resident at Canterbury in 1622. Jacques married a girl called Isabeau (family name not known); their children were Edouard (23); Jeanne (24) born at St Gain, who married at Canterbury in 1625 Philippe DE NEW; and Françoise (25) who married at Canterbury in 1631 Nicholas DANDRINNE.

DU QUESNE of Ath

A family related by marriage to the DE LA FORTERIE. Jean DU QUESNE (1) fled to Canterbury in 1568. His son Jean (2) was probably born in London about 1575; he married at Threadneedle Street in 1600 Sara DE FRANQUEVILLE (the sister of Anne who married Jean DE LA FORTERIE about the same time, see above; the sisters were born at Antwerp about the time of the sacking of the city; their father was Jean DE FRANQUEVILLE). Jean (1)'s daughter Marie DU QUESNE (3) married in 1613 Pierre HOUBLON (his second wife); Pierre's family had fled from Alva's persecution to London in 1567, when he was ten; he was the HOUBLON known by the nickname of "The Confessor".

Jean (2) and Sara DE FRANQUEVILLE had three sons Jean (4), Paul (5) and Pierre (6) and a daughter Marie (7); Paul seems to have died young, and Jean the elder died before 1636.

Jean (4) was born at London in January 1601. He was an elder of the Walloon church at Canterbury in 1638, and died at the ripe old age of 83. His first wife was Françoise (family name unknown) who witnessed the baptism of Marie DE LA PIERRE at Canterbury in 1635. In September 1642 Jean married as his second wife Ester, daughter of Samuel DE LA PLACE, a minister.

Pierre (6) was born in London in 1609. In 1636 he married at Canterbury Jeanne the daughter of Elias MAUROIS and Elizabeth DES BOUVERIES (see above). The marriage contract (9 June) mentions Pierre's late father Jean (2), and his uncles Jean and Jacques HOUBLON; among Jeanne's supporters were her brother-in-law Philippe DELMÉ (the minister at Canterbury), her sister Marie (widow of Jacques DE NEW), her brother-in-law Jean DE LILLERS, and her uncle Pierre DE LA FORTERIE (see above). Pierre and Jeanne MAUROIS had many children: their seventh son Peter (8), born in 1646, was the founder of the DU CANE family.

Marie (7) was born in London in 1602. In 16?? she married there Jacques the son of Pierre HOUBLON by his first wife: Jacques was born in London in 1592. Marie and Jacques had ten sons and two daughters. Jacques was the HOUBLON who later became known as the "Father of the Royal Exchange"; one of their sons became Sir James HOUBLON, the close friend of Samuel Pepys.

Thus, in two or three generations after the first arrival in England of Jean DE LA FORTERIE, the DES BOUVERIES brothers and Jean DU QUESNE, the following families in England were connected by marriage.

ADYE, BISCOP, BOUTRY, BULTEEL, DANDRINNE, DE FOURMES-TRAUX, DE FRANQUEVILLE, DE LA FORTERIE, DE LA PLACE, DE LA TOMBE, DE LA TOUR (OR DE LATFEUR), DE LILLERS, DELMÉ, DE NEW, DES BOUVERIES, DU QUESNE, EVE, GUESQUIER, HOUBLON, HUGESSEN, LE THEILLIER, MAUROIS, PASSET, PIPELART, THIEFFRIES, VAN DEN HOVE (OR VAN NYNOVE), VAN DER PUT.

The Second Exodus

During the 1590s, the Strangers' congregation at Canterbury was swollen by new arrivals, many of whom had earlier taken refuge from Alva in parts of France as close as possible to their former homes, but had then been driven out again by the fighting between France and Spain in the Calaisis and the Boulonnais. Possibly because they had already been uprooted twice, these families tended to stay in Canterbury and not move on to London; they also tended to marry into other families of the same sort, as the following examples show.

CARON of Estaires and Clainleu-en-Boulonnais.

A classic example of such a family were the CARON. Some thought that they were related to Antoine KARON who was burnt as a heretic at Cambrai in 1561, but the family which arrived in Canterbury in the 1590s had started out from Estaires-sur-la-Lys and had brought up a brood of children in the Boulonnais.

The patriarch was Guillaume CARON (1), born at Estaires about 1550. His first wife was Elaine DE LA PIERRE, possibly of the family at La Gorgue, who died at Canterbury in 1595; Guillaume married his second wife Marguerite RICARD at Canterbury two years later. He was an elder of the Walloon Church in 1596. His brother Jacques (2), born at Estaires, married at Canterbury in 1587 Leonora DE CALES; he died there ten years later.

Guillaume (1) and Elaine DE LA PIERRE had two sons, Moyse (3) and Israel (4); and five daughters, Françoise (5), Marie (6), Judith (7), Jeanne (8) and Susanne (9).

Françoise (5) and Marie (6) were born at Estaires; and both were married at Canterbury, Françoise to Denis FOURNIER about 1590; and Marie in 1598 to Henri HAIGNEREL from Vimy-en-Boulonnais; later, after the death of Henri, Marie married Jan LE MOR.

Moyse (3) was born after the family had settled at Clainleu-en-Boulonnais, in the 1570s. In June 1593 he married at Canterbury Salome, daughter of Pierre DES MARETS and Guillemette MASQUELIER (see below).

Israel (4) was born at Clainleu; and married at Canterbury in 1595 Jeanne DE VILLERS who was born in the Boulonnais at Huberson.

Judith (7), born at Clainleu like her brothers, married at Canterbury in 1593 Antoine DE BOULOGNE: he was born at Questreques-en-Boulonnais.

Jeanne (8), described as "jeune fille" in 1591, married Jean DE LA PORTE. (He was the son of Jean and of Mary DE VILLERS, and so related to Jeanne by marriage on his mother's side. His sister Jeanne married Jean BECQU in 1619 and his brother David married Elizabeth LAOUSTE in 1626).

In 1622, Israel CARON (4) was listed among the Strangers at Canterbury, which suggests that he was then the senior surviving member of the family there. He and his wife Jeanne DE VILLERS had many children baptised at Canterbury: Israel (10) (1596), Noe (11) (1599), Samuel (12) (1602), Marie (13) (1606), Susanne (14) (1609), and twins Judith (15) and Jacques (16) (1612).

Israel (10) married at Canterbury in June 1619 Mildred BULLOCK "entre les Anglais", which made him one of the first members of a second exodus family to marry outside the Walloon community. Some of their children (Jean (17) (1622), Thomas (18) (1623)) were baptised at Canterbury and some at the French church in Threadneedle Street: the latter included Berthelemé (19) (1620); and twins, Lea (20) and Rachel (21) (1630).

DES MARETS of Sailly-sur-la-Lys and Cormont-en-Boulonnais

A family with many connections among the Strangers. The DES MARETS came originally from the Pays de l'Alleu on the Lys: some members of the family were condemned at Sailly after the troubles, some were living at La Gorgue in the next century. Mahieu DE LE PIERRE, who fled from the *pays* to Southampton in the First Exodus, was married to Elizabeth DU MARET, possibly one of the family; those who later settled in Canterbury had stayed for a while in the Boulonnais.

The patriarch was Pierre DES MARETS (1), born about 1550, who married about 1575 Guillemette MASQUELIER; he died before 1593, she survived him. They had two sons, Esaie (2) and Jean (3); and six daughters, Salome (4), Judith (5), Marie (6), Susanne (7), Anne (8) and Bersabée (9). All these children were born at Cormont-en-Boulonnais.

Esaie (2) married at Canterbury in May 1595 Marie daughter of the late Jean TROUSSAC; she was born in the Boulonnais, at Vimy.

Jean (3) married twice: first in January 1602 to Marie daughter of the late Maxis PERLIN, born at Canterbury; second in April 1604 to

Françoise daughter of Nicholas DU VETTE, born at Merville-sur-la-Lys. Jean was listed among the Strangers resident at Canterbury in 1622, which suggests he was the senior surviving member of the family there at that time.

Salome (4) married at Canterbury in June 1593 Moyse CARON (see above), who was born in the Boulonnais.

Judith (5) married at Canterbury in October 1593 Jonas LE ROY, born at Armentières, son of the late Nicholas. (Very recently late: Nicholas, his wife Josephine and three of their children died of the plague at Canterbury in August the same year; this must have cast a gloom over Judith's marriage — but they were used to disasters.)

Marie (6) married at Canterbury in August 1602 Thomas HEDBAULT, born at Houplines-sur-la-Lys.

Susanne (7) married at Canterbury in August 1606 Esaie, son of the late Pasquier LE CHANTRE, born at Canterbury.

Anne (8) married twice: first Philippe DE MORTAGNE, second in March 1611 Jacques OGIER who was born at Cormont-en-Boulonnais.

Bersabée (9) witnessed one of the CARON baptisms at Canterbury in 1595; there is no record of her marriage.

DE SANTHUNS of Cambrai and Middelburg-in-Zeeland; and LOMBART of La Gorgue and Middelburg-in-Zeeland.

Many families came to England from Flanders after a stay in the Boulonnais or the Calaisis. Others went from Flanders to the northern provinces and raised families there before making the final move to England. Two such families, who may have met first during a stay at Middelburg-in-Zeeland, were the DE SANTHUNS and the LOMBART.

The starting point is at Cambrai in 1588, when Catherine BUQUET (who also married Pierre LE CANDLE and Gilles DE LOBEL; she must have been wealthy or attractive as well as lasting better than her menfolk) married a DE SANTHUNS and they had four sons, Guillaume (1), Jacques (2), Nicholas (3) and Tobie (4). The first three brothers are listed as heads of family at Canterbury in 1622, and served as elders of the Walloon church there six times between 1615 and 1646, so they were people of importance in the community. Guillaume (1) married Barbe (family name unknown) and died in 1624. Nicholas (3) married twice: first Antoinette DE NEW they had five children before she died at Canterbury in 1623); and then in February 1625 Jeanne DESPAGNE, the widow of a man called FRELEU. Tobie (4) married Marie, daughter of Jean DE SALOME.

Guillaume (1) and Barbe had at least one daughter, Rachel (5). She was born at Canterbury and married there in August 1626 François VAN DEN BUSCHEN.

Jacques (2) (his wife's name is not known) had a son Ezechiel (6), an elder of the Canterbury church in 1645 who married twice: Ezechiel's second wife was Marie LOMBART. She was the daughter of François LOMBART of Estaires and of Anne CHIROUTRE, the sister of Susanne CHIROUTRE (wife of Pierre DE LA PIERRE) and of Philippe CHIROUTRE (husband of Jeanne BECQU): Marie's great-aunt Jeanne CHIROUTRE had married Adam ROUSSEL, which provided a rich crop of relations: the ROUSSEL family, also of the second exodus, had come to stay at Maninghem-en-Boulonnais, and were related to the GUERLEIN, MARTIN, RICQUART and DES MASUR families at Canterbury, among others. So when the marriage contract was drawn up in January 1639 there were plenty of relations to be whipped in.

Ezechiel DE SANTHUNS was assisted by his father Jacques, his uncle Nicholas and his friend Arnout DE LILLERS. Marie LOMBART was supported by her brother Philippe (who later married Marie MAHIEU), her uncle Philippe CHIROUTRE, her uncle Pierre DE LA PIERRE (now described as "Maître" in the register), and her great-uncle Adam ROUSSEL; the contract mentioned her property at La Gorgue, and her grandparents Mahieu CHIROUTRE and Florence LE ROY.

Ezechiel and Marie had a daughter Marie (7) in 1642. When she was baptised there was a wide choice of witnesses. Those chosen were Jeanne LE CANDLE, the baby's step-great-aunt; her great-aunt Susanne CHIROUTRE; her uncle Philippe LOMBART; and her grandfather Jacques DE SANTHUNS. It was not uncommon to have a grandparent at a christening or even four generations; when Adam ROUSSEL's wife Jeanne CHIROUTRE died in her nephew Pierre DE LA PIERRE's house at Canterbury on 29 September 1654, her great-granddaughter Susanne BUCQUET was already ten years old.

Thus in two or three generations after the arrival at Canterbury
in the 1590s of Guillaume CARON, Pierre DES MARETS, the DE
SANTHUNS brothers and their wives and families, the following
families at Canterbury were connected by marriage.

> BOURGEOIS, BUCQUET/BECQU, BUISSON, BULLOCK, CARON,
> CHIROUTRE, DE BOULOGNE, DE CALES, DE LA PIERRE, DE LA
> PORTE, DE LESPINE, DE LILLERS, DE LOBEL, DE MORTAGNE,
> DE NEW, DES MARETS, DE SALOME, DE SANTHUNS, DES
> MASUR, DESPAGNE, DE VILLERS, DU VETTE, FOURNIEL, GAL-
> MAR, GUERLEIN, GUENIN, HAIGNEREL, HEDBAULT, LAOUSTE,
> LE CANDLE, LE CHANTRE, LE MOR, LE ROY, LOMBART,
> MAHIEU, MARTIN, MASQUELIER, NOTTE, OGIER, PERLIN,
> RICARD, RICQUART, ROUSSEL, SNELLART, TROUSSAC, VAN DEN
> BUSCHEN.

The list includes a number of families who arrived during the third
exodus; by then the Walloon community at Canterbury was both
extensive and deeply-rooted.

The Third Exodus

By the time that the third large wave of migration from Flanders was
set going by the prospect of renewed war between France and Spain
and the partition of the southern provinces of the Netherlands,
there was already an elaborate network of related families living in
the main Walloon communities in England, in which the new
arrivals were soon enmeshed. One such family was the DE LA
PIERRE, who when they arrived at Canterbury in 1635 had a
number of friends and relations to receive them.

Because of the frequent movement of people between the
Netherlands, France and England at the time of the main migrations, it is sometimes difficult to sort out the date of first
permanent settlement in this country. A typical third exodus family
is one which had some property (those who arrived at Dover in
1635 told the authorities that they were anxious about the security
of their lands and tenements in France and Flanders), but whose
head is not in the list of Strangers at Canterbury in 1622, which
included all the men of substance except the ministers and doctors.
One such family was the DE WINDE.

DE WINDE of Merville-sur-la-Lys and Neuve-Eglise in the Calaisis.

Like the DE LA PIERRE, the DE WINDE came to England from the Pays de l'Alleu through Calais. The founder was Robert DE WINDE (1) who inherited lands at his birthplace Merville-sur-la-Lys, married about 1610, and was dead by 1638. One of his sisters married a DORNION from Estaires; another sister, or cousin, had arrived earlier in England because in 1590 she married at Canterbury Jacques SNELLART, also born at Merville, who was listed among the Strangers at Canterbury in 1622.

Robert DE WINDE (1) had a son Robert (2) who was born at Neuve Eglise in the Calaisis about 1615, and married at Canterbury in 1639 Marie CLODORE. This marriage contract (17 January) mentions Robert's land at Merville, and Marie's inheritance in France and Flanders. Robert is shown as the son of the late Robert; and is assisted by his cousin Paul DORNION and his friends Pierre DE LA PIERRE and Jacques DE LA MERE; Marie is shown as the daughter of the late Jacques CLODORE, assisted by her brothers Pierre and Jacques, her uncle Pierre LE CLERCQ and her friends Antoine LESTIENNE and Isaac DU CASTEL.

By this time the Third Exodus was practically over; and the network of related families was becoming so complicated that it is possible to identify some sort of family connection between nearly all those mentioned; for example, as witnesses to a baptism. Perhaps it is just as well that by this time the younger generations were beginning to marry outside the Walloon community: otherwise everyone would have ended up related to everyone else, as is still the case among some French Protestant families to this day.

SELECT BIBLIOGRAPHY

Many of the sources used in this book are old or obscure, or both, and are hard to come by outside antiquarian bookshops and specialist libraries. But there are a number of excellent books in print, many of them in paperback, for those who are interested in the general history of the Reformation and the political development of western Europe in the sixteenth and seventeenth centuries; and for those engaged in the closely related pursuits of local history and family history.

Primary Sources

Agnew, D. C. A., *Protestant Exiles from France*, I, II (1866)

Bulteel, J., *Relation of the Troubles of the Three Foreign Churches in Kent* (London, 1645)

Burn, J. S., *History of the French, Walloon, Dutch and other Protestant Refugees settled in England* (London, 1846)

Calvin, J., *Ecclesiastical Ordinances* (1541)
——*Institution of the Christian Religion* (Basle, 1536)

Carson, P., *The Fair Face of Flanders* (Ghent, 1969)

Cooper, W. Durrant, *List of Foreign Protestants and Aliens Resident in England 1618–88*, Camden Society (1862)

Cross, F. W., *History of the Walloon and Huguenot Church at Canterbury*, Huguenot Society of London (1898)

de Brès, G., *Confession of our Faith* (1556); *Confessio Belgica* (1561)

de France, R., *Histoire des Troubles des Pays-bas*; otherwise, *Histoire des Causes de la Désunion, Révoltes et Altération des Pays-bas* (1606–15), Commission Royale d'Histoire (Brussels, 1886)

de Schickler, F., *Les Églises du Refuge en Angleterre* (Paris, 1892)

Durand, Edmund, *Scènes et Tableaux de la Reformation en Belgique 1520–1830* (Brussels, 1909)

Gostling, W., *A Walk in and about the City of Canterbury* (Canterbury, 1774)

Hovenden, R. (ed.), *Registers of the Walloon or Strangers' Church in Canterbury*, Huguenot Society of London (1891)

Josselin, R., *The Diary of Ralph Josselin 1616–83*, ed. A. Macfarlane (Oxford, 1976)

Lestoquoy, J., *Histoire de la Flandres et de l'Artois; Que Sais Je?*, paperback (Paris, 1966)

Meyhoffer, J., *Martyrologie Protestante des Pays-bas* (1865)

Poujol, D. F., *Histoire et Influence des Églises Wallonnes dans les Pays-bas* (Paris, 1902)

Somner, W., *Antiquities of Canterbury* (1640); repr. by Nicholas Battely (1703)

Verheyden, A. L. E. (ed.), *Correspondence inédite par des familles protestantes des Pays-bas à leurs co-réligionnaires en Angleterre 11 novembre 1569–25 février 1570, Bulletin de la Commission Royale d'Histoire*, CXX (Brussels, 1955)

—— (ed.), *Le Conseil des Troubles*: liste des condamnés 1567–77 Commission Royal d'Histoire (Brussels, 1961)

Manuscript Sources

Peters, G. F., Journal 1932–1962, Genealogical Notes
The library of the Huguenot Society of London contains a large amount of useful manuscript material, such as the genealogical collections of Henry Wagner FSA. A descriptive catalogue has been compiled by Irvine Gray (HSL Quarto Series LVI).

Periodical Publications

Camden Society, Publications

Cartes Touristiques, No. 1, Abbeville/Calais; No. 2, Lille/Dunkerque, Institut Géographique National

Green Michelin Guide to the North of France, 4th edn (1976)

Huguenot Society of London, Proceedings and Publications

Société de l'Histoire du Protestantisme Belge, Proceedings and Publications

Société de l'Histoire du Protestantisme Français, Proceedings and Publications

Telephone Directories, Département du Nord, and Département du Pas-de-Calais

Topographer, 1 (1789); 11,111 (1790); and one more vol. (1821)

Archives and Antiquarian Societies

Archives of the city of Tournai (*Régistres de la Loi and Régistres aux Comptes Généraux*)

Archives of the Kingdom at Brussels (*Papiers de l'État et de l'Audience*)

Archives de la Département du Nord, Lille

Archives de la Département du Pas-de-Calais, Arras

Canterbury Diocesan Record Office
Public Record Office
Registers of Canterbury Parishes, especially St Alphege and St George.

Secondary Sources

Aubrey, J., *Brief Lives*, ed. R. Barber (1982)

Braudel, F., *The Mediterranean in the Age of Philip II*, 2 vols (London, 1972, 1973)

——*The Structures of Everyday Life* (London, 1981)

Bridenbaugh, C., *Vexed and Troubled Englishmen 1590–1624*, paperback (Oxford, 1976)

Briggs, R., *Early Modern France 1560–1715* (Oxford, 1977)

Brill, E. J., *Leiden University in the Seventeenth Century: an exchange of learning* (Leyden, 1975)

Campbell, J., *The Walloon Community in Canterbury 1625–49* (1972) (unpublished theses, in the Huguenot Society library) 1972

Cox, J., and T. Padfield, *Tracing your Ancestors in the Public Record Office* (London, 1983)

Defoe, D., *The True-born Englishman*

Elliott, J. H., *Europe Divided 1559–98*, paperback (London, 1968)

Elton, G. R., *Reformation Europe 1517–59*, paperback (London, 1963)

Howard, M., *War in European History* (1976)

Keevil, J., Hamey the Stranger, The Stranger's Son (London, 1955)

Lasure, F. (ed.), *La Renaissance dans les Provinces du Nord* (Paris, 1956)

New Cambridge Modern History, atlas, ed. H. C. Darry and H. Follard (Cambridge, 1978); companion vol. XIII, ed. P. Burke (Cambridge, 1979)

Official History of the First World War, IX

Ollard, R., *This War without an Enemy* (London, 1976)

Pardon, J. M., *Comment Rechercher ses Ancêtres* (1978)

Parker, G., *The Army of Flanders and the Spanish Road* (Cambridge, 1972)

——*The Dutch Revolt* (London, 1977)

——*Europe in Crisis 1598–1648*, paperback (London, 1979)

——*Spain and the Netherlands 1559–1659* (London, 1979)

Parker, R., *The Common Stream* (London, 1975)

——*Cottage on the Green* (Foxton, Cambs., 1973)

Pepys, S., *The Diary of Samuel Pepys*, ed. R. C. Latham and W. Matthews; especially companion vol. X (London, 1983)

Ravensdale, J. R., *History on your Doorstep* (London, 1982)

Rye, W. B., *England* (1865) *England as seen by Foreigners*

Steel, D., *Discovering your Family History* (London, 1980)

Underwood, E. Ashworth, *Boerhaave's Men at Leyden and After* (Edinburgh, 1977)

Wedgwood, C. V., *The King's Peace*, 5th edn (London, 1974); paperback (1983)

——*The King's War*, 5th edn (London, 1974); paperback (1983)

Yourcenar, M., *Archives du Nord* (1977)

INDEX OF
NORTHERN FRENCH AND
WALLOON NAMES

Note – Names beginning De La or De Le are listed as De La. References to De La Pierre/De Le Pierre or Peters are not included because they occur throughout the text. fn = footnote.

AUBER, Jean, pastor, murdered 111, 112

BARNABAS, Jean, pastor 15
BECQU, Jean 204, Jeanne 147
BÉROT, Agnes, David, Jacques 95
BEZAERT, Mahieu 74
BONARDEL, Jean 167
BOUHART, Eloy and wife 167
BOUSIN, Helène 39, 198
BOUTRY, Melchior 198
BRIXIS, Charles, Jehan 65
BRULLY, Pierre, pastor, executed 38, 39, 54
BUCQUET, Susanne, Catherine 205, 206
BULTEEL, Jean, pastor 155, 159, 161, 162, 164, 171, Anne 201, Pierre 199

CAMBRELING, Charles and child 64
CAPPRON, Jean 124 fn
CARON (KARON), Antoine, executed 39, François, chaplain 74, Guillaume 123, family 108, 203
CASTEL, Jeanne 94, Michel 200
CAULIER, Jehan 76, Philippe 94
CAULLET, family 108
CAUTRE, Jehan 71
CHIROUTRE, Anne 125, 147, Catherine 147, Esther 184, Jeanne 124, Joddine 147, Philippe 125, Susanne 18, 131, 134, 146–8, 151, 152, 157, 158, 175, 182, 187, 206, family 134, 206
CLODORE, Jacques², Marie, Pierre 208
COUCHET, Abraham 3
COURONNEL, commissioner 93
COUSIN, Michel 198

CROCHEROY, Mahieu, eschevin 74
CROES, Cornelius, bailli 58

DANIAU, Lambert, professor 124
DANDRINNE, Nicholas 201
D'ARANDE, Elie Paul, pastor 182
DASSONVILLE, Christophe 81, 82, family 141
D'AUXY, baron, commissioner 93
DE BARBIGANT, Jean, executed 39
DE BOULOGNE, Antoine 203
DE BRÈS, Guy, pastor, executed 44, 54, 64, 83, 99, 104, 112, 130
DE BRUYNE, Jacques, hanged 71
DE BUSNES, Henri, courier 89
DE CALES, Leonora 203
DE FIEF, Peronne 145
DE FOURMESTRAUX, Marie 200
DE FRANQUEVILLE, Anne, Sara 109 fn, 199–201
DE GRIMAUPONT, Roland, executed 39
DE JONGHE, Eleazar, elder 163
DE LANNOY, Antoine, Judith 109, Philippe 3
DE LATTRE, family 144
DE LAURIÈRE, Jean 175
DE LEZENNE, Corneille, pastor, hanged 65, 76, 77
DE LICQUES, Judic 111
DE LILLERS, Arnout 206, Jean 201, 202, family 108
DELMÉ, Philippe, pastor 159, 161, 162, 168, 171, 172, 201, 202
DE LOBEL, Gilles 205, Jehan, Jehane 118
DE LON, Vital, pastor 182
DEMAIN, Jean and his brother 91

DE MONCHEAU, Louis, fort commander 89

DE MORTAGNE, Philippe 124 fn, 205

DE NEW, Antoinette 206, Jacques 201, Jane² 110 fn, Judith 178, 'Moser' 2, Philippe 201, Samuel 110fn, 183, family 108

DENGUIN, Pierre 113, 121

DE ROBECQ, Balthasar 167

DE ROME, Jenne 124fn

DE SALOME, Jean, Marie 206

DE SANTHUNS, Nicholas, elder 163, family 108, 205, 206

D'ESPAGNE, Jean, elder 163, Jeanne 206

DE VILLERS, Jeanne 203, 204, Mary 204, family 108

DE WARENNES, Jehan, seigneur, condemned 75

DE WASTEPASTE, Jehan, Pierre, Philippe, condemned 74, 75

DE WINDE, Robert 208, family 108

DE LA BECQUE (DELBECQUE), Antoine, eschevin 64, Charles 65

DE LA BUISSIÈRE, Charles, commissioner 69

DE LA DICQUE, Hugh, Jacques hanged 66

DE LA FORTERIE, Jean, Leah, Nicholas, Peter 87, 98, family 108, 197–9

DE LA GRANGE, Peregrine, pastor, executed 64

DE LA HAYE, Jacques 94

DE LA MERE (DE LA MARE), Jacques 208, Rebecca 167

DE LA NOY, family 190

DE LA PLACE, Esther, Samuel, pastor 202, family 141

DE LA PORTE, Jean², Jeanne 204

DE LA PREE, Jehan 72

DE LA QUENELLERIE, Christian, pastor 101

DE LA RIVIÈRE, François,² pastor, 99, 159, doctor 166

DE LA RUE, Abraham 3, family 141, 143

DE LA RUELLE, Marie and son 89, family 141

DE LA TOMBE, Jacques, beheaded 39, Loys, beheaded 188, Jeanne, Thomas 201

DE LA TOUR, Catherine 199, 200, Jacques² 199

DE L'ESCLUSE, François, executed 76

DE L'ESPIENNE, Antoine, hanged 66

DES BOUVERIES, Antoine 87, Jacques 119, Jean 87, Laurent 86, 109, Leah 87, Samuel 94, family 108, 199–201

DES CAMPS, François, Mahieu, Nicholas, Philippe 147

DES MADRY, Jean² 89

DES MARES, Pierre, commissioner 69

DES MARETS, Anne, Esaie, Jean, Judith, Pierre, Salome, Susanne 123, 124, 203, family 108, 203–5

DES MASUR, family 206

DES NULESCAMPS, Arnould, hanged 71

DES PRES (DE PREZ), Jean, executed 38

DES RUMAUX, Jacques 23, 24

DES RUMUAULT, Jehan 65

DORNION, Catherine, Nicholas 111, family 108, 208

DU BACQ, wife of Luc 167

DU BOIS, Jean, doctor 159, 167, Jeanne 178, 182, 187, Samuel, elder 163, family 108, 141

DU BUIS, Pierre (made-up name) 89

DU CASTEL, Isaac 208

DU CROQUET, family 141

DU HEM, Jehan, siegneur, condemned 75

DU MARET, Elizabeth 94, 98, 109, 124fn

DU MOND, Mathys, *officier criminel* 46, 47

DU PIRE, Michie 167

DU QUESNE, Jean 109fn, 197, Nicholas 118, family 108, 201, 202

DU VETTE, Françoise, Nicholas 205

ESTALLUFRET, Arnould, executed 39

FAVRE, Berthelemé 3

FERROT, Vincent, elder 163

FLÉCHICOURT, soldier 111, 112

FLÉEL, Henri – See DE BUSNES, Henri

FOURMANOIR, Martin 198

FOURNIER, Denis 203

FREMAULT, Fleurus, hanged 66, Guillaume 3, Pierre 122, family 108

FROSSARD, Charles Louis 77

GALMAR, Quintin, elder 163, family 108

GARÇON, Robin 167

GORIS, Salmon 199

GOURDIN, Jean 167

GROMM, Lambert 175

GRUELS, Pierre and his niece 96

GUENIN, family 207

GUERLEIN, family 206

GUESQUIER, Pierre 198, family 108

GUISELIN, Jeanne 6, 142, 145, 187, Louis 111, family 111, 113, 'great-grandfather' 19, 158fn, 187

GUY, Monsieur 134, 135

HADOUX, Jean 92, 93
HAIGNEREL, Henri 203
HALLUIN, Jacob 171
HAMEY, Baldwin, doctor 114, 158, son
  Baldwin 189
HAMON, Hector, pastor 101, 104
HAUWYS, Pierre 70
HAZARD, Pierre, pastor, burnt 76
HEDBAULT, Loys 118, Thomas 205
HERLIN, Michel, executed 64
HONER, Jacques 167
HOUBLON, Jacques, James, Jean, Pierre
  201, 202
HUCQUEDIEU, family 26
HUGESSEN, Jean, John 198, 199

JANNON, pastor 181, 182
JEROME, code name, see DE BRÈS
JUIRE, Guy 91

LAFFROY, David 167
LA FORT, Jan 174
LAIGNIEL, Jean 119
LAMBIN, clerk to the Count of Flanders
  138
LANSTIER, family 26
LAOUSTE, Elizabeth 204
LE BOIDE, Catherine 121
LEBRUN, Marguerite 145
LE CANDLE, Florence 145, Jeanne, Pierre
  205, 206, family 145
LE CHANTRE, Esaie, Pasquier 205
LE CHEVALIER, Samuel, pastor 104
LE CLERCQ, Pierre 208
LE COCQ, Anne 119
LE COMTE, Jean, executed 39
LE DEN, Jeanne, Thomas 95
LE FEBVRE, Harmon 37
LE GILON, Dominique, executed 38
LE GRAND, Jeanne 122
LE GROSE, Marie 199
LE KEUX, Philippe, pastor 178, 181, 182
LE MESURIER, Michel 119
LE MOR, Jan 203
LENGHON, Marie 91
LE NOBLE, Pierre 178
LE PLAT, Jehan, hanged 66
LE ROUGE, Peronne 125
LE ROY, Ester 94, Ezechias 94, Florence
  206, Guillaume[3] 81, 92–4, 108,
  119fn, Jonas 205, Louis and daughter
  167, Mahiette 93, Pierre 93, Susanne 93
LESTIENNE, Antoine 208, Catherine 200

LE THEILLIER, Jean 199, 200
LEZAIRE, Jacquemine 109
LIENARD, Jan 37
LOMBART, François 125, 147, Marie 125,
  Philippe 206, family 108, 206

MAHIEU, Jean, executed 64, Jean 119,
  Marie 206
MARKIET family 26
MARS, Marie 146
MARTIN, David and wife 167, family 206
MASQUELIER, Guillemette 203, 204
MAUROIS, Elias[2] 200, 202, Elizabeth 161,
  200, family 108, 200, 201
MERTZ, Monsieur 131
MINY, Pierre, wife of 167
MULLIER, Nicholas 144fn

NICHOLAS, family 108

OEILS, Charles 158fn, 187, Sarah 114,
  158
OGIER (OUGIER), Charles 123, Jacques
  124, 205, Robert, executed 39, 123,
  family 39, 108, 123

PARE, Marie 119
PASSET, Elizabeth 198
PERLIN, Marie, Maxis 204
PETIT, Marguerite 167
PIET, Gilles and brother 91
PILIZE, Peronne 146
PIPELART, Catherine 200
PLENNART, Annette, Marie, Martin and
  wife 95
POUJADE, Joseph, pastor 109, 171, 171fn,
  172, 181
POUT, Bartholemy, Jacob 167
PROOST, Jacques, prior 34, 35

RAMERY, Peronne 110, 118
ROMERY, Denis, Guillebert 118, 119
RICART (RICARD, RICQUART), Jacques,
  Judith, Philipette 125, Marguerite 203,
  Susanne 125, family 108, 206
ROSE, Antoinette 198
ROUSSEL, Adam 125, Jacquet 92, 93,
  Judith 125, Pierre 125, family 108, 206
ROUZÉE, Jean, boatman 89

ST RAVI, Sir William 163
SALENGRE, Nicholas, eschevin 74
SAUMON, Jeanne 145

SAUSE, Christian 93
SCHERLYM, Jacques 46
SIX, Catherine 118, Guillaume 109,
    Jacques³ 109, 110, Jean² 109, 110,
    Pasquier 110, 118, Pierre 167, family
    109, 110
SLINGHE, Jean 124fn
SNELLART, Jacques 208
SPRINGHE, family, notaries 159
STUF (STURFE), Jan 93, Louis 94

THIEFFREY (THEIFFRY, THESSIES,
    THIEFFRIES), Anne 87, Antoine 109,
    Guillaume (William), 39, 87, Quentin,
    executed 39, Valentin 109, family 198
THOREN, Lambert, burnt 35
THORIUS, Raphael, doctor 157, 158
TITELMAN, Pierre, inquisitor 45, 46, 53,
    58, 95

TKINT, Josse, executed 46
TRAISNEL, Antoine, Christophe 65
TROUILLART, Pierre, pastor 182
TROUSSAC, Jean, Marie 204
TRUPIN, Jeanne 123

UTENHOVE, Jean, pastor 99

VAN DEN BUSCHEN, François 206
VAN DEN HOVE (VAN NINOVE), Annelise,
    executed 35, Barbara 86, 200
VAN DE PERRE, Bache 73
VAN DER HULST, François, grand
    inquisitor 35, 46
VAN DER PUT, Jane 199
VAN ESSCHEN, Henri, burnt 35
VIGNE À LA, Marie 183
VOES, Jean, burnt 35

INDEX OF PLACES

Aa, river 21
Aire-sur-le-Lys 113
Alembon 119
Amboise 36, 52
Amiens 122
Amsterdam, New 3
Antwerp 34, 55, 59, 61, 62, 66, 76, 93, 98, 113–5, 117, 125, 148, 158, 201
Ardres 121, 122
Armentières 25, 59, 64, 83, 91, 92, 95, 101, 109, 136, 138, 139, 205
Armijden 82
Arras 26, 38, 39, 88, 116
Asti 67
Ath 39, 201
Authie, river 20

Bailleul 47, 128
Baisieux 110
Barreaux, Des 111
Basle 36, 99
Basseé, La 28
Bazinghem 113, 121
Berchem, forest of 55
Bergerhout, forest of 55
Béthune 76
Blankenberge 150
Bondues 66, 115
Boulogne 111, 121
Bouvines, chateau of 86
Bremen 35
Bruges 21, 25, 48, 62, 115, 117, 124, 150
Brussels 18, 26, 35, 45, 53, 57, 59, 63, 65, 75, 126, 150

Calais 1, 2, 50, 83, 84, 89, 91, 98, 110, 121, 122, 125, 132, 208
Cambrai 39, 107, 120, 203, 205
Cambridge 99
Canterbury – Blackfriars 5, 12, 15, 103, 173, 179, 183, 184, 187
    Cathedral/Diocese 5, 14, 62fn, 99, 101, 110, 155
    City 11, 13, 14, 73, 87, 94, 100, 102,

104, 106–8, 110, 111, 120, 162, 198, 200–8
    Strangers' Church 14, 32, 86, 94, 98–107, 109, 110, 123–5, 142, 147, 156, 157, 159–72, 202, 203
Castile 49
Cateau-Cambrésis 49, 53
Celle, La 71
Cinque Ports 1
Clainleu (Clenleu) 84, 123, 203
Colchester 98, 159
Cologne 99, 200
Commines 48, 64, 76, 115fn.
Cormont 84, 123, 204, 205
Courtrai 46, 118, 119

Danube, river 83fn
Delft 124
Deule, river 28, 109, 118, 144
Douai 26, 28, 124
Dover 1, 15, 51, 103, 152, 207
Dunkirk 23, 82

Earl's Colne 160, 164, 169, 186
Emden 112
Erquinghem 73
Escaut, river – See Scheldt
Espierre, tributary to Scheldt 144
Espierres – See Spiere
Estaires 61, 65, 69, 70, 73, 123, 124, 128, 136, 137–9, 203, 206, 208

Ferrara 36
Fleurbaix 73
Flushing 53, 82
Foxton 162
Frankfurt 54, 86, 87, 142, 199
Frelinghem 75

Geneva 36, 54, 64, 71, 99
Ghent 22, 25–7, 29, 46, 55, 58, 67, 69, 114, 115, 117, 150
Givenchy 61
Givry 41

Gorgue, La 61, 64–6, 69, 70, 73, 75, 76,
    133–40, 142–5, 147, 148, 151, 157, 163,
    174, 205, 206
Gorne 12, 19, 29, 43, 131–4, 179, 194
Gravelines 50, 82
Grove, manor of 5, 183
Guînes 52, 110, 111, 122, 149, 151, 182

Hague, The 116, 124
Heidelberg 64
Heiligerlee 19, 75
Henuin, fort 89, 106
s'Hertogenbosch (Bois-le-Duc) 88, 148
Hollain 71
Hondschoote 57, 89
Hoorbeke-Sainte-Marie 77
Houplines 200, 205

Jemmingem 19, 75

Langies 61
Lannoy 65
Laventie 61, 73–5, 93, 94
Lawe, river 28, 128, 136
Leie, river – See Lys
Lens 120
Lestrem 73, 76, 109
Leullinghem 121
Leyden 5, 124, 158fn, 162, 173–6, 199
Liège 120
Lille 28, 38, 41, 45, 54, 55, 63, 66, 71,
    76, 77, 81, 92, 107, 115fn, 118, 119,
    123, 134, 148, 198
Linselles 115fn
London 64, 73, 81, 82, 85, 86, 94, 96–9,
    107, 109fn, 159, 198, 201, 202
Louviers 84
Lynsted 11, 13, 87, 184
Lys, river 21fn, 26, 28, 45, 47, 48, 62, 65,
    70, 83, 107, 114, 118, 128, 138

Maas, river 59, 128, 150
Maastricht 23, 117
Maidstone 159, 162
Main, river 83fn
Malta 59
Maninghem 84, 124, 206
Marcq 52, 110, 111, 122, 149, 151
Mechelen 84, 115
Menin 61, 119
Mercy-Le-Haut 38
Merville 48, 64, 70, 73, 94, 128, 136, 208
Messines 70
Metteren 61

Middelburg, in Zeeland 15, 62, 82, 88,
    112, 124, 125, 142, 205
Milan 62
Mongeham 181
Mont Hulin 121
Montoire, chateau de la 122
Mouscron 115fn, 144

Namur 67, 116
Nancy 26
Nantes 5, 32, 41, 126, 182
Naples 62, 67
Nérac 111
Neuve Église (Nouvelle Église) 89, 92,
    111, 208
Nieullay, fort 51
Nieupoort 82
Nordlingen 149
Norwich 86, 96–8, 109fn, 159
Noyon 36

Ostend 128
Oxford 99

Paris 25, 41
Peruwels 38
Pyrénées, treaty of the 134, 137

Quesnoy-sur-Deule 71, 118, 119
Questreques 203

Reninghulst 89
Réty 111, 112
Rheims 26
Rhine, river 26, 83fn, 128
Richebourg 61, 64
Rigalles 110
Rijsbank, fort 51
Ripple 14, 184
Rotterdam 26, 124
Roubaix 39, 115fn
Rupelmonde 150
Rye 101

Sailly 65, 73, 93, 108, 124fn, 204
St. Agathe, fort 51
St. Amand 107
St. Etienne 122
St. Gain (Sainghin)-en-Melantois 86, 119,
    199–201
St. Omer 22, 26, 89
St. Pierre 122
St. Pol 120

St. Quentin 50
Sandwich 81, 82, 87, 93, 96, 98, 102, 103, 106, 110, 159, 162, 200
Scarpe, river 28
Scheldt, river 20, 21, 28, 144
Simancas 72
Southampton 86, 94, 96, 98, 106, 109, 156, 159, 204
Spiere 144
Steenvorde 70
Stour, river 105, 177
Strasbourg 36, 99

Thérouanne 26
Thiel 87, 98
Thionville 67
Tournai 28, 37, 38, 42, 45, 48, 55, 59, 70–3, 75, 81, 91, 92, 107, 115fn, 117, 131, 132, 198
Tournehem 122
Tourcoing 107, 115fn
Trent, council of 38fn, 41, 57, 69
Tripoli 53
Trois Rois, inn in Calais 89, 92

Utrecht 116, 199

Valenciennes 38, 54, 64, 65
Verdun 129, 133
Vervins 122, 126
Vieille Chapelle 61
Vilvoorde 72
Vincennes, Bois de 53
Villers-Cotterets 41
Vimy (Vimille) 124fn, 203, 204

Wambrechies 109, 110, 118
Wartburg 34
Wasquehal 66
Winchelsea 101, 110
Wissant 26, 111
Worms 34

Yarmouth 98, 159
Ypres 34, 93, 97, 98, 124, 150

Zeeland 53
Zwijn, river 21